BICENTENARY ESSAYS

BANK OF IRELAND
1783-1983

BICENTENARY ESSAYS

BANK OF IRELAND
1783-1983

Edited by F.S.L. Lyons

Gill and Macmillan

First published 1983 by
Gill and Macmillan Ltd
Goldenbridge
Dublin 8
with associated companies in
London, New York, Delhi, Hong Kong,
Johannesburg, Lagos, Melbourne,
Singapore, Tokyo

7171 1291 8

Layout and Design by Jan de Fouw, Dublin
Typesetting by Healyset, Dublin
Origination and Platemaking by Graphic Reproductions Ltd, Dublin
Printed in the Republic of Ireland by
The Ormond Printing Co., Ltd, Dublin
Bound by John F. Newman and Son Ltd, Dublin

Contents

Sources of Illustrations

The editor and publisher wish to thank the Bank of Ireland for supplying illustrations for this book from their archives and art collection. Illustrations from sources other than the Bank are listed hereunder:

Plate 1	National Gallery of Ireland, Dublin
Plate 2	Leeds Art Galleries
Plate 7	Bank of England
Plates 34 and 38	Sir John Soane's Museum, London
Plates 67, 68 and 70	John Donat Photography, London

A list of the illustrations accompanying Dr McParland's essay, 'The Bank and the Visual Arts', appears on page 138.

Abbreviations

(These relate to the archives of the Bank of Ireland, except where otherwise stated)

AOP   Audit Office Papers
Fanning   R. Fanning, *The Irish Department of Finance, 1922-58*, Dublin 1978
Hall   F.G. Hall, *The Bank of Ireland, 1783-1946*, Oxford and Dublin 1949
IBSC   Irish Banks' Standing Committee
PRO   Public Record Office, London
SPO   State Paper Office, Ireland
TCOD   Transactions of the Court of Directors of the Bank of Ireland

Plate 1

Portico of the House of Lords, 1797, from a watercolour by Samuel Wooley

Plate 2

The Irish House of Commons, 1780. On the right, Henry Grattan is urging the claim of Irish rights

Notes on Contributors

Dr Ronan Fanning is a graduate of the National University of Ireland and obtained his Ph.D. from Cambridge in 1968. He taught at Exeter University before returning to University College, Dublin in 1968 where he has since taught modern Irish history and Anglo-Irish relations. He is joint editor of *Irish Historical Studies*, the premier journal in its field, and is at present engaged upon a history of British policy in Ireland in the twentieth century. His principal publication is *The Irish Department of Finance, 1922-58* (1978) and in 1983 he will be publishing *Independent Ireland: the first fifty years.*

Professor F.S.L. Lyons is a graduate of the University of Dublin (Trinity College, Dublin). He taught history there as a Fellow of Trinity College, Dublin, between 1951 and 1964 and then became first Professor of Modern History at the newly founded University of Kent at Canterbury from 1964 to 1974. He was Provost of Trinity College, Dublin, 1974-81 and is now Professor of History in the University of Dublin. His publications include *The Irish Parliamentary Party, 1890-1910* (1951), *The fall of Parnell, 1890-91* (1960), *Internationalism in Europe, 1815-1914* (1963), *Ireland since the Famine* (1971), *Culture and anarchy in Ireland, 1890-1939* (1979), as well as two biographies, *John Dillon* (1968) and *Charles Stewart Parnell* (1977).

Professor Dermot McAleese is a graduate of the National University of Ireland and obtained his Ph.D. at Johns Hopkins University in 1971. His teaching career has been spent mainly in the University of Dublin, where he is now Whately Professor of Political Economy. His special field of interest is international economics and he has published numerous papers on foreign investment, the balance of payments and industrial policy in journals such as *Oxford Economic Papers*, the *Oxford Bulletin of Economics and Statistics* and the *Economic and Social Review*. He is a director of the Central Bank of Ireland and a member of the National Economic and Social Council.

Professor Oliver MacDonagh is a graduate of the National University of Ireland and obtained his Ph.D. from Cambridge in 1952. He was Fellow in History at St Catharine's College, Cambridge from 1952 to 1964 and from 1964 to 1968 was Foundation Chairman of the School of Social Sciences at Flinders University of South Australia. From 1969 to 1973 he was Professor of Modern History at University College, Cork and since then has been W.K. Hancock Professor of History and head of the Department of History in the Institute of Advanced Studies at the Australian National University. His principal works include *The pattern of government growth, 1800-1860* (1961), *Ireland: the Union and its aftermath* (1968 and 1977), *Early Victorian government* (1977), and *The Inspector General: Sir Jeremiah Fitzpatrick* (1981). His study of the ideology of Anglo-Irish conflict, *States of Mind,* will be published in 1983.

Dr Edward McParland is a graduate of the National University of Ireland, taking his M.Sc. degree in 1964, and obtained his Ph.D. from Cambridge in 1975. He has been a Lecturer in the History of Art in the University of Dublin for the past ten years

3

and has published extensively in such periodicals as the *Burlington Magazine, Country Life*, the *Journal of the Royal Society of Antiquaries of Ireland*, and the *Quarterly Bulletin of the Irish Georgian Society*. His book, *James Gandon*, is to be published in 1983. He is an expert on Irish architecture of the eighteenth century and is particularly interested in setting it in a European context.

Professor James Meenan is a graduate of the National University of Ireland and was Professor of Political Economy and the National Economics of Ireland at University College, Dublin from 1961 to 1980. He was a director of the Central Bank of Ireland between 1949 and 1958 and a director of the Bank of Ireland from 1958 to 1978. He has published many papers on economic subjects and his major works include *The Irish economy since 1922* (1970) and *George O'Brien* (1980).

Dr T.K. Whitaker obtained an M.Sc.(Econ.) degree of the University of London by private study. He was elected Chancellor of the National University of Ireland in 1976 and was a member of Seanad Éireann from 1977 to 1982. He was Governor of the Central Bank of Ireland from 1969 to 1976 and is at present a director of the Bank of Ireland. As Secretary of the Department of Finance between 1956 and 1969, he was closely associated with the planning and development which made that period one of exceptional importance in recent Irish history, and his report, *Economic development* (1958), is generally regarded as a major influence on policy during those years.

Foreword

TO mark, in a special way, the bicentenary of the Bank of Ireland in 1983, the previous Governor, Dr.W.D. Finlay, suggested to the Court of Directors that a written work about the Bank should be commissioned which would be of interest to all the Bank's stakeholders.

Because the chronological sequence of events in the history of the Bank is amply and accurately reported up to 1946 in *The Bank of Ireland, 1783 – 1946* by F.G. Hall, we felt that a rewritten or updated history would not be suitable.

It has been decided that a number of recognised experts in various fields be asked to write essays dealing with specific aspects of the Bank's development and, in particular, to relate the development of the Bank to the social and economic development of Ireland.

The Governor and Directors are deeply grateful to Dr Finlay for the work he has done in initiating and developing this concept and presenting it in a form which has made it an easy task to see through to completion.

For bringing the writers together, editing the work and adding his own introduction and concluding essay to it, we are indebted to Dr F.S.L. Lyons. We are grateful also to Professor Donal McCartney, who kindly acted as consultant.

We thank also the writers for their lively and enlightening contributions which, while preserving the proper historical perspective, have given new insights into the history of Ireland and the Bank of Ireland over the past 200 years.

The Governors and Directors of
the Bank of Ireland

May 1983

Introduction

Each generation, it is said, rewrites history in its own image. This is an admirable arrangement, which not only guarantees historians a reasonably secure livelihood, but also enables us continually to look at the past in a fresh light. That fresh light comes partly from the accumulation of new knowledge and partly from the longer perspective in which the passage of the years allows, or obliges, us to view the knowledge we have inherited from our predecessors.

It is our hope that this volume will throw fresh light upon the history of the Bank of Ireland in both these different ways. Much new knowledge has accumulated in the thirty-four years since the standard work, F.G. Hall's *The Bank of Ireland, 1783–1946*, was published, both about the period covered by that book and of course about the period since 1946, and one of the functions of the present work is to make at least some of this new knowledge available. But the old knowledge, too, has to be seen in a modern context. In the case of an institution such as the Bank this means that the historian, while continuing to be interested in the institution for its own sake, has necessarily also to concern himself with the environment in which that institution has to function. We have found, therefore, that the relationship of the Bank with the society it serves has emerged as one of the principal themes, if not the principal theme, of our book.

This is not to say that Hall's history has become redundant. On the contrary, these essays make abundantly clear how great a debt their authors owe to it. It remains the most authoritative account of the development of the Bank in the first century and a half of its existence. Moreover, as any serious study of banking must do, it went beyond the story of the particular institution to say a great deal that is still valid about the financial and economic structure of the country at large. In its use of the Bank archives it was a pioneering work and these archives were judiciously supplemented by reference to a great variety of printed material. The result was a very large and very solid book which, like much Bank architecture, seemed designed to inspire in equal measure confidence and awe. Nevertheless, it was a book for the specialist, and since specialists in the field have always been rather scarce in Ireland, it did not set the Liffey on fire, a form of combustion from which Hall himself, it is fair to say, would have recoiled in horror. Indeed, in my own early days as a research worker in Irish history, Hall's book was relatively easy to obtain at bargain prices from second-hand booksellers. But if it was then a depreciated currency, time has brought its just revenge and its very rarity has now made it something of a collector's item.

This in itself would be a reason for supplementing it with something that is rather more accessible. And to supplement rather than to replace is our intention, for in fact this new book cannot attempt to replace that which is, in the most exact sense of the term, irreplaceable. On the contrary, while covering some of the same ground, and much more that Hall could not have covered, it has been deliberately designed to take a different shape and to achieve a different object. It consists of a series of essays which, while fitting into a broadly chronological scheme, do not not attempt to give the continuous treatment of the Bank's affairs which was the essence of Hall's work. These essays represent a series of attempts to isolate, and in so doing to illuminate, important aspects of the Bank's evolution. While there has been close consultation among all concerned in establishing the ground plan of the volume, the individual contributors have been encouraged to follow their own bent and to use their own judgment in deciding what was significant and what was not. Obviously, we do not claim that everything significant is included in this relatively short book, but we are confident that the reader will find nothing in it that is not significant.

The contributors include both economists and historians well grounded in economic and administrative history. To me, as editor, one of the pleasures of this enterprise has been in watching how closely these two species, often thought of as poles apart, interacted with each other in discussion, revealing in the process how much they had in common. A notable example of one who almost effortlessly demolishes academic barriers between economics and history is our first contributor, Dr Whitaker, who, despite having himself played a notable part in the making of modern Ireland, undertook to write about the founding and early history of the Bank. However, since his essay also covers the period when a separate Irish currency continued for a generation after the Union between Britain and Ireland, some of the problems he deals with will not seem altogether unfamiliar to the present-day reader.

He is followed by Professor Oliver MacDonagh, now resident in Australia, but one of the most distinguished Irish historians of his generation, with experience equally balanced between economic, social and administrative history. His wide-ranging contribution emphasises the continuing preoccupation of this volume — that the history of the Bank cannot be considered apart from the history of Ireland and that an integral part of the institution's history must be an assessment of its contribution towards the development of Irish society and the growth of the Irish economy. Professor MacDonagh is followed by another historian, Dr Fanning, also a graduate of the National University and, like him, moving easily between different kinds of history which are often regarded as distinct but which, especially in a small country like Ireland, overlap so much that virtuosity becomes a necessity rather than a luxury. As one of the editors of *Irish Historical Studies*, Dr Fanning is well placed to observe, and in a measure to direct, the currents of research into our recent history. His own interests lie mainly in the decades after independence and his book, *The Irish Department of Finance, 1922–1958*, makes it peculiarly fitting that he should deal with the Bank's history during that crucial period.

The main emphasis of these bicentenary essays is upon the institutional Bank, its working, its problems, the national and international framework within which it has to operate. In particular, the later essays discuss the modern Bank and its rôle in the new Ireland it has helped to bring into being. All of this marks a radical departure from Hall's history, which dealt with the period since 1922 merely in an epilogue which occupied thirty-two out of the book's 523 pages. In one respect, however, it may appear to a superficial glance that we are treading the same ground, for this volume contains, as Hall's did, a contribution dealing with the architectural history of the Bank. But there are some fundamental differences between the two. The earlier work included an account by C.P. Curran both of the 'parliament house' and of the fitting of the Bank into that setting. But, despite Mr Curran's liveliness as an architectural historian and the undoubted charm of his narrative, his account was in three respects deficient. First, he did not have, could not have had, all the relevant materials at his command and recent research has thrown up a great deal that needs to be incorporated into any historical survey of what was for so long the Bank's headquarters. Second, it was no part of his brief to consider subsequent architectural developments, not just in Dublin but throughout the country, for which the Bank was responsible. And finally, it was again no part of his brief to consider the Bank in its function as encourager and patron of the arts, which function has assumed an increasing importance in recent years with the comparative decline of private patronage.

These various aspects loom large in Dr McParland's original and strikingly illustrated essay. Dr McParland, who lectures in the history of art in Trinity College, Dublin, is himself a specialist in eighteenth-century Irish architecture and is the author of a forthcoming book about James Gandon. He brings a highly professional eye to the subject, but in this essay he is at least as stimulating in what he has to say about Baggot Street as in what he has to say about College Green. His analysis of the new head office is, indeed, one of the most penetrating accounts so far given of that notable addition to the modern architecture of Dublin. Further, his remarks on the building up of the Bank's collection of modern Irish art are a valuable reminder of a public rôle played by the Bank which has not always had the recognition it deserves.

With the next two contributors we move from historians to economists, though one of these, Professor Meenan, besides being an eminent academic economist, has always been one with an historical as well as a practical bent. As director of the Central Bank of Ireland for a number of years and of the Bank of Ireland between 1958 and 1978, he has first-hand experience of his subject, and as author of *The Irish economy since 1922*, and of a recent study of George O'Brien, the doyen of Irish economic historians, he is well placed to put the modern Bank in historical perspective. But as important as perspective is environment. Properly to understand the functioning of the Bank at the present time, we should have a grasp of the milieu within which it now operates, a milieu so different in so many respects from that depicted in Hall's history as to belong virtually to another world. To describe this vastly changed environment, not only in national terms but in international terms as well, is the task of Professor McAleese, Whately Professor of Political Economy in Trinity College, Dublin. Professor McAleese's special interest is in international economics, and his essay is important not least for its appreciation of the international factors which now play such a decisive rôle in our affairs.

Hall's book was described on its dust-cover as 'an official history of the Bank of Ireland'. The word 'official' was perhaps unfortunate, suggesting what in reality was quite untrue — that it was a history purveying the Bank's corporate viewpoint. If that was not true of Hall, it is equally untrue of these essays. This is not a 'house' production in the sense of representing a particular establishment attitude. The contributors, it is hardly necessary to state, have had complete freedom, both of access to materials (except, naturally, where the confidentiality of the Bank's relations with its clients was involved) and of comment upon or interpretation of what they have found. That said, all of us gratefully acknowledge the virtually unlimited help we have received from the officers of the Bank, ranging from the use of the archives to various kinds of assistance in the prosecution of our research. A special debt is due to the archivist, Miss Sarah Ward-Perkins, who not only provided us with a most helpful guide to the relevant material in her charge, but also did much to smooth the paths of individual contributors.

This generous help has been given to us at every level. In his preface to Hall's history, the late Professor George O'Brien referred to the survey of the Bank's archives which was made as a prelude to that work. 'In the course of this inquiry', he wrote, 'Mr W.D. Finlay was employed to copy, calendar and index the relevant contents of the Court Minute Books which have been preserved from the foundation of the Bank. Mr Finlay's assiduous performance of this onerous task greatly facilitated the later stages in the preparation of the present volume.' Now, some thirty-five years later, it is a pleasure to record that the same Mr (now Dr) Finlay, during his term as Governor of the Bank, was the inspiration for this sequel to Hall's book and it is scarcely too much to say that it might never have appeared at all had it not been for his energy and enthusiasm. The invaluable support given by his successor, Dr D.S.A. Carroll, has reaffirmed the importance attached by the Bank to the successful — and punctual! — completion of the project.

I should like in conclusion to add my own tribute to the essayists who rose to the occasion and met a particularly stringent deadline with remarkable *sang froid*, to Professor Donal McCartney for his wise advice on numerous occasions, and also to our publisher, Mr Michael Gill, his colleague, Mr Fergal Tobin, and his designer, Mr Jan de Fouw, who responded so positively to the challenge of this particular opportunity. It only remains to congratulate the Bank upon its two hundred distinguished years and to wish it continued success and prosperity in the centuries still to come.

F.S.L. Lyons

Plate 3

David La Touche, first Governor of the Bank of Ireland

Origins and Consolidation, 1783-1826

T. K. Whitaker

THE Bank of Ireland opened its doors in Mary's Abbey, Dublin on 25 June 1783, in modest premises rented for a year for £27 and then purchased for £850. Today the assets of the Bank of Ireland Group are £6,000 million, with premises alone worth well over £100 million. The two centuries during which the Bank has grown have seen significant change in Irish political, economic and social conditions. The Bank has influenced the transformation and, in greater degree, been influenced by it. The earliest period of the Bank's life, from 1783 to 1826, was perhaps the most exciting of all. It was the period of Grattan's Parliament, the French Revolution and Napoleonic wars, the rebellion of 1798, the Act of Union, and finally the suppression of a separate Irish exchequer and currency. It is a period of special interest because it saw the newly-established Bank of Ireland reluctantly undertake and yet competently discharge various central banking duties, including that of stabilising the external value of an independent national currency.

Only a Bicentenary!

Two hundred years of service to the Irish public merit recognition, congratulation and commemoration. The hindsight thus afforded brings many interesting features to light, some still topical but also others now seen as curiosities, ironies or blind spots. The first curious thing about the Bank of Ireland is not that it is two hundred years old, but that it is not nearly a hundred years older still. After all, the Bank of England was founded in 1694 and the Bank of Scotland only a year later and Dublin was then the second city in these islands, much larger than Edinburgh. Why was it that the Irish sister's birth was so long delayed, so that it was only in 1783 that the Bank of Ireland, with a charter similar to that of the Bank of England, saw the light of day? The explanation must be sought in the peculiar conditions of eighteenth-century Ireland.

State Finances

Most of the great national banks of the world, including the Bank of England, owe their origin to a monarch's financial need. So perhaps one of the reasons for the late arrival of the Bank of Ireland may be that, for most of the eighteenth century, successive monarchs were doing quite well out of their Irish revenue, even to the extent of being able to charge pensions for their mistresses to it, and had no pressing need to charter a bank to augment their resources. Many Irish legislators would, in any case, have been reluctant to confirm an instrument which passed money, free of parliament's control, to crown or government.

Revenue held up so well against expenditure that no national debt accumulated in the first half of the century. For much of the second half surpluses were avoided and deficits created, at the deliberate instance of the Irish parliament, by resort to what we would now call 'capital services' — development grants for private enterprises, mills, canals, roads, street-widening, piers, quays, collieries, hospitals and even churches. The deficits had grown to create a national debt of over £1 million by 1780 but, despite the tight financial grip exercised by Grattan's Parliament, the debt had reached £2.25 million before war broke out between Britain and France in 1793. The French wars and the 1798 rebellion pushed the national debt to over £23 million by the end of the century. In the 1780s, therefore, the substantial permanent credit available to government at one stroke in return for the granting of a bank charter was not to be disdained.

Plate 4

The charter of the Bank of Ireland

Plate 5

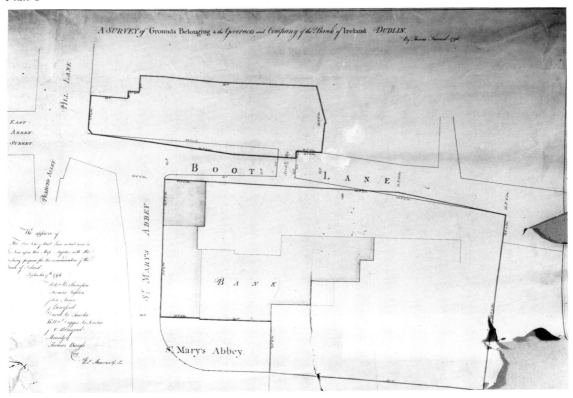

Thomas Sherrard, Survey of the site of the first premises of the Bank of Ireland in Boot Lane and Mary's Abbey, 1796 (north lies to the right)

Private Finances

A more fundamental reason for the Bank's tardy appearance must be that the financial needs of the country for most of the eighteenth century were modest, though increasing, and were being met, however unsatisfactorily, by the motley coinage in circulation, by an inflow of capital, and by the credit and money transmission system provided by private banks and traders.

In Ireland the eighteenth century, particularly the second half, was an age of growth, if not of enlightenment or equity. The population more than doubled to reach five million by 1800 but it remained predominantly rural, and in rural Ireland, outside the eastern maritime counties and the hinterlands of Cork and Limerick, smallholders, cottiers and labourers made up most of the population. The result of the confiscations and other changes in ownership in the previous century was that only one-seventh of the land of Ireland was left in Catholic hands and, since Catholics predominated in numbers, it was they who were crowded in the poorest regions either on holdings of less than five acres or as labourers. Poverty was, therefore, commonplace and universal and a subsistence economy prevailed over large areas. It was a society in which there was limited need for money, though it was not as much dominated by barter, or 'commutation of wares', as it had been when the English martyr, Edmund Campion, described the scene in 1571. Money was needed to pay wages and rents, though the latter were in places paid wholly or partly in kind by way of labour and produce; to have grain milled into flour or meal or even to buy

Plate 6

Deeds of Conveyances of the Bank's first premises at Mary's Abbey

grain at times of harvest failure; to deal in livestock and wool at fairs; to pay for the butter made, the yarn spun and the cloth woven in rural homes; and to purchase household needs, including tobacco, salt, soap, candles and clothes, at markets or in the village shops which were becoming more common towards the end of the century. It was by those few who regularly had surplus money arising from rents or profits — landlords and their agents and the larger merchants — that banking services were first provided.

Conditions improved markedly from mid-century on as roads were built, canals started, domestic spinning and weaving spread even to remote areas, supplementing the income of farmers and labourers, and trade generally expanded, though remaining a small proportion of national income. Exports, which were less than £1 million at the beginning of the century, had topped £3 million by 1780, with beef, linen and butter as major components. Irish salted beef used to go mainly to the English and French slave colonies until demand slackened at the time of American independence and the shipment of live animals to the British market took over. The growth of economic activity, supported by a favourable balance of payments, was accompanied by a significant increase in the supply of money. The amount of cash is thought to have expanded tenfold in the course of the century.

The Currency Situation

Nevertheless, the Irish public had to make do throughout the century with a varied assortment of debased coins, supplemented by tokens, tallies, IOUs and forgeries of all kinds.

From the beginning of the century until the Union was completed on 6 January 1826, all transactions in Ireland were conducted in Irish pounds. The Irish pound, however, was merely a *numéraire* or unit of account: there was no Irish currency of a denomination exceeding one penny. For most of the century — until the Irish pound followed sterling off gold in 1797 — a fixed relationship, established by royal proclamation, existed between the incorporeal Irish pound and sterling; thirteen Irish pounds were equal to twelve pounds sterling or, in practical terms, thirteen Irish pence were equal to an English shilling.

Coinage was highly important at a time when wages were less than a shilling a day — averaging 6½d. a day for a labourer in the 1770s when a wife and a couple of children might earn nearly as much again by spinning linen yarn in the home. The chaotic state of the Irish coinage is vividly described by the economic historians. There was no Irish mint. The patent, admittedly profitable, granted in 1722 to an English iron merchant, William Wood, to coin halfpence and farthings badly needed by the Irish public was relinquished in 1724 after a storm of opposition fomented by the *saeva indignatio* of Dean Swift's *Drapier's Letters*. The shortage of copper coin was acute for the rest of the century. Obtaining small change of a gold guinea (worth 273 Irish pence from 1717 on) at a fair or market was a difficult matter, likely to involve loss. For silver coins, the main reliance had to be placed on British sixpences, shillings, half-crowns and crowns, all, like gold coins, clipped or 'sweated' to the minimum weight at which they would pass muster. There was a prohibition since the time of Henry VIII on the export of English gold and silver coin to Ireland. A wide variety of degraded foreign gold and silver coins circulated. Proclamations attempted to fix their local value at defined weights and, in 1775, to end their acceptability as legal tender. The lists of these coins read like treasure-trove inventories — ducatoons, Peru and Mexican pieces of eight, pistoles, crusados, louis d'or, new gold of Portugal, and even the gold moidores of Masefield's poem 'Cargoes'. To make up the deficiency of coinage, merchants issued silver and copper tokens in great quantities. Counterfeit money was not uncommon. The Cronebane halfpenny struck by the Irish Mining Company in 1789 was circulating widely at the end of the century.

In rural Ireland tallies were more frequently used than either tokens or coins. Tallies were small sticks, split symmetrically and notched across the split, so that each half bore a similar record of a debt to be paid by a certain date. Interest arose through the original loan being less than the specified repayment. The lender kept one half of the tally, the borrower the other. Discharge of the debt was signified by the integration of the two halves in the hands of the borrower who could then destroy the evidence of his debt. Tallies, repayable from specified revenues, had been a favourite money-raising device of Charles II and were later exploited to excess by William III; the Bank of England came to his relief by purchasing unredeemed royal tallies as one of its first major investments.

Plate 7

Tally sticks, 1824-5

The Private Banks

In a largely subsistence economy, with money in limited and infrequent use amongst the great majority of the people, special financial services were required only by a few, and their interests did not always coincide. For some time, absentee landlords were so concerned to have access to bills on London as a means of recovering rents out of Ireland that they tried to obstruct the availability of such bills to merchants. This was the thought behind an act of 1756 which required bankers to cease being traders but still allowed traders to issue notes.

The two principal groups which had access to surplus funds — landlords or their agents and merchants — were interested primarily in safe and efficient transfer of credits and discharge of debts. They wished to effect monetary settlements with minimum resort to the dangerous and expensive movement of gold and silver from place to place. The principal services sought were, on the one hand, the discounting (immediate purchase for cash) of bills of exchange, on Dublin or London, received in payment for domestic sales or exports and, on the other hand, the provision for cash of similar bills of exchange which could be used to discharge debts incurred for purchases at home or abroad or provide resources for high living in London. The discount was a compound of interest and commission, charged by way of reduction of the nominal amount of a bill, in return for cashing at once a payment due only in twenty-one or thirty-one days' time. The 'cash' paid out by the discount houses and private banks consisted mainly of their own notes, which since 1709 had been made transferable by endorsement.

The issuers had every incentive to circulate as many of their own notes as they could and to economise in their outlay of gold and silver, though the less reckless recognised the need to hold a prudent proportion of gold and silver coins with which to redeem such notes as from time to time might be presented for payment.

The predominant function of banking at the time has been described as the transfer of payments between regions (and countries) rather than the transfer of resources between lenders and borrowers. The taking of deposits and the making of advances, in today's sense, were minor activities. Overdrafts were unknown. There were only a few specialist banks, though a large number of merchants also issued notes. A typical note had print on the front — the back was left blank for endorsements but rapidly became a mass of signatures and ink blobs; the notes themselves were often cut in half, each half being sent separately through the post to avoid theft.

In the first quarter of the eighteenth century there were only a few banks in Ireland, concentrated in Dublin and Cork. By the early 1750s the number in these cities had scarcely reached ten but banks had opened in Belfast, Waterford, Clonmel, Athlone and Galway. Belfast was still at that time a small city, with a population only about one-tenth that of Dublin, and its first bank came to grief within a few years, so that the north of Ireland continued for decades to trust far more to gold than to bank notes or credit.

The second half of the 1750s saw the collapse not only of the Belfast bank but of most of the Irish private banks, leaving eventually only four or five in Dublin of which the most prestigious and prominent was La Touche's, the only one, indeed, to last another century. The development of strong banks had been inhibited by the Partnership Act of 1741 which limited the capital of a bank to £10,000. The smaller private banks were not only vulnerable to 'runs' — the presentation of large amounts of notes for encashment at the one time — but also to trade vicissitudes such as the harvest failures which occurred every fifteen or twenty years or a slump in the export market for linen or butter. The illiquidity of bankers coincided unhappily with the liquidity exigencies of their customers. Most of the successive banking crises were a consequence of bad harvests which, by depleting exports and necessitating increased grain imports, caused an external payments drain, general financial stringency, and, worse still at times, widespread famine.

Absentee landlords have already been mentioned as interested customers of banks and jealous protectors of their own interests against those of merchants in foreign trade. At mid-century absentee rents may have been in the region of £500,000 a year, a not inconsiderable sum when exports of goods were under £2 million. Arthur Young, in 1779, estimated absentee rents at £732,000.[1] Visible exports were then about £3 million, so the ratio remained the same.

Proposals for a National Bank

Absentee landlords as well as the larger merchants were to the fore amongst the early petitioners for a national bank. However, all attempts in Dublin in the first half of the century to set up an Irish counterpart of the Bank of England were thwarted by political agitation. The most vigorous opponent of the first project (1719-21) was the redoubtable Dean Swift whose virulent anti-Whiggism found an outlet in factious criticism of the project and of the subscribers, as well as later of Wood's coinage patent. There was plenty of distrust, jealousy and apprehension to play upon — ill feeling about the restrictions which had been placed by the English parliament on Irish manufactured exports, suspicion of the intentions of the commercial interests supporting the English government, fear that the charter might be revoked if these interests were harmed, resentment towards absentee landlords, and lack of confidence in financial institutions after the bursting of the South Sea Bubble in 1720. Enough popular agitation was generated to cause rejection of the confirming bill by the Irish parliament.

Later, another Irish figure to achieve world renown, the philosopher Bishop Berkeley, anticipated socialist doctrine by insisting that any such chartered bank should be publicly, rather than privately, owned and controlled — a bank 'whereof the public alone is proprietor and reaps all the benefit'. He queried 'whether the bank proposed to be established in Ireland, under the notion of a national bank, . . . be not in reality a private bank . . . as those of England and Scotland, which are national only in name, being in the hands of particular persons and making dividends on the money paid in by the subscribers'.[2] Berkeley's ideal finds expression in the present constitution of most central banks, including our own.

Experience accumulated over the decades of the instability of the private banks and the inadequacy of the financial system to cater for the needs of an expanding economy. It was, however, only in the new patriotic atmosphere of Grattan's Parliament, about to gain its independence from Westminster, that the demand for a national bank, 'with public security', was revived and, not without some opposition, received legislative approval in May 1782.

Establishment of the Bank of Ireland

The act authorised the establishment, on the model of the Bank of England, of the Governor and Company of the Bank of Ireland and prescribed that its paid-up capital of £600,000 be lent to the treasury at 4 per cent per annum, made its stockholders personally liable for borrowings by the Bank in excess of £600,000, and fixed the maximum interest to be paid or charged at 5 per cent. No other corporation or partnership exceeding six persons could issue notes payable on demand or for less than six months. The Bank was prohibited from lending to the government without the sanction of parliament and was also forbidden to lend on the security of land. A way was soon found around the former restriction but the latter persisted until 1860. Because all of its original capital had to be lent to the treasury the Bank started short of working capital but a further £120,000 was subscribed by the stockholders at 5 per cent interest. A royal warrant of June 1783 directed that all public funds in Ireland were to be paid into the Bank of Ireland. It thus became the government's banker and later was given charge of the management of the national debt. Almost from the beginning the authorities looked to the Bank as an independent source of financial advice.

The principal partner of La Touche's bank, David La Touche, who had been one of the foremost promoters of the new bank, became its first Governor. Indeed, four of the La Touche family each subscribed the maximum sum of £10,000 to the Bank's capital. The original La Touche was a Huguenot refugee who had fought on William's side at the Battle of the Boyne in 1690 and, having first become a poplin manufacturer, later concentrated on banking, with capital supplied originally by fellow Huguenots. The La Touche bank itself was taken over by the Munster Bank in 1870. The Bank of Ireland acquired, and restored in College Green as an 'honoured heirloom', the Venus and Cupid ceiling from the first Governor's private house in Castle Street before it was demolished in 1946. William's victory at the Battle of the Boyne is itself commemorated in a tapestry which hangs in the old House of Lords chamber in College Green.

Among the subscribers to the original capital of the Bank were Robert Emmet's father; the Theobald Wolfe after whom Wolfe Tone was named and whose son wrote 'The Burial of Sir John Moore'; a founder of the Kildare Street Club, William Conyngham; and a man who was killed in the Robert Emmet rising, Lord Kilwarden. There were a few wealthy Catholic subscribers, notably members of the Sweetman brewing family. The subscription list included lawyers, physicians and merchants as well as nobility, clergy and country gentry. All the members of the first Court of Directors were drawn from this list.

The name given to the Bank by the charter was 'The Governor and Company of the Bank of Ireland' and the charter established the terminology of Court of Directors and General Court of Proprietors. The by-laws of the Bank provided for the formation of committees of directors, one of which, the daily committee, attended each day at the Bank from 11 to 2.30 o'clock to manage its affairs, only executive functions being delegated to staff. To ensure punctual attendance a system of fines, increasing with the degree of lateness for meetings, was imposed, the fines being deductible from a deposit which each director had to make at the outset with the Secretary of the Bank.

The staff originally appointed consisted of nineteen persons, the highest paid having £150 per annum, the lowest £25. These were the precursors of the present staff of over 7,300 in the Bank itself and 8,800 in the group.

The first Court of Directors was entirely Protestant, mirroring in this respect Grattan's Parliament. The parliament, though it had no control over government, was progressive and patriotic but by no means representative. A Catholic had no right to sit in it. The parliamentary oath described the Catholic religion as 'superstitious' and 'idolatrous'. Catholics were still excluded from state and judicial offices. In such conditions of civil and political inequality, the prescription in the charter that all members of the Court of Directors should subscribe to the declaration contained in the penal legislation of 1704 — 'An Act to Prevent the Further Growth of Popery' — and take an oath of 'allegiance, supremacy and abjuration' is scarcely to be wondered at. Not only Catholics but Quakers were thus debarred. It is to the credit of the original directors that a large minority — a majority with reference to Quakers — were embarrassed by these relics of penal legislation and voted to have them removed. The discriminatory provisions continued to prevent Catholics from becoming directors and even from voting at general meetings until 1829 when, despite the failure of the Catholic Emancipation Act to remove the restrictions, the Court of Directors decided to treat them as a dead letter. The first Catholic joined the Court in 1830 and the restrictions were repealed by the Bankers (Ireland) Act of 1845.

Some of the promises which have been required on oath from directors for the past two hundred years are expressed in language which now has a quaint ring: 'I will be indifferent and equal to all manner of persons . . . I will faithfully and honestly demean myself according to the best of my skill and understanding.'

The Early Years

For its first ten years the Bank was not troubled by fresh exchequer demands for money: the national debt scarcely rose. But in 1793 war was declared on France and five years later rebellion broke out in Ireland. Government expenditure increased enormously, giving rise to deficits which the public became increasingly reluctant to finance by taking up government debentures. The needs of the exchequer were so exigent that all scruples about the illegality of the Bank lending to the government without parliamentary authority were overborne.

Meanwhile, the Bank's normal business was growing, principally in the form of rediscounting trade bills for the reputable private banks. Taking deposits and keeping current accounts transferable by cheque were minor activities and overdrawing of accounts was not allowed. Even for private customers, the discounting of a bill was the only route to bank credit. The issuing of notes was, of course, an important function from the outset. Printing of the notes in Dublin was arranged as early as 1784. Notes were issued in large denominations both in Irish pounds and in guineas (from five guineas to £500) the values in both currencies being shown on their face. The Bank's note issues came on the scene in really significant quantity only from the turn of the century; notes for under £5 were issued only after 1797, when gold payments were suspended. The Bank eased the coinage problem by issuing silver tokens for ten pence and five pence — forerunners of a decimal system officially installed only in 1971! The fixed relationship of thirteen to twelve between the Irish pound and sterling was ended when sterling, followed by the Irish pound, went off gold in 1797. Grattan took strong exception to the intervention of the lord lieutenant to forbid gold payments by the Bank of Ireland before the Irish parliament had authorised this course.

During the Napoleonic wars the Irish pound 'floated' in relation to sterling. It fell at one time as low as sixteen shillings — an experience repeated by its modern counterpart in November 1980 — and on occasions was at a small premium. Whether the depreciation was due to changes in the balance of payments or the over-issue of notes became a matter of formal parliamentary inquiry in 1804. In 1821 the old thirteen to twelve ratio was restored and there was for a few years a managed currency exchange standard, with the Bank of Ireland performing the stabilising rôle appropriate to a central bank. It took the Bank some time to realise that the volume of its own note circulation affected the exchanges and, as explained later, the Bank was drawn only by degrees into exercising its exchange management function.

The confusion and inconvenience associated with a chaotic coinage and an erratic exchange rate were probably more tolerable in the boom war years than in the

Plate 8

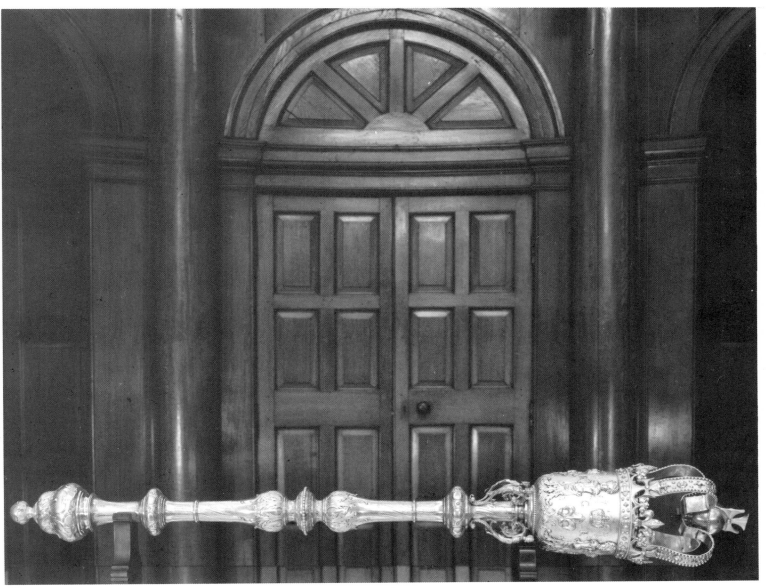

The Mace of the Irish House of Commons. Made in England in 1765, it is fifty-eight inches long and weighs 295 ounces

recession that followed. Even in England in the early nineteenth century coins were scarce and untrustworthy. To alleviate the shortage the Bank of England was putting overstamped Spanish dollars and tokens into circulation; tradesmen's tokens of 6d. and 1s. were popular. It was not until 1816, under Liverpool's Act, that gold was made the only standard, the sovereign being introduced at 20s. (£1 1s. 8d. in Irish currency), and silver being minted into merely representative coins of limited legal tender.

Exchange Rate Management

The main groups interested in the exchange rate between the Irish and British pounds were merchants in British-Irish trade, absentee landlords and, of course, the two exchequers. The more inflationary climate of the Napoleonic wars had provided scope for the spread of private banks, thus adding to the note circulation. Concern about the relatively rapid expansion of note issues and the depreciation of the Irish pound led to a call in 1803 for the imposition of a statutory obligation on the Bank of Ireland to redeem its notes in Bank of England notes. As already mentioned, a committee of inquiry was set up to report on the causes of the depreciation and to recommend remedies. This committee was, in essential respects, a preview of the famous bullion committee of 1810. Though John Foster chaired the earlier committee, Henry Thornton was the guiding spirit of both inquiries. His pioneering work in the theory of money, credit and interest is reviewed at length in J. A. Schumpeter's *History of economic analysis.*[3]

The spokesman for the Bank of Ireland, with the corroboration of Bank of England witnesses, maintained that the exchange rate was determined by the balance of remittances (trade, rents and capital) between the two countries and could not be affected by the size of the note issue in Ireland, which could not be excessive so long as it was based on sound security. They were unwilling to acknowledge any connection between the money supply and the demand for imports. The committee did not accept this argument. They considered that the over-abundant issue of paper had raised prices in Ireland as compared with Britain and thus caused the exchange rate to fall. The payments balance, they found, was normally favourable to Ireland. Surprisingly, however, they supported the view that a depreciated exchange rate 'has not the smallest influence on the trade of the country, either by encouraging its exports or checking its imports'.

For a remedy, the committee looked chiefly to the restoration of the old fixed parity between the two currencies and their eventual amalgamation. Meanwhile, they recommended that the Bank of Ireland should arrange for its notes to be redeemable in British sterling and should establish a fund in London for that purpose.

The committee's report was not even discussed in the parliament of the United Kingdom until five years later, and then without result in Ireland, possibly because, with the help of tighter note issuing and credit policies, the exchange rate stayed close to the old parity from 1805 to 1813; indeed it rose to a premium from 1812 to 1815. When the Irish pound did fall again for a while the depreciation was welcome for the relief it brought, at a time of depression and scarce money, to Irish agriculture and trade.

The directors of the Bank of Ireland, in any case, had advanced many reasons for not formally undertaking a responsibility to stabilise the exchange rate. By degrees, however, they were drawn into the smoothening of the rate to facilitate transfers of public funds and, having opened an account in the Bank of England in 1821, pursued an active policy of stabilisation between the restoration of the old parity and the amalgamation of the two currencies in 1826. This policy involved the seasonal building up of funds in London on which drawings could be made to provide sterling at par for customers needing to transfer funds to England. This was the first instance of a sterling exchange standard. As Dr G.L. Barrow says, the Bank's 'undertaking to give bills on London at par for its notes (and deposits) had transferred the critical fluctuations from the exchange to its London funds' and 'the idea that its own circulation had no bearing on the exchanges was thus finally laid to rest'.[4]

Even after the merger of the two currencies in 1826, the Bank of Ireland continued to exercise various central banking functions, including the provision of 'last resort' facilities for other banks, and it is only in recent years that it handed over to the Central Bank its functions as the government's banker and the registrar of government stocks.

Abolition of the Irish Pound

In Ireland, the abolition of a separate Irish currency as from 6 January 1826 meant that a distinction which had lasted for over a century was suddenly ended. The historic event was noted by Amhlaoibh Ó Súilleabháin, the Callan schoolteacher, in his *Cín Lae* or diary: 'an toirtín, nó an trí pingine déag, níl ann anois ach scilling mhaol no lom .i. dhá phingin deag' (the 'toirtin' or thirteen pence has been replaced by the bare shilling or twelve pence). The Bank of Ireland was shut on 5, 6 and 7 January to enable it to cope behind closed doors with the changeover, which of course also meant

Plate 9

Bank of Ireland note for one and a half guineas (£1 14s. 1½d.), 1806

that its own notes had henceforward to be issued in pounds sterling rather than Irish pounds. No immediate withdrawal of its Irish currency notes was, however, prescribed. Dublin Corporation did not change its accounting system to sterling until 1829 and on the Dublin Stock Exchange quotations in Irish pounds for stock denominated in Irish currency continued up to 1830.

Bank of Ireland as central bank

Apart from its responsibility for stability of the exchange rates and its functions as government banker and fiscal agent (much reduced after the Irish exchequer was abolished in 1817), the Bank of Ireland discharged other central banking duties as well.

Very early in its life the Bank adopted a 'minimum cash ratio' principle — deciding to hold at least 20 per cent of its current liabilities (notes, post bills and deposits) in gold during the peak demand season and about 16 per cent at other times. The associated decision to maintain these reserve ratios by selling or buying government securities whenever necessary has been described as an unconscious anticipation of open-market operations.

Plate 10

Bank of Ireland note for one guinea (£1 2s. 9d.), 1813

Private bankers kept part of their reserves in Bank of Ireland notes and regarded the Bank of Ireland, though a competitor, as also being a protector in times of trouble. The Bank of Ireland normally came to the rescue of private banks in difficulty. All the Dublin banks, including La Touche's, were supported during a particularly critical week in mid-1820, but one Dublin bank 'went under without a cry' and, while some country banks were helped, others whose links with the Bank of Ireland were weaker had to close down. The government itself intervened in 1822 to make loans from the exchequer to business firms. This unusual initiative did something to revive economic life in a country which had recently lost half its banks.

The Bank of Ireland never attained the dominant regulatory position which the Bank of England held in the British banking system. There was no foreign exchange market in Dublin, all financial dealings with the continent being cleared through London, except for certain transactions with Portugal. The Bank of Ireland itself had a 'last resort' relationship with the Bank of England, from which it was able to draw gold or notes in time of crisis.

Plate 11

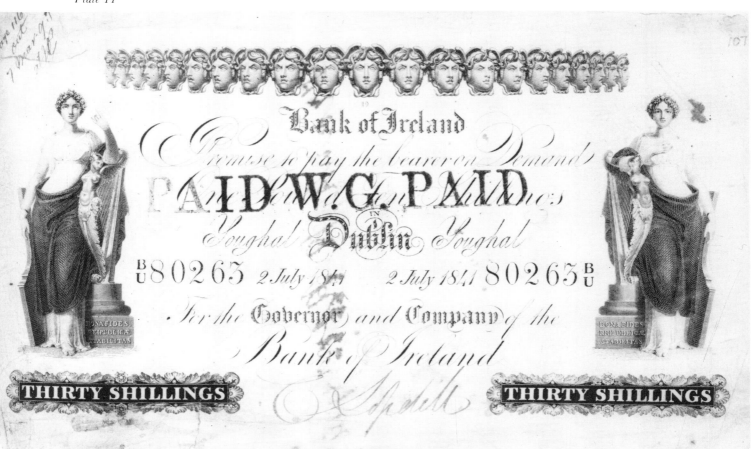

Bank of Ireland note for thirty shillings (£1 10s. 0d.), 1841

The Price of Parity

The monetary stringency required, first to screw the Irish pound to the old thirteen to twelve parity and then to move it up to its new identity with the pound sterling, was, undoubtedly, deflationary. The effects both in Ireland and Britain of the return to gold aggravated the general recession which followed the ending of the Napoleonic wars. There was here a forewarning for Mr Churchill (which if heard went unheeded) of the distress likely to accompany the restoration of the gold standard in the mid-1920s at the pre-war parity.

In Ireland, before the resumption of gold payments in 1821, a drastic contraction of the money supply was being enforced. The Bank of Ireland's note circulation was cut by one-fifth between 1819 and 1820. The shortage of money coincided with a severe economic crisis and was accentuated by the collapse of many of the private banks, leaving most districts in Ireland without any banking facilities. These banks had accounted before the crisis for about one-third of the total circulation; after it, Bank of Ireland issues of notes and post bills represented nearly three-fourths of the national currency. This dominance was, however, short-lived.

Mention of post bills brings to mind that security of money transmission was a problem even in those days. Post bills sought to answer this problem by specifying that payment would be made only after a certain interval, so that they would be valueless while in transit and payment could be stopped if they were stolen.

It is curious that, for a short period, Bank of Ireland notes were at a premium over gold and the Bank, interested in keeping up its note circulation, could refuse to accept gold coins in lodgments or in payments for its own notes. This occurred during the lead-up to the restoration of the gold standard in 1821 at a time when, outside the north of Ireland, there was virtually no demand for gold for internal circulation in Ireland. The inferior status of gold currency was due partly to the greater convenience of bank notes but also to the risk of receiving less than full value for an underweight coin. It is ironic that the Governor of the Bank of Ireland in the 1820s was the second Arthur Guinness who may never have fully appreciated that the stringency he imposed as a banker was cramping his trade as a brewer.

The perhaps over-severe verdict of Lynch and Vaizey is that 'the ultimate consequences of the revaluation of the currency and the restoration of specie in Ireland were of the greatest political and economic significance. It is possible, indeed, that the reduction of the circulating medium in this period was a major factor in limiting the growth of the use of money in rural Ireland and that the depression of demand was a cause of many of the ills attributed later — and mistakenly — to the Union'.[5] Even without a deliberate squeeze, Waterloo would have been a disaster for the Irish economy. The victory over Napoleon ushered in depression in Britain and an inevitably sharp fall in prices for Irish exports of beef, grain and textiles. It is true that monetary policy operated to accentuate rather than relieve the depression.

Development of Commercial Banking

Through various statutory extensions granted on condition of corresponding loans to government, the issued share capital of the Bank had risen to £3 million by 1821. For the extension which carried it to this figure the Bank not only had to grant the usual government loan but also to agree to a limitation of its monopoly. The Bank's note issue in Irish pounds reached a peak of £3.66 million at the end of 1824. Private and public deposits at this time exceeded £2 million. On these deposits no interest was paid. The Bank made its money largely by investing these free resources in government securities and by its private discounting and rediscounting operations. In 1824, for instance, the Bank's total income was over £400,000 — almost nine times the annual income of its initial years — and, of this, discounting provided £52,000 while most of the rest came from holdings of government securities and from the annuities paid by the government on charter-related loans from the Bank. Discounting business was contributing a shrinking share of Bank income and both lending by way of advances and overdrafts and money transmission by cheque had yet to become of major significance. Dividends paid to shareholders for the year amounted to £300,000, staff costs were a mere £32,000, note printing cost £4,000 and the government received £15,000 in lieu of stamp duty on the Bank's notes.

The Bank's dominance of the depressing Irish financial scene began to be diluted in the 1820s, first by the restriction in 1821 to within a fifty miles radius of Dublin of its note-issuing monopoly as a bank of more than six partners, and then by the emergence of the new Irish joint-stock banks, the Northern Banking Company, the Hibernian and the Provincial, all in 1825, with the Belfast Banking Company following in 1827, the National in 1834 under O'Connell's chairmanship, the Ulster and the Royal in 1836. It was the initiative of Belfast merchants which led to the Irish Banking Act of 1824 under which the Northern Banking Company was the first to be established. The Hibernian Bank was formed by a combination of Catholics and Quakers to 'put down' the monopoly of the Bank of Ireland and in a reaction against the illiberal and anti-Catholic clauses of its charter.

Apart from presiding for many years over the National, O'Connell had earlier supported the establishment of the Hibernian but, as a politician, had no compunction in the early 1830s about inciting runs on banks for gold — a piece of mischief-making to which the Provincial, being foremost in branch banking, was particularly vulnerable — or about leading the opposition to the last five-year extension (1839) of the privileges of the Bank of Ireland.

To meet the competition of the new joint-stock banks, much stronger than that of the now mostly defunct private banks, the Bank of Ireland set up, between 1825 and 1830, its first twelve branches in the principal cities and business centres of Ireland. With central banking hauteur, however, it still disdained to pay interest on deposits, although the new joint-stock banks did so from the outset, and it succumbed to the forces of competition only in 1864. After the 1820s the Bank no longer had a monopoly position but it retained its leadership and a not unimportant rôle as a bankers' bank.

The Move to College Green

A feature of the Bank's history in this opening phase which will always be remembered with pride is the move from the original brick premises in Mary's Abbey, beside an open sewer, to the classical grace of the vacated houses of parliament in College Green, adapted aesthetically to banking use by Francis Johnston, who completed the windowless façade. The Mary's Abbey premises had very soon proved inadequate and had to be extended by neighbouring acquisitions; but in this area of narrow streets and sugar refineries fire was a perpetual hazard. The Bank had, indeed, decided to move to the east side of Westmoreland Street, opposite the parliament building, in 1799 but, in the end, possession of the full site could not be secured. Consideration of the purchase of the parliament building began soon after the passing of the Act of Union — an act opposed, it is right to say, by the four La Touche members of the Irish parliament — and negotiations were completed in August 1803, the purchase price being £40,000. It is particularly gratifying that, despite a requirement to obliterate all traces of the building's parliamentary function, the Bank managed to maintain virtually intact the old House of Lords chamber and to re-instal the original chandelier and the tapestries, dating from 1733, which represent King William's victory at the Boyne and the 'glorious defence of Londonderry'. An almost equally venerable institution — the Royal Irish Academy in Dawson Street — still preserves the Lord Chancellor's chair and some of the benches, while the chandelier of the House of Commons, having first crossed the road to St Andrew's Church, now hangs over the heads of examinees in Trinity College. The original silver mace of the House of Commons was bought back by the Bank at a sale in Christie's in 1937; that of the House of Lords is now in the National Museum.

The Changing Economic and Social Scene

Though it came belatedly on the Irish scene, the Bank of Ireland was fortunate in the timing of its founding and in the buoyancy of trade and finance in its formative years from 1783 to 1815.

The second half of the eighteenth century was a period of well-sustained economic growth, with few and only temporary setbacks. Population growth and the incipient industrial revolution caused markets to expand both for foodstuffs and textile manufactures. The circumstances of war added to demand. Professor Cullen has described the years from 1793 to 1815 as the 'culminating phase of a long wave of expansion going back to the 1740s'.[6] In the final decades of the century linen accounted for well over half of all Irish exports and cotton mills were being built, with the aid of parliamentary grants, throughout the country.

The second part of the period with which this opening essay deals, 1815 to 1826, was anything but fortunate. All prices fell steeply after 1815. Both Britain and Ireland were hit by major economic crises in 1819-20 and again in 1825-6. Even if the protection afforded by Grattan's Parliament had not been removed, the cotton and woollen industries would have suffered decline. Agricultural output and exports took up again in the 1830s but, as the long Victorian era commenced, social and economic trends were increasing the vulnerability of Irish society. Between the time the Bank was established and 1841, the population doubled to over eight million. Dublin, Belfast and some well-situated towns continued to expand but most of the population increase took place in rural areas amongst labourers and smallholders. As the numbers grew, more and more subdivision of holdings had to take place and reliance on the potato crop for food increased. Meanwhile, the important income supplement once provided by domestic spinning and weaving was rapidly disappearing as steam power and factory organisation took over and the textile industry contracted into the north-east corner. The scene was being set for social disaster. Much the same combination of circumstances led to harrowing crises in Silesia and Flanders in the 1840s, but coal and iron came to their rescue later. Despite the opening up of Ireland by roads, canals and railways, the spread of a monetary economy was slowed down by the general poverty of the rural population, the prolonged depression in maritime Ireland after the Napoleonic wars, and the tragic disruption caused in the 1840s by the Great Famine.

References

1   George O'Brien, *The economic history of Ireland in the eighteenth century*, Dublin and London 1918, p. 62.

2   The quotations are from *The Querist*, as cited in Joseph Johnston, *Bishop Berkeley's Querist in historical perspective*, Dundalk 1970, pp. 50, 177-8.

3   J. A. Schumpeter, *History of economic analysis*, New York 1954, especially pp. 718-24.

4   G. L. Barrow, *The emergence of the Irish banking system, 1820-45*, Dublin 1975, pp. 51, 44.

5   Patrick Lynch and John Vaizey, *Guinness's brewery in the Irish economy, 1759-1876*, Cambridge 1960.

6   L. M. Cullen, *An economic history of Ireland since 1660*, London 1972, p. 100.

Plate 12

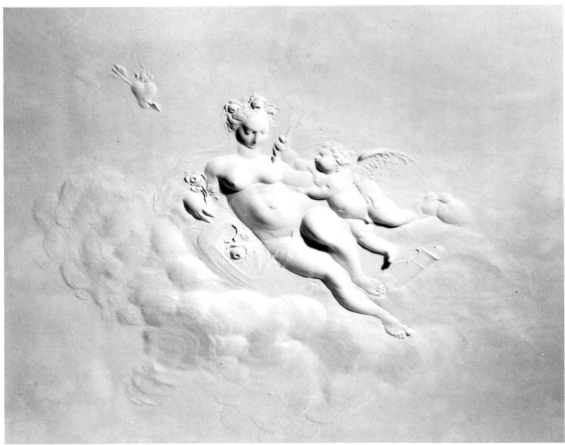

Detail of the La Touche Venus and Cupid ceiling

Plate 13   The Flaxman/Smyth model for 'Commerce', College Green pediment

The Victorian Bank, 1824—1914*

Oliver MacDonagh

IN the decade following Waterloo, the Bank of Ireland lost several of its advantages. The union of the British and Irish exchequers in 1817 robbed it of its intimate connection with government. The Bank of England now dominated the combined national finances, and Ireland was reduced to a branch office of the British treasury. Indeed, there were but three transactions, all of a humdrum character, between the treasury and the Bank of Ireland (hereafter the Bank) in the quarter century before the Great Famine. Meanwhile, the renewal of the Bank's charter in 1821 cut into its virtual monopoly of Irish public banking. Joint-stock banking with the right of note-issue was now permitted outside a radius of fifty miles (Irish) of Dublin. However, the renewing act (1 & 2 Geo. IV c. 72) laid down that the members of an Irish joint-stock bank must reside both in Ireland and outside the radius, and earlier legislation had settled that each member of such a bank must sign every note issued. There were further legal obstacles, but these two between them seemed to assure the Bank that no rival could in fact be constituted; and it continued to preside serenely and alone for three years more, resting upon the guarantee contained in the 1821 act that no further concession would be made before 1 January 1838.

But there were two weaknesses in the Bank's situation. First, the private banking system had largely collapsed in Ireland in the financial crisis of 1820 — outside Belfast and Cork, only two small private banks in minor inland towns survived. As the Bank resolutely refused to establish branches, this meant that the reason for contracting the monopoly in 1821, the provision of provincial banking facilities, remained unsatisfied. Secondly, the Bank lacked, or at least neglected to build or maintain, political influence at Westminster; whereas there were other people with such influence eager to fill what looked like a profitable vacuum. In 1824 assaults were launched from three different directions. A group of Belfast merchants petitioned for the withdrawal of the disabilities holding them back from establishing a joint-stock bank in the north; a group of Catholic merchants in Dublin petitioned similarly, with the added aims of the right of note-issue within the fifty-mile radius and also perhaps the right to establish branches close to Dublin; and a group of London capitalists, supported by leading Irish Whigs and Tories, proposed a branch bank system after the Scottish pattern, again to be free from the fatal existing restraints.

At first the Bank was unalarmed. But it rapidly discovered that trust in princes — now that they had been constitutionalised at least — was misplaced. During 1824-5 all the protections (extra-radius Irish residence for shareholders, joint signatures on notes, and the various technical difficulties) were removed by legislation. The

---

* Purists may cavil at the use of the term 'Victorian' to describe a period which begins before 1837 and continues after 1901. But Professor MacDonagh is viewing the Bank in the context of Victorian business administration and finding it in some ways a very Victorian institution. His title, therefore, though chronologically inexact, expresses a true historical perception and for that reason I have preferred it to the other available alternatives (Ed.).

Northern, Hibernian and Provincial Banks were the outcomes of the respective petitions of 1824. The Northern was comparatively small and localised, although it was, of course, strategically well-placed to take advantage of the country's principal centre of economic growth. The Hibernian was also comparatively small, and it lacked influence in parliament. Its crucial request, the right to issue notes in Dublin, was rejected by government, though with the promise (later repudiated) that it would be granted when the Bank of Ireland charter came up for renewal in 1838. On the other hand, it had a sure base in the Dublin Catholic mercantile community who had established it in the belief that the Bank discriminated against them: they would continue to support it despite its disadvantages. The Provincial, however, represented a real threat to the Bank. It had capital, expertise, organisational ability and the ear of government.

In the last quarter of 1824 the Court reached the painful decision that it must compete immediately with the Provincial, and set up branches where its prospective rival proposed to do. The race was on. In 1825 the Bank established seven branches against four set up by the Provincial, but by 1829 the proportions were 9:15 and by 1833, 12:21. In Cork, Limerick, Waterford, Belfast, Derry, Galway, Sligo, Armagh, Wexford and Clonmel, they were direct rivals. The Bank had Westport and Newry to itself, but the Provincial could counter this with Athlone, Kilkenny, Ballina, Tralee, Youghal, Enniskillen, Monaghan, Banbridge, Ballymena and Birr. The Bank had opened no branches within the radius, relying on its monopoly to protect it there. Although several of the Bank's branches, such as Cork and Belfast, were successful from the start, there can be little doubt that the Provincial was victor in the opening round. Its profits and dividends grew steadily, from £28,000 and 4 per cent in 1826-7 to £61,000 and 8 per cent in 1834-5. Meanwhile, the Bank's dividend was unchanged at 10 per cent from 1809 to 1829 and fell to 9 per cent in 1830, while its reserves were practically stationary between 1821 and 1832. The explanation would appear to be the superior management of the Provincial. The Bank, in setting up branches, sought to delegate them to local businessmen or bankers, on a comparatively small retaining salary and what might be a considerable income from discounting commissions. The local agents employed their own staffs and made their own office arrangements initially. In places this worked satisfactorily: Wexford, where the Redmond brothers in effect transformed their well-run private bank into a Bank branch, is one example. But generally it failed because neither the untrained agents nor their employees fitted into a large, centralised, expert organisation. By the early 1830s, the Bank was sending its men from head office to instruct the clerks — perhaps some agents and sub-agents, too — in the provinces. This, however, proved insufficient, and in 1834 it was decided to take over all the branch employees and replace both them and the agents, in time, with men regularly recruited and experienced in head office or efficient branch work. Perhaps it was not until 1860 or even later that the original agency system and its appendages had worked their way through completely to death or retirement. The Provincial, on the other hand, recruited its first managers from Scottish branch banking and similar areas of expertise, put them on a level with the local 'directors' and connected them effectively to London, where the major decisions were taken. It was, moreover, an aggressive and innovative business. When the Bank refused to exchange notes with it and demanded payment in gold, the Provincial set up a legal action which soon brought the Bank to heel. When the Provincial suffered from 'runs' in Munster in 1826 and 1828, while the Bank escaped because it was required to pay gold only at College Green, Thomas Spring Rice, a leading Whig and director of the Provincial, successfully carried a bill to remove the Bank's exemption. The most serious clash occurred in 1827 when the Bank claimed that the Provincial's promise on its notes that they would be paid in Dublin by its agent, a private bank, broke the prohibition on note-issuing by joint-stock banks within the radius. The Provincial resisted, and the Bank took legal action, which it won first before a jury and then on appeal. The Provincial re-appealed, but meanwhile Spring Rice asked the ministry to intervene. Under government pressure the Bank agreed to a compromise whereby the wording on the Provincial notes was altered and its Dublin agent was required to keep a special account at the Bank through which all the disputed notes would pass. But the Provincial secured its primary objective — the ability to pay its notes anywhere within the radius — and insisted that this be statutorily enacted in 1830. Contrariwise, the Hibernian lacked political weight. The right of note-issue was of critical importance at this time. In effect, banks could borrow at $1\frac{1}{2}$—2 per cent by issuing notes, whereas other borrowing cost 5—6 per cent. Operating within the radius, the Hibernian could not issue notes, but it did issue rough equivalents which it named 'tokens', justifying them on the ground that they contained no specific promise to pay. When the Bank protested in 1827, the government intervened *against* the Hibernian, and its critical battle was lost.

Politics also affected banking in a more ordinary Irish way. In 1830, 1831 and 1833 O'Connell launched runs for gold on the Bank, the Provincial and the savings banks in Waterford, Cork and other Munster towns in order to bring pressure upon the government in various crises. None was especially damaging financially. In fact, they may have increased confidence in the banks' stability, and they certainly led to some 'counter-strikes' by merchants refusing to buy from farmers until the run was called off. But it was costly and laborious to carry and distribute sufficient quantities of gold to meet these sudden demands. O'Connell himself, however, was no enemy to banking: the Provincial had, in fact, retained him as counsel in the Bank's actions of 1827-9. Having failed to beat them, he proceeded to join the banks in 1834.

The prospectus of the National Bank issued in that year recognised the remarkable achievements of the Provincial, but discerned two weaknesses, over-centralisation and what might nowadays be termed multinationalism, the failure to 'unite itself with a body in Ireland, with whom to share its profits, as well as fortify itself in principle'. It had, moreover, opened a mere twenty-one branches in nine years. The National would remedy this first by devolution — subsidiary local banks, half owned locally and half by the London parent company, which would, however, retain both 'supreme control' and a veto over proposed local directors — and, secondly, by extending banking facilities much more widely geographically and much deeper socially. It lived up to its word. After little more than a year's operation, it already ran twenty-seven branches, and several of these in places without any existing bank. In Kerry, for example, not only Tralee but also Cahirciveen, Listowel, Killarney and Killorglin were already being served by the National. From the start it set out to attract small capital as well as large, by interest on current accounts, by preferential interest on deposit accounts below £30, by offering extra-banking financial services for a small commission and by waiving charges for religious and charitable institutions. By the beginning of 1836, it had already more shareholders than the Provincial (773 to 644). 'National' was really meant in two senses: it set out to provide both a comprehensive network for the whole island and a financial organisation for repealers. Seven of the original committee were Repeal MPs and three of the first directors were O'Connell himself (as Governor), his son, Morgan, and his son-in-law, Fitzsimon. At the same time, the committee included some city MPs and the board some London moneymen, among them T. Lamie Murray, an able disciple of Thomas Joplin, the celebrated banking reformer of the 1820s. Thus, despite its nationalism, the National had access from the beginning to London capital and expertise, and these must have contributed something to its early success. It was not therefore as different from the Provincial as the prospectus had foreshadowed, and it rapidly moved back to 'over-centralisation' too. By 1837 the subsidiary company system had proved so cumbersome that all these companies except two (Clonmel and Carrick-on-Suir) were amalgamated with the London parent; and nineteen years later even the two survivors were swallowed up.

The Bank responded to the challenge of the National by opening ten new branches during 1834-40 — but several of these were in its protected area of the radius — and the Provincial by opening seventeen (five of which, however, were soon withdrawn). But these were really holding operations. The Provincial's profits and reserves were higher in 1835 than they were to be again for twenty years; and the Bank's story is much the same. By 1850, the National branches totalled forty-eight as against the Provincial's thirty-eight and the Bank's twenty-four.

In the two decades, 1825-45, then, the Bank's response to the challenge of the joint-stock banks was adequate in the sense that it almost held its ground, but unimpressive in that Irish banking business had grown prodigiously without any increase in the Bank's profits or reserves, despite the fact that it still enjoyed a monopoly within the radius. Various reasons can be ascribed for this. Its initial agency system generally provided poor local management and organisation, and even in the years 1835-45 these weaknesses were only gradually being eliminated. After its initial burst, it was slow to establish new branches, and refused several requests to do so from quite substantial towns. It would not allow any interest on deposits — this was regarded as 'not respectable' in Dublin — although the Provincial and the National did so from the start. It was slow to innovate: it did not enter the important field of railway financing until the end of 1847, which was very late. It may have suffered from being labelled the 'Protestant' and 'unionist' bank, as its rivals set out to project the opposite images. Not least, its Court was drawn from small segments of Dublin businessmen and lesser landowners without either financial or political connections in London.

On the other hand, it is unfair to compare the Bank directly with its joint-stock rivals. As, in several respects, a central bank, it was under some disadvantages. It was required to lend the bulk of its capital to the government at a comparatively modest rate, $3\frac{1}{2}$ per cent. It was prohibited from making mortgages on land: it had been felt originally that a state bank should not have money tied up in long-term ventures, and this hereditary caution may explain the Bank's reluctance to enter the railway field at first. Above all, it took on, in the 1820s and 1830s, the rôle of bank of last resort in Ireland, and this, while adding to its status and influence, placed burdens and charges upon it which, by definition, all other Irish banks escaped. This rôle was adopted in a piecemeal, *ad hoc* manner. It had come to the rescue of many of the private banks during the crisis of 1820. Even the *Freeman's Journal*, no friend, reported, 'The liberality of the Bank of Ireland has had much to do in softening the extremity of the distress'.[1] The joint-stock banks were at first coldly treated. The Provincial was afforded accommodation only on the strict financial merits of its case, and the Hibernian's drafts were accepted in lodgments only on condition that it kept a substantial credit at the Bank. A suggestion from the Deputy Governor of the Bank of England in 1829 that its sister Bank should stand behind the Irish joint-stock banks and in return supervise note circulation and the system generally was roundly rejected. But during the 'run' of 1833, it assured the Provincial that its own stock of specie was sufficient to support all the Irish banks; and three years later, in the very grave crisis produced by the collapse of the mushroom Agricultural and Commercial Bank, it gave a clear lead to all the other Irish joint-stock banks and freely provided them with accommodation even on the security of commercial bills. The National and Provincial received £249,000, roughly half the total of the advances. This decidedly established the Bank as lender of last resort. In the course of the post-mortem, the governor of the Bank of England, rather unfairly, accused it of speaking

> as if the preservation of your credit as an individual Bank were almost your only object ... The elevated position, however, occupied by the Bank of Ireland as the Chartered Bank ... imposes on it not the care of its own credit only, but the protection of the banking and commercial security of Ireland generally.

In reply, the Bank agreed that its primary business 'as a National Bank' was the upholding of the general credit in Ireland.[2]

The implicit identification of the situations of the Banks of England and Ireland was not altogether just. The Bank of Ireland was a private corporation with duties to its stockholders. It was statutorily limited to an interest rate of 5 per cent and could therefore not act — profitably at any rate — as the bankers' banker. After 1825, it gained much less than its counterpart from being government banker. Its work in this sphere was very much smaller than the Bank of England's, fixed in scale, mechanical in nature, only moderately rewarded and not even exclusive outside the radius, for as early as 1828 the Provincial had, through its political pressure, won the right to act as banker there for the excise, post office and stamp revenues. Thus the Bank had to act

Plate 14   Money-chest brought to Ireland by William III

as a commercial as well as a central bank if it were to survive in post-1825 Irish banking. Still, after all allowances are made for the difficulties which its second rôle created for its first, it still seems fair to adjudge its commercial performance between 1825 and 1845 as only mediocre.

The Bank's charter ran out in 1838, but with few alterations it was renewed from year to year down to 1845, by which time the English Bank Charter Act of 1844 enforced some fundamental changes in the Irish system. The essential purpose of this statute was the control of note-issues, and this could not be effective if any part of the United Kingdom were exempt. The Bankers (Ireland) Act of 1845 withdrew the Bank's monopoly within the fifty-mile radius, and permitted the Irish banks which already issued notes to continue to do so at their 1844-5 levels, with any excess issue to be covered by specie actually in their hands. The basic (or fiduciary) levels were fixed as follows:

Bank of Ireland	£ 3,738,428
Provincial Bank	927,667
National Bank	852,269
Ulster Banking Company	311,079
Belfast Banking Company	281,611
Northern Banking Company	243,440
	£ 6,354,494

The Bank also failed in its attempt to have the restriction on its lending on land mortgages repealed. Goulburn, the Chancellor of the Exchequer, argued that a state bank should not enjoy the licence of a fully commercial one. On the other hand, the Bank successfully resisted attempts to permit public funds to be paid into *any* bank in Ireland, and to allow the unlucky Dublin-based Hibernian and Royal Banks to join in note-issuing. It was confirmed as government banker, though without any payment for its services: the interest rate of $3\frac{1}{2}$ per cent on the Bank's capital deposited with the government was deemed by Goulburn to be a sufficient recompense. Nor was the Bank on a par with the Bank of England in note-issuing. The latter was ultimately to take over the entire issuing of notes in England and Wales, whereas the Bank was but one of six banks of issue in Ireland, though much the largest.

Paradoxically, the 1845 act enhanced in several ways the Bank's rôle as a central bank. Its leadership of the Irish banks became more formal and specific. It had always been the main channel for the import and export of specie. Now this function became more pronounced, and the Bank set up stocks of coin in each of the provincial capitals, giving discretion to the local agents to advance specie for short periods to the other banks as occasion arose. Again, it had early established a note clearing system in Dublin, which it had developed *pari passu* with the development of the joint-stock banks. Now it created a more elaborate and efficient machinery for clearing the cheques as well as notes of all six Irish issuing banks (it also arranged to act itself as clearing agent for the non-issuing Hibernian and Royal Banks). Each member of the new exchange deposited a fixed sum in exchequer bills; and if after the daily balance, the share of any bank exceeded its agreed limit it had to sell the surplus to the banks in deficit. The proportions required — the Bank 38 per cent, the Provincial, 22, the National, 17, and the three northern banks, 11 each — may give an indication of the relative business conducted by the six in 1846. The exchange worked admirably, and preceded its English counterpart by nearly twenty years. Finally, the Bank, freed from limitation upon the rate of interest which it charged, became the 'bankers' bank' for all the Irish joint-stock banks other than the Provincial and National, affording them set overdraft facilities upon the deposit of securities at the current rate charged by the Bank of England. At the same time, the Hibernian and Royal agreed to issue Bank of Ireland notes exclusively in return for accommodation to the amount of notes circulating at 2 per cent below the usual overdraft rate. Thus, the Bank established its domination of the Irish banking system. The Provincial and National were indirectly but none the less effectually governed by the Bank's policy operating through the major sector which it controlled.

As a commercial concern however the Bank fared comparatively poorly. In 1864 the Court, through a committee, conducted a protracted inquiry into its performance since 1845 which presented sorry reading for the directors. It found, first, that the Bank's note circulation, despite the arrangement with the non-issuing banks, had fallen to some 54 per cent of the 1846 level. The other issuing banks had collectively held their own — mainly because the National had actually *increased* its issue by over 50 per cent — so that the Bank's proportion of the total Irish note issue had declined from 59 to 43 per cent. Secondly, it was found that the Bank's proportion of private deposits in Irish banks had fallen from 34 per cent in 1846 to 12 per cent in 1864: 'the whole private deposits in Ireland had increased by about £7,500,000, and . . . very nearly the entire of that increase went into the hands of the joint-stock banks.' More generally, the committee was concerned by the Bank's failure to share in the remarkable progress of the joint-stock banks since 1845. True, the years 1861-4 had shown some faltering, but this was seen, like the setbacks of 1847 and 1851, as a brief interruption; and it was gloomily anticipated that pressure for re-allocating note issues to correspond to the long-term trends would soon make itself felt: 'there can be little doubt but that before long a legislative alteration in the proportions of circulation allowed to each bank will be applied for'. The committee concluded that 'some decided action' by the Bank was absolutely necessary 'at least to arrest any further injury to its interests if not to recover . . . its former position'.[3] In only three years since 1830 had its dividend reached the 10 per cent which had been normal in the early nineteenth century.

Thus the Bank had actually fallen back as a commercial concern while most of its competitors, and in particular the National, had surged ahead, increasing profits, dividends, deposits and capital. No doubt, it had made modest gains from its new activity of bankers' banker (although it seems to have run the Dublin note and cheque exchange for nothing); but these could have counted for comparatively little in the balance. One reason for its slowness to react to its retardation was undoubtedly the survival of the prohibition on its lending money on land mortgages. After its failure to have this removed in 1845, the Court came to assume that it denied them a highly important section of Irish business. When the Encumbered Estates Bill was in passage in 1849, they again made strenuous efforts to have the prohibition withdrawn, and throughout the 1850s they rehearsed this grievance and tended to ascribe their lack of progress to it automatically. It was not only that land dealings increased significantly after 1849, but also that capital was being borrowed extensively for the Irish 'agricultural revolution' of the 1850s and that many Irish businessmen and manufacturers were now buying into land, and presumably banking where they could get money for its purchase or management. At last, in 1860, the Bank, though with considerable difficulty and in the teeth of opposition from the veteran Spring Rice (long since ennobled as Lord Monteagle), succeeded in having the offending clause repealed.

But it was then found that the change had little effect upon the Bank's fortunes. Hence the eventual alarms of 1864. Of course, the committee found the first explanation of the lack of progress in the withdrawal of the monopoly within the radius, although the fact that it opened only two new branches within this considerable region between 1845 and 1870 does not suggest any very resolute effort to defend its business there. But the committee also gave great weight to two other factors, the rapid increase in the branches of the joint-stock banks, and their granting interest on deposits. Again both courses had always been open to the Bank, and since 1845 at least obvious expedients in the light of their rivals' activities. In fact, the Bank had opened as many new branches as any of its rivals, other than the Provincial, in the 1850s. The difficulty was that its base in 1845 had been very small for so dominant an institution, so that in 1860 it still accounted for a mere 15 per cent of Irish branches as against the National's near 30 per cent and the Provincial's near 25 per cent. Interest on deposits had ever been anathema to the Bank, probably because it traditionally enjoyed a considerable body of them free, and the change would lead immediately to new outgoings. The committee calculated that it would need over £1 million of fresh deposits before it would begin to gain significantly from the turnabout in policy. None the less, it firmly recommended that interest on deposits be forthwith granted, and it also supported the rapid expansion of branches if — but only if — this were done.

The Court showed unusual reluctance to adopt a committee report in this particular instance, some directors clinging to the argument that the Bank of England granted no interest on its deposits. But in the end the bullet had to be bitten, and on 1 October 1864 interest on deposits was announced, and a new programme of branch creation undertaken.

The programme was certainly pursued with vigour. Over the next twelve years twenty-four new branches were established, almost doubling the Bank's total. Certainly this improved the Bank's relative position in terms of country outlets. But the improvement was not marked — from 15 to 16.6 per cent of the whole by 1880 — because it formed part of a general wave of expansion. During 1860-80 the number of bank branches grew from 180 to 479 (sixty-four of these sub-branches). In particular, a new star arose in the form of the Munster Bank, which was not even in existence when the Bank's decisions were reached in 1864, but which possessed three-quarters as many branches as the Bank itself by 1880.

The leap in the number of bank branches was one expression of the golden age of Irish commercial banking, as we might term the mid-Victorian years — 1858-79, to speak precisely. The Bank shared moderately in the wave of prosperity. Its branch profits increased from £78,000 in 1860 to £100,000 in 1870 and £127,000 in 1875. But this was well below the average performance. To look, for example, at its later marriage partners, the Hibernian's net profits rose from £24,000 in 1860 to £38,000 in 1870 and £62,000 in 1875, while the National's increased from £102,000 in 1869 to £116,000 in 1870 and £197,000 in 1875. Both were, moreover, adding considerably to their reserves, while the 'Rest' fund of the Bank remained practically stationary. The general pattern may be summarised thus: that from the late 1850s to the late 1870s

Irish banking business doubled, with matching — or better — aggregate profits, while the Bank's business (including new deposits) and profits increased by roughly 60 per cent.

But the late 1870s represented a sort of apogee in nineteenth-century Irish banking. The disastrous harvests of 1877-9 and the concomitant land war plunged Irish agriculture into prolonged turmoil and distress, and this also took a distant toll in several important business failures in the succeeding decade. Herein undoubtedly lies the fundamental explanation of the lower profits and reduced dividends of 1880-1900. But an important contributory factor must have been the continued expansion of branch banking. Nearly 200 branches and sub-branches were added to the system in these gloomy years. It is noteworthy that apart from an initial faltering in the early 1880s the volume of banking business in Ireland did not decline but continued to grow rapidly for the remainder of the century. Of course it was advantageous socially that banking services should have become more widely available and more extensively employed — and possibly cheaper too as competition intensified. From the industry's point of view, however, this advance was made at the expense of its profitability. At most, the expansion into new places, the attraction of new classes of customer and the consequent considerable increases in staff and *matériel* enabled the Irish banks to stay at or near the point to which they had declined by the early 1880s.

In this phase of recession the Bank appears to have fared relatively well. Its net profits did not fall greatly in the years 1875-85, and thereafter they remained comparatively stable. By contrast the Hibernian's fell as low as £17,000 in 1885 and had recovered to only £43,000 by 1900. Moreover, its reserves were exhausted by 1885 and never replenished in the remaining years of the nineteenth century. The fortunes of the National, however, followed much the same pattern as the Bank's; if anything, its history was the happier. Its net profits fell to £176,000 in 1885 — some 20 per cent below its record of the previous decade — but had recovered to £232,000 by 1900. In general, the National and the Bank had come to resemble each other remarkably by the late nineteenth century. The National had more branches — by about one-fifth — and its average profits were higher, again by approximately one-fifth. Their respective totals of deposit and current accounts together mounted more or less in step, with the Bank's always slightly in advance. (The National's totals of deposits alone, however, were always considerably the higher.) The National was the more conservative in adding steadily to its reserve. The Bank's was to remain unchanged down to 1910. Correspondingly, the National's dividends were kept comparatively low for a longer period. But the two were identical in policy in opening fewer new branches and sub-branches than other Irish banks in 1880-1900: indeed, the National pruned its sub-branches most severely. This may indeed help to account for their relatively better performances.

Overall the National was probably the most successful concern in the later as well as in the mid nineteenth century. But they were not strictly comparable institutions. The Bank was still to a degree the state's bank. Between 1858 and 1865, under the influence of 'treasury reform' and Gladstonian candle-end saving, its official rôle was diminished. The government funds and unclaimed dividends at its disposal were very greatly reduced, while at the same time the interest rate which it received on the £2.6 million compulsorily lent to the government was reduced from $3\frac{1}{2}$ to 3 per cent. Traditionally, the Bank had, in true eighteenth-century fashion, regarded the use of government funds as its primary reward for managing government business. Henceforward it was to be paid fees for this work upon agreed scales. The Court expressed its satisfaction when these matters were finally arranged in 1865: indeed it was obsequiously grateful. It is very doubtful, however, whether any institution bargaining with the ferocious mid-Victorian treasury held its ground. And there was worse to come. In 1892 the Chancellor, Goschen (all the more a Gladstonian in finance for having abjured the master as home ruler) lowered the government's interest rate to $2\frac{3}{4}$ falling to $2\frac{1}{2}$ per cent, as well as effectively reducing the scale of fees for the management of government business. The late nineteenth-century Bank could surely have employed its 2.6 million to better advantage than the 3 or $2\frac{3}{4}$ per cent return afforded by the exchequer; and the government work, ever expanding in type and complexity, was very costly in terms of labour. Moreover, the assumption that the state bank needed extraordinarily high reserves was never modified, and the Bank's were always in excess of £1 million, several times larger than those of any of its Irish rivals. Overall then it seems likely that the Bank's governmental rôle was decidedly and increasingly disadvantageous to it as a commercial concern. At the same time, the solidity of its governmental bases may help to explain why the Bank did not fall so far as most others during the phases of depression, as well as to explain its relative sluggishness in the more prosperous years.

The three most remarkable features of Irish banking in the final years 1900-14 were a further rapid expansion in the number of branches and sub-branches, a continued steady increase in the volume of business conducted, and stationary, or more exactly slightly lower, profits, upon the whole. The three may be in fact interconnected. These were years in which one particular form of agricultural revolution was gathering pace in Ireland. At last the ownership of land was passing on a very considerable scale from the landlords to the small — often very small — tenant farmers. This created much potential new business for the banks and prompted the expansion of at least occasional banking services to ever smaller and more remote centres. But the new business was probably unremunerative. Current and deposit accounts were often tiny in the country branches, and advances of less than £10 were quite common. Indeed, the Bank itself advanced sums as small as £2-3. Often these loans were but slowly re-paid and swiftly renewed, if possible. Thus, it does not seem at all implausible to connect the further growth in commercial banking with lower profitability — at least immediately. True, this was nothing new. As early as the 1870s and 1880s the Bank's branches in poverty-stricken Co. Mayo, for example, with practically no landlord, professional or mercantile business of significance, had had to turn to the poor tenant farmers to furnish customers. But the land purchase act of 1903 vastly increased the numbers and needs of such a clientele.

Perhaps surprisingly, in view of its origins and governing ethos, the Bank participated fully in this popularisation. In fact it was spoken of as probably the leader in 'cater[ing] for the needs of the small rural classes'. At the same time, the Court was fully aware that the extension of services was unprofitable. They were not disturbed. The Bank's self-image was still to a degree that of a great public utility as well as a commercial enterprise. Correspondingly, it also saw itself as *primus inter pares* among Irish banks if not as ultimate controller of the entire system. Nor was this a mere illusion of grandeur. When, for example, in 1903 the Irish banks, in the heat of the new competition, began to offer different interest rates on deposits — characteristically, from its entry into the field in 1864 the Bank had effectively laid down the standard —

the Bank by persistent pressure and negotiation soon restored the old uniformity. Negotiation with its companion-rivals was always necessary. The Bank had no warrant to command. But it none the less invariably took either the initiative or the headship in all joint action. In short, the Bank was accepted as the natural hereditary leader among banks. But this proud station could not have been established or maintained without considerable sagacity and tact.

Administratively, the Bank was an archetypal Victorian office of the better sort. The directors were active, and therefore informed, managers. Almost all were members of one or more of the six specialised committees which divided the day-to-day work of the Court; and many acted on the 'deputations' — or branch inspections by directors — which continued throughout the nineteenth century. The head office, little changed in staff numbers (they increased from 170 to 200) during our period, was divided into twenty or so 'departments'; some consisted of a single officer, but others, the cash, transfer, ledger and agents 'offices', for example, were comparatively large. This division of labour and function was already substantially established by 1825. Rational and effective, it was little altered until the age of 'management studies' dawned in 1910, with reports on the operations of all sections by the Bank's auditors.

The main area of change and growth was, of course, the branches. These were subject to three successive major changes during the half-century 1825-75. First, their subordinate staffs became employees of the Bank rather than of the agents; secondly, the agents also became direct employees of the Bank rather than individuals or partnerships to whom the Bank's business was farmed out; and thirdly, the branches ceased to be treated as essentially separate from head office in terms of staff, and transfers between the two 'systems' ceased to be exceptional. Thus centralisation, professionalism and uniformity advanced steadily in the Bank in the middle quarters of the nineteenth century, just as they were doing contemporaneously in the public administration in general. Numerically, the staff in branches steadily overhauled the head office staff during our years. By 1840, it was (in round figures) half as large; by 1870, equal; and by 1914, 350 as against 200. This meant of course that the staff as a whole more than trebled in size between 1825 and 1914, ending at 550 officials.

Employment in the Bank was eagerly sought, and for good reason. Salaries were minute in the probationary and early years — the need for a protracted period of family support ensured a degree of 'gentlemanliness' — but thereafter attained a respectable clerkly competence even for those who never reached responsible office. Moreover, the stipends for the middle and senior grades increased steadily — by nearly 100 per cent in all — between 1830 and 1900. This was far in advance of the increase in living costs (even allowing for a more expensive *style* of living) during the period. By the end of the century, an agent's emoluments averaged some £400 per annum, to which we should add perhaps £100 for a house and other perquisites and £50-£60 for his commissions as insurance agent — for the Bank had agreed formally to agents acting for both life (1870) and fire (1891) companies. Of course the principal branch managers and the most senior officials at head office earned much more, between £900 and £1,200 in general. Thus the Bank provided a solid middle and upper middle-class occupation — if one could survive the initial penury — and the spasmodic but repeated bursts of branch-opening meant that reasonable careers were constantly opening up to talent: doubtless luck or favour assisted in many an ascent.

The Bank was also truly Victorian in its paternalism. From very early in its history, staff were permitted to retire upon 'annuities'. For long this was allowed only for ill-health or 'infirmity', and the amount of the annuity depended on the Court's estimation of the recipient's worth, moral as well as in terms of service rendered. None the less any such concession was gracious by the standards of early Victorian Ireland. Still more so was the allowance, from 1806 onwards, of widows' pensions and education money for orphaned children — disarmingly, the Court persisted in the belief that these would encourage the clerks 'to a continued exertion in the discharge of their respective duties'![4] Not only were such grants unusually generous by contemporary standards; their rules were also generously interpreted. Maiden sisters were sometimes equated with widows; education grants were sometimes extended for a year or two; dead clerks' arrears — borrowing against salary was understandable in the days of quarterly payment — were sometimes written off. The sums involved would seem miniscule to us, but the 'respectable' often did live then at or near the Micawberian margin. By the same token, the Court attempted to help in the struggle for genteel survival by inculcating habits of thrift and prudence. It gave preferential interest rates on staff deposits, especially for small sums and for junior clerks. Thrift and prudence on the Bank's own account were served by limiting the amounts of the favoured deposits strictly, lest the relatives of staff members should take advantage of the Smilesean carrot.

The Bank's paternalism wore another face; that of the awful Victorian *paterfamilias*. The order books evidence ever more elaborate regulations to ensure attendance by 9.30 a.m., to counter early departures, to stamp out the reading of newspapers or the pursuit of private affairs in the office 'or any like mode of creating inattention',[5] to eradicate from the service those who contracted debt or signed promissory notes or dealt in 'speculative' stocks — even to outlaw match-boxes from clerks' desks! Departmental heads and agents were not merely encouraged but even enjoined to delate offenders to the Court. This bred obsequiousness, at least on paper. Erring officers almost welcomed the rod; certainly some fell over themselves to acknowledge that they deserved it. 'I have neglected my duties', wrote one peccant agent in 1847, 'which must shake all confidence on the part of the Board in my judgment as a man of business'.[6] Correspondingly, Jove's frowns were expected to be feared. It seemed enough to the Court, when anathematising match-boxes in 1857, to pronounce that any guilty clerk 'will incur their displeasure'.[7] A few years earlier an agent who had allowed further bills against an overdrawn account was told that, since 'experience will prove an impressive lesson ... they do not mean to visit the transaction with any heavier mark of their displeasure than the expression of their extreme disapprobation'.[8]

As time passed however so did the Court's hand appear to lighten. Increasingly, the staff, even the most junior, were regarded, and treated, more like responsible men and less as arrested schoolboys. In several of the inspections of the 1870s and 1880s, for example, each member of a branch appears to have had the opportunity to give his judgment of the local situation; and these views were really given a weight. *Pari passu*, a combination of growing staff numbers and the general late nineteenth-century passion for codification led to the regularisation of pensions and allowances of all types. This meant a loss of flexibility. But it was more than compensated by substantial increases in amount and the practical certainty of receipt (the Court reserved the right — rarely exercised — to withhold a pension or education fees wherever it regarded the pensioner's conduct as opprobrious or the school chosen as unsatisfactory). The modern 'career structure' of forty-five years service, with generous retirement, widows and education provisions, was fully formalised in 1889-90. The age of rights had finally displaced the age of grace and favour.

In many ways, the Bank Guarantee Fund, to which officials were required to contribute in order to make good defalcations, epitomised these several characteristics. The total sum demanded for the fund increased steadily as both branches and instances of embezzlement grew markedly after 1865. The staff were informed in detail of each case of fraud and told whether the fund could safely bear it or whether a fresh 'levy', graded according to rank, would have to be deducted from their salaries. In certain respects, the Court's attitude was highly authoritarian. The members were given no voice in determining either the total, or the fate of surpluses, of the fund. They were ordered to report in confidence any indications that a fellow-member might be in or heading towards financial difficulties, and punished, sometimes severely, for failures in vigilance or precautions. A Court Order of 1 July 1890 ran:

> Had some of the members of the Fund at the branches where the defalcations now in question took place, followed this course [reporting their suspicions], and otherwise discharged their duties faithfully, those unfortunate losses could not possibly have occurred, as you will probably have gathered from the fact with which you are, no doubt, acquainted that an official who had been in one of the branches was called upon to resign, and one who had been in another, has had his retiring allowance reduced by £100 a year, which sum is being applied to recoup the Guarantee Fund the loss it has sustained at that branch. It will, therefore, be seen that any omission on the part of a member to protect the Fund, is not only likely to result in a loss to it, but also to be disastrous more or less to himself.[9]

On the other hand, the decision on the continued membership of an indebted official, or the personal responsibility for the loss where a member had been negligent, was left to the vote of the staff in general. When one sub-agent declared that he was now clear of his notorious 'pecuniary difficulties' apart from his Bank loan, each officer was 'distinctly asked whether they have any objection to his [the sub-agent's] name being continued as secured by this Fund for the future'.[10] Correspondingly, when an agent's carelessness had led to a clerk rifling £62 — 'I plead guilty to allowing the Bill Case at all out of my possession, and throw myself on the generosity of the Directors'[11] — it was left to the entire membership to determine whether the agent or the Fund should bear the loss. The Victorian clerk probably adjudged his Court as the legendary Victorian schoolboy had his headmaster, 'a beast, but a just beast'.

What sort of men were the bank officers? Our best — and practically our only worthwhile — single source is a collection of notes made by the Bank's inspectors during their visits to the branches between 1888 and 1903. By definition this excluded head office. It was also unsystematic. Such basic classification as religion, father's occupation and marital status was only spasmodically noted. None the less it does place some firm ground beneath our feet, all the more so as such pieces of evidence as we do have are, for all their variations of time, place and observer, remarkably consistent.

The first question in nineteenth-century Ireland — to say nothing of other Irelands — was religion. The returns indicate that at least 80 per cent of the officials were Protestant, the great majority of them members of the Church of Ireland. This is inherently probable. Banks were still Protestant strongholds. In the census of 1901 'bank service' still appears in the first rank of Protestant occupations. The Catholic proportion of this occupation was only 23 per cent as against a Catholic proportion of 74 per cent in the Irish population as a whole. To see this in perspective we might note that Catholic barristers constituted 44 per cent of the whole, Catholic doctors 43 per cent of the whole and Catholic schoolmasters 70 per cent of the whole in 1901. The reason for the striking difference between these last middle-class occupations and middle-class occupations of the banking type is doubtless that in the first open competition was a relatively significant factor both in entry and for success, whereas in the second even entry was generally closed to those outside the networks of influential connections. And if Catholics accounted for only 23 per cent of Irish 'banking service' in general in 1901, we should expect them to account for considerably less than that proportion of the Bank's staff. Traditionally, the Bank was *the* Protestant — indeed, *the* Anglican — institution among banks, at any rate outside the plantation counties. Even in the Catholic south there were fair-sized branches where, as late as the 1890s, the entire staff belonged to the Church of Ireland.

The information on 'father's occupation' is much more meagre than that on religious affiliation. Such as it is, however, it is again substantially what we might have expected, solidly middle to upward middle class: army officer, police inspector, chief schools inspector, Dublin Castle official, wholesale timber merchant, provincial newspaper proprietor, postmaster, master of a merchant vessel, gentleman farmer, 'substantial' farmer. One minor surprise is the relatively large number of clergymen's sons, almost one-third of the number specified. Most of these were, of course, the sons of rectories, but Methodist and Presbyterian ministers' sons were also represented. Another mild surprise is the relative paucity of bank officials' sons or relatives. If this last was truly representative of the Bank's staff in general, and not a mere freak or accident of meagre and random statistics, an interesting question is presented. Does it suggest a strong tendency to upward social mobility in the profession, or disenchantment with this particular livelihood by its practitioners, or some mysterious purpose of the Court's in grudging nominations to the sons of its own employees?

The numbers for whom religion and marital status happen to be correlated, though small, are not altogether inconsiderable — twenty-eight Protestants and five Catholics. The majority of the few Catholics specified were married; but the Protestant returns are startling. Exactly 75 per cent of them were returned as 'bachelors', and these included agents, sub-agents and cashiers as well as juniors. Moreover, some were recorded as having fair sums of money on deposit or private means. Does this signify anything beyond the chance of particular inspectors' jottings? There is one curious piece of matching, if not precisely corroborative, evidence. In 1878 the Bank collected, doubtless for some pension-planning purpose, the ages of some 250 of their employees and (where applicable) of their wives. The age differential of the married (who constituted only 35 per cent of the whole number) was ten years or over in one-third of the cases. In several instances it was twenty years or more! A possible explanation of the two pieces of data is that the very small stipends of the early years of service, combined with the very high level of 'respectability' expected in the occupation, practically ruled out hopes of marriage before the age of thirty or perhaps even thirty-five for most officials. This might well account for both the much younger wives and the widespread refusals to hazard familiar habits and hard-gained comforts in any matrimonial lottery. As to the second phenomenon, Protestant bachelordom,

44

however, should we altogether exclude a still wilder explanation, that of a species of 'death-wish' among the middle ranks of the *fin-de-siècle* 'Anglo-Irish'?

The inspection note books are scattered with sudden, sad vignettes. In one provincial office in 1901, the sub-agent was reported as

> Undoubtedly soured by being only what he is after 31 years. Domestic relations not improving his temper & owing to them & to his poor appearance he is socially ostracised wh causes him to see slights on all sides never intended.

He was not on speaking terms with the junior clerks, of one of whom ('quick' and 'willing' though 'not overtidy') it was said, 'Is of a rather gloomy temperament no doubt added to by being constantly ragged at by [the sub-agent]. Has unfortunately imbibed rather atheistical views'. The cashier of the same office, who suffered from a cataract in one eye, was characterised as 'of gentlemanly appearance with good address but somewhat affected in his manner'. It comes as no surprise that more than one member of this branch desired a transfer. Of the second teller in another branch, struggling to reduce a tiny overdraft forced on him by family debts, it was recorded, 'Has a widowed mother and six sisters who have to live as governesses and he has to help and so is crippled. Protestant'. An exchange clerk elsewhere was

> Very painstaking and hardworking but unfortunately for himself most nervous and absentminded: this latter complaint he tells me affects him even in his outdoor life ... He does the Exch[ange] work most correctly and satisfactorily but in the detail work of the office makes mistakes wh wd seem to be due to downright stupidity but are in reality due to his extreme nervousness... I think under another agent he wd show to better advantage but besides some hesitation on his part as to leaving his mother & sister alone here, they wd prefer him to remain in [   ] for a while & have home comforts till his health gets more established.

Nor were the surroundings always inspiriting. The natural 'gloom' of the Ballina office in 1900, arising from 'the close proximity of the adjoining & opposite houses', was accentuated by 'the dingy colour of the wall paper'; its winter discomforts, by the broken stove.

But — Ballina's interior notwithstanding — light exceeded shade in the reports. Lloyds'-like, the inspectors' favourite commendation was 'A1 hand', and they bestowed it on a very considerable body of the clerks. Most agents were highly regarded, and a few sub-agents spoken of as excellent managerial material. Many branches appear to have been happy, cheerful and pleasant. Unfortunately, though naturally, neither these reports nor the directors' often looked beyond the office walls. None mentions, for example, the houses or lodgings in which the officials lived. None mentions their wives (except for a handful of references to religion or private money) or their children. The 'bank service' in the provincial towns of this epoch must have contributed heavily to the new phenomenon of games-organisation and club life — rugby, rowing, lawn tennis, golf. But the records are silent on all this. *A fortiori* they say nothing about the more solitary consolations of fishing, shooting and the like.

Curiously, the anonymity is compounded by the near absence of reference of any kind to the profession in even the most painstaking contemporary depictions of Irish life. Joyce passes them by, and even Somerville and Ross, in all their scrupulous dissections of provincial Irish Protestantism, never advert to the bank agent or bank clerk. To some extent this is comprehensible. A bank officer was a nomad. No matter how long he stayed in a single branch, he was always liable to swift transfer. Again, the Court exerted constant pressure upon the officials *against* all public commitment or involvement, most of all political. The Bank's agents were forbidden to use the bank houses in which they dwelt to establish residential qualifications for voting in parliamentary elections. They were not even allowed to accept commissions of the peace without the Court's express permission, or town commissionerships at all. Moreover, they were required to send in 'full and explicit' confidential reports on the 'habits' and 'conduct', as well as the professional competence, of each subordinate officer. Thus the ethos (or at least the Court's ideal) of the service was that of the withdrawn and neutral citizen. Tellingly perhaps, the inspectors' supreme accolade was 'gentleman-like', their most damning judgment, 'rather common'.[12]

None the less, the extraordinary spread of branch banking throughout Ireland in our period must have had profound social effects. For one thing, although the great increase in and wider scattering of staff in the period 1825-1900 was by no means an exclusively Protestant phenomenon, it did mean that one little enclave for the middle-class 'Anglo-Irish' had been much developed — or at least extended. For another, the constant traffic with the metropolis, and the movement of people between city and provincial town, inevitably leavened rusticity and introduced novel activities and associations. The primary effect of the multiplication of branches was of course economic: the spread of the money habit, the availability of investment capital and the stimulation of savings. But we should not forget that in the wake of all this came small but, cumulatively, far from insignificant changes in social attitudes and behaviour in the country towns and vicinage. The new birds of passage did not come and go to no effect.

The Bank was one of the few Irish institutions which linked the eighteenth to the twentieth century. It was a product of the 'age of Grattan', spiritually as well as actually, and even in 1914 still bore some of the marks of its 'patriotic' ascendancy origin. It had of course changed significantly in many ways, as the world about it had changed in almost all. But the degree of continuity and unbroken development was high. Even its profits, dividends and reserves were at much the same level on the accession of George V as they had been on the accession of George IV, almost ninety years before!

The major changes in the interval had been great attenuation in the Bank's rôle as state bank of Ireland; a considerable diminution in the relative value of its rights of note-issue; the explosive growth of branch banking, with a corresponding tripling of staff; the supersession of the Bank's old monopoly by a sort of 'commonwealth' system of Irish joint-stock banks in which, as traditional leader, it served as 'mother-country'; and a gradual mitigation of its unionist, loyalist, metropolitan and Protestant characteristics with corresponding shifts in its national outlook and function.

In one sense, the Bank remained (as it had always been) as 'national' as any, and more 'national' than most of its commercial rivals. The directorate was almost entirely Irish-born and Irish-resident. A large majority of the Court were in fact Dublin businessmen, wine merchants, brewers, flour millers, paper manufacturers, general merchants, and the like. Many of these were also directors in Irish canal and railway companies. None belonged to the higher reaches of the Irish ascendancy, let alone the larger British commercial world, during our period. Their networks of connection centred in institutions like the Ouzel Galley Society or Simpson's or Cork Street Hospitals, of which large numbers were members or trustees. Thus, throughout our period the control of the Bank rested with a predominantly Protestant section of the Irish (and particularly, Dublin) mercantile community, which was deeply committed, personally and economically, to its homeland. This may have made for provincialism, complacency, over-caution and narrowness of financial view. But there could be no doubt of the thorough Irishness of the management, unless 'Irishness' be defined in the most exclusive and intolerant of terms.

It can scarcely be doubted that the members of the Court were unionists to a man, or that the great majority of the staff regarded themselves as 'loyalists'. In the very rare cases where the inspectors noted an official's politics, it was to ticket him as 'nationalist' — and Catholic, of course. The nationalists themselves, even at the close of the nineteenth century, regarded the Bank as aligned with their opponents. It was in fact a campaign by the *Freeman's Journal* and *United Ireland* (which accused the Bank of 'strangling' the Munster and threatened that 'Irish opinion would demand the stripping of the Bank of its indefensible and ill-used monopoly of public money') that compelled it to begin publication of its accounts in 1885. Two years earlier, the *Freeman's* had sourly greeted the Bank's celebration of its centenary by the hope that it would never celebrate another centenary in the same place. By its very site, the Bank still symbolised, in nationalist eyes, the loss of Irish parliamentary independence.

Yet institutionally the Bank's loyalism under the Act of Union was very moderate indeed. Its only political intervention between 1825 and 1875 not directly concerned

Plate 15

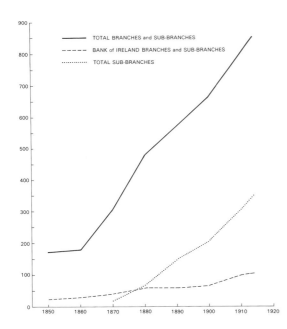

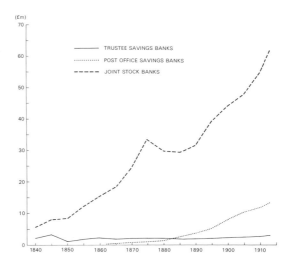

Number of Irish joint-stock bank branches and sub-branches, 1850-1914

Deposits and current balances in Irish banks, 1850-1914

with its own standing as a bank was to support the opposition to a Dublin improvement bill. The military occupation of head office was planned in 1848 and some branch offices were barricaded in 1867; but the first was a government initiative and the second a normal precaution during disturbances. Royal visits did draw unusual exertions and large contributions from the Court; but these were rare and unaccompanied by any extraordinary flunkeyism. When the Bank Holidays Act was passed in 1871, the Court promptly dropped the Queen's Birthday celebration on 25 May. In short, despite the natural political sympathies of the bulk of the Bank's members, its corporate conduct was essentially a-political, even in the nineteenth century. By the early twentieth, it was (as, for example, the negotiations over the details of the 1903 land bill clearly show) practically indistinguishable from any other Irish bank in dealing with governments and parties.

There is a rather better case for characterising the nineteenth-century Bank as 'Protestant' than for characterising it as 'unionist'. A trivial but telling illustration from the mid-century is the Court's paying for a pew at the local Anglican church for the accommodation of the 'Bank Establishment'. This was not, in any aggressive sense, a sectarian action. But it does reflect an assumption that the Bank was still by and large a Church of Ireland institution. Similarly, the Bank regularly subscribed small sums in support of a handful of Church of Ireland parish schools in Dublin throughout the Victorian epoch. Of course, the Bank had never been exclusively Protestant, let alone exclusively Anglican. Several of the first subscribers had been Catholics; and although the original charter had barred Catholics from the Court and deprived them of voting rights at stockholders' meetings, the Bank abandoned both these discriminatory provisions in 1830, fifteen years before they were (at the Bank's own urging) formally repealed.

As this clearly shows, the Bank's Anglicanism was never of the bitter, partisan, exclusive kind. It was simply the natural consequence of the Bank's originating in the conditions of late-ascendancy Ireland. Moreover, it softened imperceptibly but decisively during our period. The establishment of the other banks of the final fusion, the Hibernian and the National, may have sprung from the confessional bias of the late Georgian Bank — so their promoters averred, at any rate. But in fact the needs of money-getting and money-making could not be religiously hemmed in, either in the long run or altogether. We do not know when the Bank first recruited Catholic staff. But it must have done so regularly, if in small proportions, from 1850 onwards. Moreover, as the Catholic Church acquired Irish capital in increasing amounts in the second half of the nineteenth century, a fair proportion of it must have been vested in Bank of Ireland stock, a favourite trustee security. As the Bank multiplied its branches and sub-branches in the south and west after 1865, its proportion of Catholic customers must have risen sharply, for there were few others there to be attracted.

The process of de-anglicanisation was well under way by then. At least as early as 1877 an advance for the building of a Catholic church was recorded and there are other examples.[13] By the beginning of the twentieth century such transactions had become commonplace. A handful of extracts from the board memoranda of a three-month period in 1903-4 shows this clearly. On 11 November 1903 a particular Convent of Mercy was granted 'an advance of £1,500 . . . against the security of the transfer of £500 Bank Stock standing in the names of Ellen Burke, Frances Carroll, Mary Daly and Kate Maginnis [sisters in the convent], the ordinary collateral loan rate to be charged'. On the same day the Very Rev. M. Howley, PP was allowed a loan of £1,380 on the security of industrial shares. Two months later, the Court made a donation of £10 to the Christian Brothers' Schools, North Brunswick Street. A month later still a slightly larger donation was made to the Fermoy Christian Brothers' Schools Building Fund, albeit with the apologetic rider that the 'new school . . . is not an entirely denominational institution but is partly a technical one'.[14] Thus the Bank had integrated itself into the larger Irish community well before the new order of 1921-2 divided and reconstituted the island politically. Doubtless, the 'Catholic' element in its business, like that of its staff, was still comparatively small in 1914. But it was both considerable and growing; and more important, the last barriers (in people's minds) to the Bank's presenting itself as supra-denominational were disappearing fast.

If nineteenth-century Ireland, outside the north-east, escaped an industrial revolution on her own account, she certainly underwent a commercial one. The volume of deposits and cash balances in the Irish joint-stock banks increased more than ten-fold between 1840 (the first year for which reliable statistics are available) and 1914. In the same period the Irish population was almost halved. There could be no more striking evidence of the rapid expansion of the money economy and of business practice and cast of mind. Savings (about one-half of them in the hands of the joint-stock banks) had grown even more rapidly, and by 1914 well exceeded £30 million. The Bank had played a leading part in all these developments, first, as a major constituent of the joint-stock banks, next, as the linchpin of the banking system and finally as manager of the main part of the government's financial operations in Ireland.

At the same time, there were distinct limits to what the Bank itself, or the joint-stock banks in general, could do for the Irish economy even in the final decades of our period. Joint-stock banking was primarily an urban activity; and although the number of branches and sub-branches in Ireland grew from 174 to 809 between 1850 and 1914, the number of places in which a bank branch was *permanently* open was only 242. Thus there were still less than 250 true banking centres in Ireland — not to add rather absurd levels of 'competition' with three or four branches of different banks in towns of two or three thousand inhabitants. The Bank had probably more farmer, and especially small-farmer, customers than most of its rivals. Yet even in its case, only one-quarter of the advances of the *country* branches were made for agricultural purposes. The truth was that the joint-stock banking of the day was ill-suited to provide the type of credit needed by small-scale, penurious Irish agriculture. Three- or four-month loans were the norm; twelve months was the outermost time limit for an advance; and it was difficult to make any allowances for agrarian seasonality or capital works or natural disasters within the existing overdraft structure. Even the current comparatively small and presumably selective business with farmers could scarcely have been profitable. To have tried to multiply it a sufficient number of times to bring a quarter of a million smallholders into its orbit would surely have been ruinous in the years immediately preceding the First World War. None the less, the new banking system was soon to enjoy a golden hour in even its rural sector. In 1914 Irish farming was on the threshold of an unprecedented if brief upsurge of prosperity, and then the pre-war banking network could be turned more fully to account.

The Bank was rooted in Irish soil. This was increasingly the case, in a more or less real sense, from 1860 onwards, when its lending on land mortgages was allowed. But much more significant was the invariable truth of the proposition, metaphorically speaking, throughout our years. The Bank remained, as it had begun, a native growth. But it also adapted itself easily, almost effortlessly, to changing Irish circumstances. In doing so, it served as a bridge between Grattanism and Griffithism, between the declining and the rising ascendancies in nationalist Ireland. Overall, the nineteenth-century Bank had proved to be both a creative and an integrating force in its native land. It had few companions, let alone superiors, in either rôle.

References

1   *Freeman's Journal*, 3 June 1820.
2   TCOD, xii/109, 20 Dec. 1836.
3   TCOD, xxi/228-34, 29 Aug. 1864.
4   TCOD, xvi/55, 19 Mar. 1846.
5   *Order book, 1827-78*, p. 5 (20 Dec. 1831).
6   TCOD, xvi/405, 26 Nov. 1847.
7   *Order book, 1827-78*, p. 14 (5 Feb. 1859).
8   TCOD, xvi/110, 10 June 1846.
9   *General orders, 1889-1904* (1), p. 21.
10 *General orders, 1869-89* (1), p. 40 (2 Dec. 1871).
11 *General orders, 1869-89* (2), p. 78 (13 Nov. 1874).
12 Information concerning Bank staff is in Bank's Office Inspectors' Report Books, Nov. 1888-May 1889, Nov. 1890-Aug. 1891, Mar.-Dec. 1892 and Mar. 1900-Mar. 1903.
13 Applications for advances from agents, 5 Sept. 1877; see also Agents Memorandum Book (Feb. 1888) for an advance to Youghal Convent.
14 TCOD, xxxvi/143, 148, 217, 253, 12 Nov. 1903, 21 Jan. and 18 Feb. 1904.

Plate 16

College Green at night

Plate 17

Oisin Kelly
The Marchers 1969
Cast metal painted silver
18 × 78 × 7 cms

The Impact of Independence*

Ronan Fanning

THE quarter-century between the outbreak of the First and Second World Wars was arguably the most turbulent in the 200-year history of the Bank of Ireland. If the European cataclysm of 1914-18 ultimately exposed the flaws in the foundations of British financial might, of which the Bank was then the central Irish pillar, the localised shock of republican rebellion at first seemed still more ominous. Easter 1916 was followed by Irish revolutionary nationalism supplanting the more conservative nationalism of the Irish Parliamentary Party at the 1918 election. Guerilla war in 1919-21 led to a negotiated settlement between the Irish revolutionaries and the British government. The outcome was the dissolution of the 120-year-old United Kingdom of Great Britain and Ireland and the partition of Ireland: the six north-eastern counties, Northern Ireland, remaining in the United Kingdom; the other twenty-six counties forming the Irish Free State, an independent dominion within the British Commonwealth. There followed the bitter, if brief, Civil War of 1922-3.

Instability and disorder remained the central concerns of the leaders of independent Ireland. Only in 1927, when Eamon de Valera led his Fianna Fáil party into the Dáil, was the reconciliation of the main body of republicans to parliamentary methods of opposition materially advanced. Fianna Fáil's first entry into office in 1932 seemed to pose fresh threats to the *status quo*. Anglo-Irish financial relations were thrown into chaos by the so-called 'economic war' which compounded the effects of world-wide recession upon the Irish economy; simultaneously, de Valera set about unilaterally rewriting the constitutional relationship with Britain. The banking commission appointed by the new government appeared to offer the prospect of further change. Although 1938 saw not only the publication of what, for bankers, was a reassuringly orthodox majority report but also the Anglo-Irish financial and other agreements ending the economic war, bank and government officials alike were already beginning to bend their minds to the emergency arrangements necessary in the event of another European war.

Our period, in short, is one of change. The break with Britain clearly was the greatest change, posing as it did the challenge of whether what had been *the* Bank of Ireland in the United Kingdom could retain its primacy in independent Ireland. The Bank's response to that challenge — the impact of independence, first in anticipation and then in actuality — forms the central theme of this essay.

*My thanks are due to Margaret O'Callaghan of St John's College, Cambridge, who did the research for this essay and to Sarah Ward-Perkins, the Bank's archivist, who successfully pursued so many enquiries.

The Bank and Home Rule

The Bank's attitude towards home rule had always centred around how its prosperity and rights might best be protected if home rule were to come into effect; special clauses to that end had been included in Gladstone's bills of 1886 and 1893.[1]

That their head office in College Green had formerly housed the pre-Union parliament meant that a demand that it house the home rule parliament was never far from the minds of the Bank's directors. They were concerned at the absence of provisions safeguarding their premises in the 1914 Government of Ireland Act due to the great speed with which that act was passed at the beginning of the war, although they did obtain an assurance from 'a responsible member of Mr Redmond's party that as far as the party was concerned the premises of the Bank would not be required for the use of the Irish parliament'.[2] There matters rested until the Easter rising of 1916.

The rising itself seems to have had little effect on the Bank, other than to occasion the Court of Directors to record that it had forced the closure of the Bank's Dublin offices from Easter Monday (24 April) until 4 May and, a week later, to record their appreciation of the services rendered by their chief cashier and by the Bank's porters 'during a period of much anxiety'.[3] What did excite alarm were the negotiations conducted by Lloyd George later that summer with Redmond and Carson with a view to implementing home rule immediately. The Governor, R.F.S. Colvill, wrote to Sir John Bradbury of the treasury seeking protection — in the event of a new Irish government wishing to acquire College Green — 'from having to part with them at an inadequate price, and from being disturbed before being provided with equally suitable premises in as good a position'. Although Bradbury's reply — that the Prime Minister and Chancellor of the Exchequer did not think that special provision could be made in the bill [4] — was hardly reassuring, the collapse of the Lloyd George initiative meant the matter was again shelved, this time until the drafting of the Government of Ireland Bill in 1920.

Gold and Legal Tender

The status of Irish currency was another matter for contention between the Bank and the treasury during the war. The Bank of Ireland, like the Bank of England, had been relieved of the statutory obligation to pay in gold when the Bank Charter Act was suspended at the beginning of the war and when the Currency and Bank Notes Act of 1914 decreed that Irish bank notes were legal tender. The measure quickly won public confidence; half the £500,000 in gold transferred from the Bank of England to the Bank of Ireland in Dublin before reopening to meet the possibility of a run after the declaration of war was returned almost immediately.[5] Thereafter the Bank, acting on treasury instructions, obtained an undertaking from all the Irish banks that gold payments throughout Ireland should be restricted; the link with gold was effectively broken and in December 1915 the Irish banks released £2 million in gold to the government — the Bank's contribution was £730,000 — in response to the demand for gold for the American exchange scheme which was central to financing the British war effort.[6] By mid 1916 the mood of emergency had so receded that the treasury proposed withdrawing the status of legal tender conferred on Irish bank notes by the 1914 act. Colvill presided over a special meeting of the Irish banks which protested that such a move could precipitate a severe financial crisis: 'in the present state of political feeling, the introduction of an English paper currency, only convertible in London, as the sole legal tender, would . . . be used as a pretext for strong political action, and a serious demand for gold would probably arise.'[7] The treasury backed down, although insisting that the act would be revoked not later than the conclusion of hostilities whether or not gold circulation was restored.

The increased gold reserves needed to peg the exchange rate with the dollar continued to preoccupy the treasury. In August 1917 the Chancellor of the Exchequer, Bonar Law, asked the Governor to arrange that 90 per cent of the gold holdings of the Irish banks be placed at the treasury's disposal in the Bank of Ireland. Although the Irish banks ultimately complied with this request[8] they again argued that 'the present political condition of Ireland' made possible 'an organised rejection of British currency notes in payment of Irish bank notes (which are convertible at the head offices in Ireland of the Irish banks of issue)' and that each Irish bank should have sufficient capacity to meet its own notes in gold to defeat any such movement. Bonar Law's response — that it was not immediately intended to remove the gold from Ireland and that it would 'remain the property of the contributing bank until such time as the treasury found it necessary to ask for it to be placed at its disposal for actual use' — scarcely met the point.[9]

The Bank's concern with the possibility of a politically motivated run grew in proportion to the deteriorating political climate, as we can see from Andrew Jameson's evidence to Lord Cunliffe's Committee on Currency and Foreign Exchanges in London in 1919. Jameson, the chairman of John Jameson the distillers, had been Governor in 1896-8 and was a director of the Bank for a record period (from 1887 until his death in 1941); he was later to receive a government nomination to the first Senate of the Irish Free State. In response to some aggressive questioning — notably from Lord Cunliffe and Sir John Bradbury of the treasury — he suggested that if Bank of England (as opposed to Bank of Ireland) notes were made legal tender they would be more 'liable to be attacked by the rebellious element of the population . . . the Sinn Féin element would undoubtedly publish articles to say that England was taking all the gold out of Ireland and replacing it with an English note only payable in London, and that nobody in Ireland could get any gold at all'. Jameson referred to the collapse of Munster Bank in 1885[10] and the consequent run on Bank of Ireland notes in the south of Ireland which was stopped by the quasi-public delivery of a half-a-million in gold from London to College Green. Ireland, he suggested, was 'a great deal worse now than it was in those days . . . there is a much more intelligent lot of men at the head of affairs, and if there was anything of the kind engineered now it would be after a fearful preparation' — he referred particularly to a recent article by Arthur Griffith in *Nationality* 'written on the assumption that all the cover we keep for our excess issue was in gold' and raising the spectre of what might befall 'if they had known that the cover for the excess issues was currency certificates in London'.[11]

These, then, were among the considerations which caused Jameson and his fellow-directors to urge that there were grave risks in terminating the status of Irish bank notes as legal tender, notwithstanding their war-time agreement to the contrary with the treasury. A meeting of representatives of all the Irish banks chaired by the Governor, N. J. Synnott, on 16 September 1919 opted for the permanent retention of legal tender status, as opposed to the reversion to the pre-war position, when asked to state their preference by the treasury on behalf of the Cunliffe Committee.[12] But the committee ruled otherwise — notwithstanding the reservation of its only Irish member, the former Governor and then director of the Bank, G. F. Stewart, 'that the pre-war status should not be restored in Ireland until the government considered the time opportune' — and a proclamation withdrawing legal tender status from Irish notes, issued on 20 December, came into force on 1 January 1920.

The Bank did succeed, however, in persuading Whitehall to introduce a bill — enacted as the Bank Notes (Ireland) Act 1920 — placing Irish notes on the same footing as English and Scottish by making them payable only at the head office of the bank concerned.[13] That bill coincided not only with the Government of Ireland Bill but also with renewed treasury pressure for the transfer to London of all the gold in the custody of the Bank of Ireland; the treasury treated the Irish banks' acquiescence in the latter as a *quid pro quo*.[14] The Governor suggested that the gold should be held in Dublin by the Bank 'as custodian and on behalf of the Bank of England, and be included in the weekly returns of the Bank of England'. The political climate, he pointed out, had changed materially for the worse. The transfer probably could not be concealed 'and if the fact became generally known the knowledge might be used to increase the difficulties of the administration and undermine the credit of the banks'. He questioned 'whether the danger to public credit involved in the removal of the relatively small amount of gold held by the Irish banks would more than counter-balance the advantage, if any, accruing from the physical possession of this gold by the Bank of England'.[15] But the treasury stood firm and the practical details of the transfer were discussed at a meeting in Dublin Castle on 4 June 1920 between the new Governor, W. P. Cairnes, his predecessor, N. J. Synnott, the new under-secretary for Ireland, Sir John Anderson, and A. P. Waterfield of the treasury. Anderson and Waterfield had only just arrived in Ireland as part of the team of British civil servants hand-picked to overhaul the rotting administrative timber of Dublin Castle.[16] Cairnes pointed out that the gold weighed over seventeen tons and that six military lorries, which could be accommodated simultaneously in the courtyard at the back of the Bank, would be needed to move it. He suggested that it should be moved as secretly as possible, preferably at night under the cover of the curfew then in force because of the IRA's guerilla campaign in Dublin.[17] There was some delay in effecting the transfer due to the Irish banks' anxiety that progress should first be made with the Bank Notes (Ireland) Bill. But on 31 August Anderson informed the Governor that the bullion had arrived at its destination without a hitch; he enclosed an order for £5 to be distributed among the Bank's porters who had loaded it. He confessed that it was 'not a very large amount, but as you know the treasury practice has never been over generous in these matters!'[18] — hardly a surprising judgment given that the Bank had estimated the value of the gold as £1,968,000.[19]

The Bank and the Government of Ireland Bill

By mid 1920 the escalation in the level of political violence is discernible in the Transactions of the Court of Directors. The first hint of what lay ahead came in January 1919 in an exchange of correspondence with Brigadier-General A. W. Pagan, the general officer commanding the Dublin district, on the provision of a military guardroom.[20] By March 1920 the Bank's Limerick agent was seeking advice 'as to the advisability of his taking sporting guns and other weapons from customers for safe keeping. It was ordered that he should not take any more.' The same meeting asked the Bank traveller and Secretary to report on 'the risk of loss by robbery with violence

Plate 18

William Plunkett Cairnes

in connection with value in transit between head office and branches'. The Deputy Governor, then W. P. Cairnes, interviewed the Castle authorities and reported back to a special meeting of the representatives of all the Irish banks on 16 March (which, as we shall shortly see, was of historic significance for quite different reasons) when it was unanimously agreed 'that an armed guard for the protection of value in transit was inadvisable'. By September 1920 the directors found it necessary to order that 'anyone depositing boxes or cases in head office in future should be required to state they do not contain either arms or ammunition'[21] and Cairnes raised the same subject with Anderson at the end of October following a police visit to the Bank in connection with the possible storing of arms, ammunition or explosives in customers' safe-deposit boxes whose contents were unknown to the Bank.[22]

But the safeguarding of their College Green premises against expropriation after the enactment of the Government of Ireland Bill still loomed largest in the minds of the Bank's directors. The Governor, N. J. Synnott, had informed the treasury in March 1920 that the Bank's case was

> that although a general clause covering all buildings, etc., and machinery for reserve services would probably be necessary in any case to cover all government services, in the case of the Bank of Ireland a special clause would be necessary inasmuch as the head office and buildings here, being the old parliament house might be immediately claimed, before any substantial premises were found.
>
> The Bank do not want so much an absolute prohibition against taking the premises as a clear provision that such action should not be taken until the substituted premises and accommodation were provided. Of course no provision for mere compensation would suffice, either from the point of view of government services or the other business of the Bank. Serious interruption of government and other services for perhaps three years could not be met by any compensation. On the other hand, as our building covers about two acres in the centre of the city, and a substantial site and building might be of less area and value, the compensation clause would seem to be also necessary, and machinery provided for its adjustment.
>
> We are inclined to suggest that the tribunal to decide all such matters might be something of this kind — three persons, appointed respectively by Surveyors' Institute of London, the Royal Institute of Architects of Ireland and by the treasury. Of course all plans, etc., and proposals as to a substituted site and buildings should be submitted to the Bank for their approval.[23]

By 11 May, when the Governor put the Bank's case to the chief secretary, Hamar Greenwood,[24] a comprehensive memorandum[25] on the subject had already been drawn up. This began by emphasising that the Bank had no objection to their head-quarters being used by either of the parliaments envisaged under the terms of the Government of Ireland Bill (the parliament of Southern Ireland or the Irish parliament) provided they were not dispossessed and also provided they could carry on their business as government and private bankers in College Green until they were found a suitable site and building. They submitted that, since the circumstances under which they might be dispossessed and their business disturbed arose 'solely from the provisions and as a result of a government bill', it was 'only common justice' that the bill include the safeguards they sought:

> The Bank claim this as owners of property of which they have been in possession for 118 years, with a title based on a public statute and derived direct from the crown and His Majesty's treasury; in the interests of public credit of the public services; of their numerous customers; and of the proprietors of bank stock, whose stock has been made trustee stock by public statute.

What particularly disturbed the Bank was that in the existing political climate 'the temper of the newly elected parliament of Southern Ireland might be such that the

Plate 19

College Green, House of Lords entrance

demand to obtain possession of the Bank premises might be founded, not only on a certain amount of legitimate sentiment, but be largely promoted by a desire to embarrass the imperial government by rendering difficult, if not impossible, the carrying on of business by its financial agent in Ireland'. The result would be to 'place in the hands of a parliament largely composed of persons not favourably disposed towards the British connection a powerful instrument for discrediting the British government and for rendering its business in Ireland impossible'.

The memorandum also included a list of sites, in descending order of preference, to which the Bank might move. Their first choice was the corner of Grafton Street and Suffolk Street directly opposite the Provost's House in Trinity College and including, among other premises, Hamilton Long's chemist shop, Barnardo's the furriers, Dixon and Hempenstall's opticians and Slattery's pub; next came ground they owned in

Westmoreland and Fleet Streets followed by Foster Place (including the Royal Bank premises), Jury's Hotel, the Chamber of Commerce, the site of St Andrew's Church ('the site . . . is fairly large and the church itself is nearly always empty') and finally 'as a temporary expedient . . . the south wing of the front buildings of Trinity College, including the Regent's Hall' — it was suggested, although dismissively, that Trinity 'might be willing to sell the whole of the front of the buildings for the purpose of a permanent bank'. Not for nothing was the Bank specially 'anxious that the onus of dispossessing persons in occupation of premises to be handed over . . . should be put upon the Government of Southern Ireland'.[26] Provision would also have to be made for an office where bank notes were manufactured and printed and for destroying cancelled notes, which must be 'entirely segregated' from the rest of the building, and much stress laid on the numbers of Bank employees to be accommodated — over 300 in all: there were then 262 officials (ninety of whom enjoyed the designation 'lady clerks') working in College Green in addition to nineteen porters, nine charwomen, fourteen 'luncheon room employees' and eighteen described as families and servants living on the premises.

The Bank's representatives got no satisfaction from Anderson at their meeting on 4 June. He took the line that the provision of a new site 'was a question of administration for the future government of Ireland rather than a subject of clause in an act of parliament'.[27] Nor were the Governor (W. P. Cairnes) and Deputy Governor (H. S. Guinness) reassured by a further interview with Anderson a fortnight later when he made what they regarded as no more than 'a deliberate, stereotyped, government offer' of a clause giving the Bank compulsory powers to acquire the land necessary for the erection of an alternative building. Anderson deprecated the Bank's proposal that any such clause contain provision for delay and for compensation, insisting instead that the Bank 'trust in the goodwill of the new parliament of Southern Ireland', notwithstanding Cairnes's *cri de coeur* that 'as an Irishman living in Ireland and knowing the people about him, he felt that it was not reasonable to ask the Bank to rely altogether for its future house and future buildings on the generosity of a future parliament'. Cairnes argued that Anderson's proposal 'could only have been made in ignorance of conditions prevailing in Ireland and urged that an interview with the Prime Minister and Chancellor of the Exchequer be set up for a few of the Bank's directors 'who would probably be able to give the Prime Minister a great deal of information on the real state of the country'. Anderson opposed the idea, saying that the parliamentary situation in regard to the bill 'was so sensitive that any safeguarding of the interests of the Bank might be imperilled by a too insistent urging of the Bank's present views'; he was evasive on the subject of whether the Bank would be provided with the text of the proposed clause.[28]

This stark difference of opinion reflected the division between the optimistic neo-Gladstonian liberalism which sometimes informed treasury attitudes to Irish independence[29] and the pessimistic, entrenched unionism which frequently characterised the attitudes of the Bank's directors and which, as we shall see, emerged on other occasions in the years 1920-23. Unpersuaded by Anderson or by the other under-secretary, the Irish-born and Catholic James MacMahon, 'a silent auditor' at the meeting until called on to speak by Anderson in whose opinions he promptly acquiesced, the Bank took its case to that most powerful and sympathetic ally of Irish unionists in Whitehall, Walter Long. Long, the last chief secretary for Ireland in a Conservative government

Plate 20

College Green, daylight view

(in 1905), was then First Lord of the Admiralty and it was there that he received three of the Bank's directors — Cairnes, Jameson and George Stewart — on 5 July. Cairnes, whose father had also been Governor and who came from a family of Scottish descent, was a chairman of the Great Northern Railway and less prominent politically than either Jameson or Stewart (Governor in 1914-16, a large land-agent who was active in the Irish Landowners' Convention and vice-chairman and, briefly, chairman, of the Southern Unionist Association).[30] Long was accompanied by the staunchly unionist Irish attorney-general, Denis Henry, who later became Lord Chief Justice for Northern Ireland, and H.A.L. Fisher, the Minister of Education and the only Liberal present. Confronted by this solid unionist phalanx, the treasury representative swiftly

Plate 21

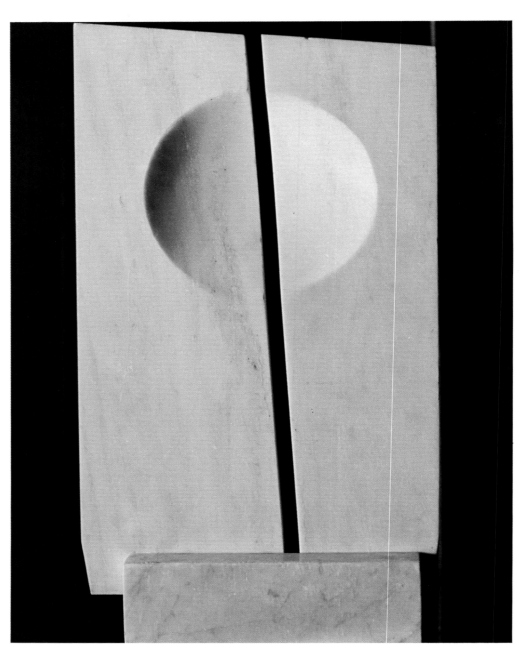

Gerda Frömel
Two piece marble sculpture 1970
Marble
560 × 310 × 100 mm
Unsigned
Exhibited at the Dawson Gallery, 1970; 'The Irish Imagination 1959-71'
Municipal Gallery of Modern Art, Dublin, 1971

back-tracked on Anderson's opposition to the protective clauses. Long, having examined the draft clause prepared by the Bank, offered to improve it and promised to take it up with the Irish Office. The deputation to London took the opportunity to rally support from such other powerful unionists as the party chairman, Sir George Younger; Walter Guinness (the cousin of the Deputy Governor, Henry Seymour Guinness) who became financial secretary to the treasury in 1923-4; and Sir Maurice Dockrell, the MP for South Dublin. Cairnes and Jameson also called on the Governor of the Bank of England who expressed his willingness to help.[31]

Long had advised the deputation that, in future, they should communicate directly with him,[32] and not with Anderson or the treasury. They took him at his word when the relevant section (passed by the House of Commons on 29 October 1920) differed slightly from the wording agreed between Long and the Bank in August. Although Long was ill his private secretary saw no difficulty in restoring the wording wanted by the Bank and this was done before the bill was finally enacted on 23 December 1920.[33] Section 66 gave the Bank all they wanted: it laid down that the government of Southern Ireland would be entitled to acquire the Bank of Ireland premises at College Green for the use of their parliament on fulfilment of the following conditions:

a) there shall be provided at the expense of the Government of Southern Ireland for the use of the Bank *a site and buildings suitable both as to situation of site and accommodation* and ready for occupation as head office of the Bank of Ireland;

b) there shall be paid to the bank compensation in respect of the bank premises and of disturbance, after taking into consideration the value of the new premises as aforesaid.

(The Bank's last-minute amendment is italicised; this replaced the less watertight phrase 'premises suitable'.) Provision was also made for arbitration in the event of a dispute.

The safeguards proved superfluous in that the Government of Ireland Act 1920 never came into effect outside Northern Ireland, but the episode was a most impressive demonstration of the Bank's political muscle in unionist circles at a time when the Conservative party held a stranglehold on the Irish policy of Lloyd George's coalition government. Still more significant was what it revealed of the profound distaste of the still unionist-dominated board for the prospect of Irish self-government. But, before we consider the Bank's relations with the first independent Irish government, it is necessary to look at certain changes in Irish banking structures which occurred in 1920 and which provided the formal framework for the conduct of those relations.

The Origins of the Irish Banks' Standing Committee

There were no arrangements before the war for regular meetings of the Irish banks. Although a 'meeting of the representatives of the Irish banks' was held at the instance and in the head office of the Bank of Ireland in December 1913 to fix and maintain deposit rates, the Bank's proposal that such meetings be held annually was not immediately implemented.[34] But the war gave some impetus to such meetings because of the treasury's sporadic requests, through the Governor of the Bank of Ireland, that the Irish banks confer together on such matters as the transfer of gold and also because of a private agreement between the banks at the start of the war that they would work together for its duration — 'that each bank would retain its existing business but would not canvass for or encourage business away from any of its competitors'.[35] But the real impetus to joint action came in 1918 when the newly-formed Irish Bank Officials' Association (IBOA) communicated with the banks individually, seeking arbitration on salaries and conditions of work. Two meetings of the representatives of Irish banks were held in November 1918 and a third in June 1919 when it was resolved not to recognise the IBOA; that, in the event of a strike, 'banking business should be carried on as far as possible'; and that no bank should take advantage of any difficulties which the strike might cause for any other bank.[36] But at a further meeting, on 4 July, the Provincial Bank broke ranks when their representatives favoured recognition of the IBOA subject to assurances that they 'would not interfere with the management' and that deputations to bank directors 'should consist only of members and staff of the bank and not of any outsiders'. The other banks continued to insist on the undesirability of recognition and drew up a seven-point memorandum for the Provincial Bank's board in an effort to restore solidarity.[37] The memorandum argued that recognition which 'is in direct opposition to the settled policy of the English banks' would lead all officials to join the IBOA; non-recognition, even if it meant a strike, would cause many to leave the IBOA. The memorandum suggested it was illusory to expect that either of the Provincial Bank's conditions for recognition would be accepted or, if accepted, implemented: 'experience amply shows that it is not the moderate element, or the wisest counsellors, who in the end control the action of unions, but generally a handful of extremists'.[38]

By 20 November 1919 matters had deteriorated to the point where the Court of Directors were informed that many of the staff intended sending in notice of resignation and a 'committee of the Board' was appointed to discuss with heads of departments 'the steps necessary for carrying on the business of the Bank' and to prepare a press statement.[39] On 25 November, at a meeting with the representatives of the other Irish banks, it was agreed that each bank would appoint two members to act on a standing committee empowered to take all necessary action in the event of a strike.[40] Although the strike was averted — a special meeting of the Court of Directors approved an agreement effectively recognising the IBOA and agreeing to arbitration[41] — the standing committee was empowered to conduct arbitration negotiations on behalf of all the banks. The arbitration award was made on 12 March 1920 and on 16 March 'the representatives of the Irish banks' met under that title for the last time when it was unanimously agreed

> to form a Standing Committee which would meet quarterly, or oftener if necessary, to decide upon steps to be taken to deal with the difficulties which were arising out of the altered conditions then existing, and to consider any matters of common interest to the banking system which might emerge in the future, including actual and projected legislation.[42]

The Irish Banks' Standing Committee (IBSC) properly so-called met for the first time on 24 March[43] and ordinarily thereafter in March, July, October and December each year. Its establishment and procedures reaffirmed rather than reduced the pre-eminence of the Bank of Ireland in the Irish banking system. Although the IBSC has no written constitution and no rules its meetings were by custom and in accordance with the precedent established at 'meetings of the representatives of the Irish banks' presided over by the Governor of the Bank of Ireland or, in his absence, by the Deputy Governor.[44] The appointment to the key post of secretary of the IBSC was 'left in the hands of the Governors and directors of the Bank of Ireland'[45] in the first instance and was traditionally thereafter a member of the Bank's staff; the IBSC's address was the Bank's College Green headquarters at which all meetings were held. Thus at the first meeting of the IBSC after the signing of the Anglo-Irish treaty of 1921 it was the Governor of the Bank of Ireland who initiated discussion of 'the many problems that confronted bankers in view of the contemplated setting up of an Irish Free State' and who was empowered to convene a special meeting if the banks were not consulted.[46] And it is to those processes of consultation between the putative rulers of the Irish Free State and the Bank of Ireland that we must now turn.

The Provisional Government and the Bank of Ireland

The provisional government was established on 16 January 1922 to take over the administration of the twenty-six counties in the interregnum before the coming into existence of the Irish Free State on 6 December 1922. Financial policy was high on its agenda as the decision of its chairman, Michael Collins, also to hold the Finance portfolio clearly reveals. The government minutes show that financial policy was first discussed on 18 January when it was immediately decided that the Bank of Ireland be asked to act as the new government's financial agents and that credit of up to £1 million be negotiated. Collins met Andrew Jameson at lunchtime that day and, later the same day, confirmed the request in writing before leaving for London, indicating that it was 'not yet possible to make any definite proposal for accommodation' pending agreement with the British on the details of the transfer of government services.[47]

On 19 January the Court of Directors approved the Governor's reply formally accepting the position of financial agent to the new government and saying that he would inform the Bank's shareholders of the appointment at the half-yearly meeting next day.[48] Although Collins told a government meeting on the 20th that he had also met representatives of the Munster and Leinster Bank the previous evening when he had 'indicated that it was probable that some of the purely commercial concerns of the government would be managed through different banks'[49] it was already plain that in banking and finance, as in the public service and most other areas other than the exclusively political, continuity rather than change was the guiding preoccupation of the provisional government.

The Bank's fears that they might lose their College Green premises thus proved groundless. Indeed the government seem to have been rather taken aback by their apprehensions. Witness the report of W. T. Cosgrave — whom Collins had arranged 'would be associated with him'[50] in managing financial policy — to his government colleagues on 19 January on an 'interview with the Bank of Ireland authorities' at which 'the question of acquiring the Bank premises was also mentioned ... and it appeared that the Bank authorities had anticipated that the premises would be required for government purposes'.[51] The impression that this came as something of a surprise to the government is confirmed by the instruction, at their meeting of 18 January, to Cosgrave and Patrick Hogan to inspect the Merrion Street premises which ultimately became Government Buildings.[52] Later inquiries in May and October 1922 by a London firm, Phoenix Industrial Services, about the rumoured reconstruction of College Green into a permanent headquarters for the Irish government met with negative replies; and the response to their final inquiry in January 1923 was that 'no such scheme is in contemplation at the moment'[53]. The present writer has found no evidence that it ever was.

The energy expended by the Bank in guarding against an expropriation that was never even attempted may be best seen, perhaps, as a tangible instance of how the fevered imaginings of wealthy Irish unionists, fearful of their fate in an independent Ireland, flawed their political judgment. The likelihood was that any native Irish government assuming power in Dublin would have wished to establish cordial relations with the Irish banks, and the Bank of Ireland in particular, in the interests of financial stability and business confidence. Likelihood became certainty in the case of a provisional government struggling to assert its authority against that large anti-treaty faction led by Eamon de Valera whose opposition was to lead to the ultimate instability of civil war. No government composed of Sinn Féin's elected representatives, moreover, whether pro- or anti-treaty, was likely to look with favour upon a proposition which had been written into the Government of Ireland Act. Ironically, the Bank's clauses inserted in the 1920 bill may have proved more preventative than protective in the face of a government which viewed that bill only with contempt.

But the speed with which the new government made the Bank its financial agents did little to allay its directors' fears. On 1 February three of their number (Cairnes, Guinness and Jameson — the last of whom was to play an increasingly prominent rôle in politically sensitive negotiations in the immediate aftermath of independence) sought solace from the treasury in London where they met Sir Basil Blackett and Otto Niemeyer.[54] Cairnes who, as Governor, did most of the talking complained that the Bank 'were kept absolutely in the dark ... in regard to the financial arrangements necessary for carrying on the government of the now* Irish Free State, neither had they been made aware of the steps — if any — which were in contemplation'. The deputation were still less happy when they discovered what was contemplated: namely that there was no intention to bring a bill before the Westminster parliament immediately ratifying the treaty and the status of the provisional government but to bring in an 'omnibus' bill later on which would approve, *inter alia*, the as yet undrafted constitution of the new state. All three directors argued that this 'would lead to chaos and have a disastrous effect on the prospects of a final and satisfactory settlement being arrived at in Ireland'. Nor were they reassured by Blackett's statement

> that Mr Collins would have to come to the Bank as an ordinary borrower for the £300,000 he required, and the Bank would have to treat his request for a loan exactly as they would act if a similar request were made to them by any other prospective borrower of similar credit and financial standing.

Nor did Blackett react helpfully when 'pressed as to the way in which the British government, in authorising the Bank to grant this loan, would safeguard the Bank's interest'. Indeed the deputation concluded that 'it appeared pretty obvious that no scheme had been thought out by the treasury' which had never considered many of the points raised by the Bank. Blackett and Niemeyer 'were completely taken aback' by the more horrific apprehensions expressed by the deputation, notably that Collins

---

* This was not strictly accurate: the Irish Free State did not come into existence until 6 December 1922.

Plate 22

Andrew Jameson

would be pressed by certain parties in Ireland to ask the [British] government to hand over to the Irish Free State the thirteen to fourteen million pounds held as cover for the excess circulation of Irish bank notes, and would be pressed to ask that this repayment should be made in gold.

They were taken aback, too, by the Governor's asking whether the treasury had 'been thinking about our charter and of the possible effect of the repayment of the government's debt to the Bank'.

Two themes of enduring significance for the next twelve months and more emerge clearly from this exchange of views. First, the Bank's concern to obtain British government guarantees for any loans they might make to the Irish government and the treasury's reluctance to promise such guarantees. Second, the less pessimistic treasury, as contrasted with the Bank's, view of the financial prospects of the new state. Blackett stressed, for instance, that the treasury

would not like to see a separate currency established in Ireland . . . [and] that it would naturally be to the interest of the British government that the future currency of the Irish Free State should, from the outset, be sound in itself and established upon a sound basis.

He further argued that, from what he knew of Collins's plans to introduce income tax at a lower rate than in Britain, 'as a bait to draw manufacturers to establish factories and businesses', a sound currency was equally in the interests of the new Irish government. The treasury's tendency to identify with those interests, which grew stronger after the outbreak of civil war, was reinforced by the close ties between treasury officials — Otto Niemeyer, who the deputation rightly concluded had effectively been designated the treasury spokesman in such matters, played a key rôle here — and their former colleagues who now worked for Collins's Department of Finance.[55] Hence their negative response to Jameson's suggestion at the end of the meeting 'that the wisest thing to do' would be for representatives of the treasury, the Bank and the provisional government 'to meet together and thrash out all these things around Sir Basil's table' — a proposal which says volumes about the Bank's perception of its powers and privileges.

Banking and currency were again discussed a fortnight later by the Governor and an economic adviser to the provisional government, Professor T. Smiddy of University College, Cork.[56] Smiddy's intention was to present a report which would 'avoid all political issues, . . . express as few opinions of his own as possible, and . . . consider the question purely from an economic angle'. Cairnes, obviously reassured, 'concurred' in these views. Having first 'expressed the hope that no change in the currency of the country would eventually be found desirable', he argued that, if change there had to be, 'either for political or for sentimental reasons', or if it proved practically impossible to keep the Irish and British coinage at parity, it would be desirable to adopt a standard ten shilling coin for two reasons; first because, if 'variations of exchange must exist, it was better that they should not be quoted as taking place between coins of precisely the same nominal value', and, second, because of 'the facility it offered for sub-division under a decimal system of coinage', this although it was some fifty years before decimalisation came to Ireland. Cairnes also advised Smiddy that, while he was opposed to any change in coinage or currency 'at the moment', he thought the new government 'were entitled to receive the profits, now accruing to the British government, arising from the excess issue of Irish notes [long a bone of contention between the Bank and the treasury],[57] from the coinage of silver and from the coinage of copper'. After Smiddy, drawing heavily on the opinions of R. G. Hawtrey of the treasury, had reviewed the state banking systems obtaining in other Commonwealth countries and the United States, Cairnes replied

> that the opinion of those occupying the highest and most responsible positions in the financial world was that you could not have one and the same bank undertaking the proper duties of a state bank viz.: the issue of its currency, the keeping of its balances, keeping the ultimate accounts of the other banks in the country, and at the same time acting as an ordinary competitive, commercial and industrial bank. It could not be expected that such a composite institution would find favour with the other banks, who would naturally consider themselves handicapped by the central bank's capacity to use the balances placed at their disposal by the government and by these other banks.

The remarks are of particular interest in that Cairnes, as he admitted, 'said things which were against rather than in favour of the interests of the Bank of Ireland' in his capacity as the government's financial agent. His deprecation of Smiddy's opinion that there should be but one issuing bank on the grounds that 'sentiment would probably be against such a unification' falls into the same category. That Smiddy, for his part, not only drew so heavily upon accepted treasury wisdom but 'thought that the Irish banks were in a sound financial condition, that their banking system was a good one, and . . . that there should be as few changes as possible in their banking laws' must have gone some way towards reassuring the Bank.

The deteriorating political situation, on the other hand, caused growing unease as the number of raids by the irregulars on various Bank branches mounted. On 1 and 2 May 1922 no fewer than twenty-six branches were raided, receipts being issued by the raiders in all cases. The amounts taken ranged from £143 0s. 11d. in Bagenalstown to £20,910 0s. 0d. in Tipperary; the other towns where more than £10,000 was taken were Ballina, Clonmel, Ennis, Mitchelstown, Tuam, Waterford, and Wexford (there were no raids in Cork or Galway on this occasion). In Tipperary, Claremorris, Charleville and Ennis the raiders also took cancelled notes which, in the last two cases, they later returned. All told and excluding cancelled notes, the Bank's losses came to £156,392 12s. 6d. and a special Court meeting decided that Cairnes and Jameson should see Richard Mulcahy, the Minister for Defence.[58] The outbreak of civil war at the end of June made matters worse and on one occasion, 6 July, when there was fighting in Dublin, a meeting of the Court had to be abandoned because there was no quorum.[59] On 3 August the Court approved a government request 'to withdraw signing powers from all their officials in the city of Cork' (then controlled by irregular forces) and empowered the Governor to do likewise in other branches if necessary.[60] It was not necessary, as government troops quickly gained the upper hand and signing powers were restored in Cork, again at government request, on 24 August.[61] Although the civil war did not thereafter make so dramatic an impression on the day-to-day business of the Court it reinforced the ties between the government and their bankers. One illustration will suffice: namely the controversy which arose when the treasury wrote to both Bank and government saying that the register of British government stock maintained at the Bank of Ireland in Dublin would be moved to the Bank's principal office in Belfast[62] and the accounts of stockholders domiciled in Northern

Ireland transferred there; the accounts of those domiciled south of the border would be transferred to the books of the Bank of England.

The Bank were 'quite taken by surprise' by the treasury's letter and the new Governor, Henry Guinness, immediately contacted Michael Collins. Guinness also began co-ordinating joint opposition to the proposal with the Dublin Stock Exchange and Chamber of Commerce and the Incorporated Law Society; and he urged Andrew Jameson to arrange a meeting in London with Winston Churchill as he felt that 'the treasury have been working this business on their own account without any reference to the political situation or the high contracting parties concerned'.[63]

Jameson was unable to set up a meeting with Churchill but he and Guinness, accompanied by the Bank's first auditor (Newman Thompson, who attended many such sensitive interviews of which he seems to have prepared the record and who was also the first secretary to the IBSC) saw Sir Basil Blackett at the treasury on 16 June.[64] The meeting was stormy and Guinness accused Blackett of not treating the Bank 'with proper consideration; the treasury had adopted Irish methods [a phrase redolent of the schizophrenia affecting the Bank's unionist establishment in this period] and presented a pistol at their heads'. Guinness also pointed out that, even if such legislation had to be introduced at a later date

> the present was the most inopportune moment that could have been suggested; at a time when it was peculiarly necessary to maintain at any rate apparent confidence in the mutual good faith of Great Britain and Ireland, the contemplated action that manifestly implied the want of faith in the Bank, that had served the treasury for nearly 150 years, and in the provisional government soon to become the actual government of Ireland. If the treasury persisted their action would be resented by the whole community and would be regarded as a calculated act of unfriendliness.

Blackett's admission that the treasury had acted in the first instance at the request of the Northern Ireland government added fuel to the flames. Although he claimed that when they agreed to the Belfast register proposal they had not realised its wider implications, Michael Collins, for one, had already concluded it was 'another of these moves calculated to strengthen enormously the position of the north-east'.[65] Guinness expressed his support for the provisional government in still more trenchant terms in a memorandum handed to Blackett on 19 June:

> The withdrawal of the register of British government securities from Dublin would be seized upon by the republicans as a confirmation of their propaganda that under the alleged friendly treaty between England and Ireland, England's attitude, far from being conciliatory, was that of an unfriendly creditor exacting the last farthing from a debtor in temporary difficulties of reconstruction.
>
> It would add most seriously to the already immeasurable difficulties of the provisional government in their genuine attempt to reconcile Ireland to the treaty and to the establishment of an orderly government.
>
> The country is in a distracted condition, and throwing sand instead of oil on the wheels of the provisional government is directly playing into the hands of the insurgent party and exasperating those who are doing their best to restore order.
>
> If the registers were retained in Ireland as a dominion, no action of the new government could operate to confiscate the physical property of an owner of

Plate 23

Henry Seymour Guinness

inscribed stock. The register might be taken, but that would be ineffectual, as duplicates are kept in London.

Any questions of capital, interest, tax and exchange are capable of friendly adjustment without cutting the painter at the very moment when the most delicate negotiations are pending on the main issues.[66]

71

These arguments were elaborated in a formal five-page memorandum of 6 July which was approved by the Court and signed by Guinness and which argued that treasury policy can

> certainly be attributed to a favoured nation treatment of Northern Ireland and would further embitter the present unfortunate relations between south and north and the movement of the remaining stocks to London would have the appearance of pre-judging the financial arrangements between Great Britain and the Irish Free State, to the detriment of the latter state.[67]

Reference was also made to the 'most serious' effect on the Bank 'as a business corporation ... The relations of the Bank with the imperial exchequer would be reduced to their having made a loan to the British government of £2,630,769 4s. 8d.'. The memorandum suggested that the Bank might demand repayment of this debt as they were entitled to do under statutory amendment to their charter (Vic. 8 and 9, 37, 4). Coupled with 'the complete determination of the Bank's present position as managers of the national debt in Ireland' this was 'the most economic solution for the Bank of Ireland as a commercial corporation'. But 'animated by the feeling that in the new conditions arising from the establishment of the Irish Free State individual interests should not be pressed to the possible disadvantage of the body politic', the Court deemed it 'a wiser and more patriotic course to merge their interests in the general financial interests of the nation at large'.

The treasury agreed to postpone action, but only briefly, and their draft legislation was ready by the end of October. Again Guinness immediately enlisted the government's support, this time from W.T. Cosgrave, head of government since Collins was killed in August.[68] Dublin's case, Cosgrave revealed, had not been helped by the delivery in error to A. P. Waterfield, the treasury's man on the skeleton British staff still in Dublin, of a memorandum drawn up by Collins for his own officials in the Department of Finance which stated, *inter alia*, that the transfer of the registers to England 'was not an unreasonable proposal'. Cosgrave duly made representations in London both to the treasury officials and to Churchill's successor as Colonial Secretary in the new Conservative government, the Duke of Devonshire.[69] But it was that government's appointee as the first governor-general of the Irish Free State, Timothy Healy, whose influence proved decisive in blocking the transfer of registers. Devonshire admitted to 'a great regard' for Healy who, he said, 'put flowers once a year on the grave of Lord Frederick Cavendish on the anniversary of his death'.[70] Healy was Devonshire's 'sole nominee as governor-general'[71] notwithstanding the reservations of the Prime Minister, Bonar Law, that 'he was impulsive and he drank too much whisky at night'.[72] But Bonar Law's reservations, reinforced by his party's dislike of Healy, were overcome by the force and eloquence with which Healy had argued the case for retaining the register in Dublin. Law was 'satisfied from his argument that it would injure British interest on the Irish market if the treasury proposals were carried through' and this 'turned the scale in favour of his appointment'.[73] Guinness duly reported Healy's key rôle to the IBSC on 13 December (within a week of the establishment of the Free State) and a grateful committee voted that he be paid £160 for out-of-pocket expenses and professional services — £55 to be paid by the Bank of Ireland, £55 by the other Irish banks and £50 jointly by the Stock Exchange and Incorporated Law Society.[74] The outcome was a British order-in-council providing that only holdings of stockholders domiciled in the north who did not object to the transfer would be registered in Belfast; procedures bringing the Bank of Ireland register in line with the procedures governing the United Kingdom debt were not finally agreed until the Anglo-Irish talks of 1964.[75]

The Bank and the Irish Free State 1922-32

But matters did not always run so smoothly between the Bank and Cosgrave's government. Government borrowing in general and the launching of the first national loan in 1923 in particular was a cause of dissension.[76] Joseph Brennan, the Secretary of the Department of Finance, wrote to Henry Guinness on 13 March that the government needed £2,750,000 to meet the deficit for the current financial year and, in the likely event of the deficit continuing to grow, another £750,000 to £1,000,000 a month for the next eight or nine months. The banks expressed unanimous outrage when Guinness informed them of the government's demands at an IBSC meeting next day. They were especially irked that they were being given so little notice, as a British government guarantee for the loan might otherwise have been sought. But, although all agreed they would rather *not* advance the initial £2,750,000 'there seemed to be no alternative left as a large proportion of the money was required for the army, and if the advance was not granted they could not see how the army was to be paid'. They were unanimous, however, that they would make no further advances without a British treasury, or some equally acceptable, guarantee.[77]

The Bank's difficulty, as Andrew Jameson succinctly explained some weeks later in London to W. Ormsby-Gore, the parliamentary under-secretary to the Colonial Office, was that 'only the Free State government stands between Ireland and complete anarchy'.[78] Although, having accepted a government nomination for the Senate from Cosgrave, Jameson was 'forced to take an optimistic view', his optimism was wearing thin. He told Ormsby-Gore that although relations between the government and 'the bankers' committee headed by Henry Guinness' had 'started by being intimate but are so no longer, and that the bankers have no idea where the Free State government are now looking and they are rather apprehensive'. Guinness, too, had been made a senator by Cosgrave — as had another future Governor of the Bank, Sir John Keane — and senators had particular cause for apprehension when they became targets of the irregulars' campaign of arson and murder in the early months of 1923. Jameson in fact was first on the list of those to be shot on sight but went on to act as intermediary between Cosgrave and de Valera in the abortive negotiations which prefaced the ceasefire at the end of May. On 24 March Guinness's home at Burton Hall, Stillorgan, was attacked by armed men, who, having turned out him and his family, planted gelignite in the basement and set fire to the upper floors which they had first sprayed with petrol. Although the gelignite failed to explode, the house was badly damaged by fire.[79] Such was the background to Jameson's insistence to Ormsby-Gore that Whitehall ought to be in touch with Guinness ('who is in a better position to speak for the banks, and commercial community than any man in Ireland').

But Otto Niemeyer of the treasury reacted negatively to Ormsby-Gore's report arguing that

it would be a fundamental mistake for us to intervene in the matter. We have no power to do so effectively if we wanted to; and our interference would probably have quite the opposite effect to what we wished. The Free State is now a dominion. It must make its own experience in currency matters as in others. The business of the Irish banks is to make their influence felt by their own government and to give that government sound advice. The government will need the banks' assistance and will probably be not at all unwilling to listen to them.

On the other hand, if the Irish banks come over here and particularly if they are known to be coming over here, they will at once deprive themselves of exercising their proper influence in their own country.

The Free State has its financial troubles before it and it would be foolish to pretend that they are not considerable: but they are by no means insuperable and in fact are far less than those of the greater number of countries in Europe. On the whole, the Free State has hitherto shown no inclination to panic legislation and their own interests seem to me to be entirely in favour of reasonably sound monetary policy. But they clearly must be left to run their own affair.

Mr Guinness, the Governor of the Bank of Ireland, writes to me not infrequently on bank business and is naturally in touch with the Bank of England. He has the natural channel for discussion, if he wishes to take it privately. I think he has been wise in not asking our advice so far.[80]

Niemeyer was convinced of the 'soundness' of the financial policies of Cosgrave's government, formulated by Brennan and other former treasury officials, and did not think 'they will levy on their banks if the latter are reasonable . . . But Irish banks must be prepared to support their government, as they well can, without thinking too much or solely of their immediate profits'.[81]

However, the mood of the Irish banks was very different from the Olympian detachment of Niemeyer's Whitehall perspective. Indeed, when on 13 June 1923, the two senior officials in the Department of Finance, Brennan and J.J. McElligott, went directly to the Bank of Ireland and sought personally to address an IBSC meeting then in progress on the additional accommodation of £7 million needed by the government before October,

> several members . . . expressed dissatisfaction with the way in which the banks were approached in regard to government borrowing. They felt they were entitled to know if the two young men [Brennan was then 36, McElligott 33] who waited on them spoke with authority. Many things were said that would not be said by the President himself and the impression was created that the Minister of Finance had no conception of the responsibilities attaching to banks in regard to their investors.

When Brennan and McElligott were admitted to the meeting they were told

> that if the public could be induced to subscribe to a Free State loan that would be a voluntary action on the part of the subscribers; to ask the banks to utilise their depositors' money in subscribing to such a loan was asking the banks to use, without their consent, the monies of depositors unwilling to assist the government financially.

McElligott's objection that the banks had invested in British government securities without their depositors' prior consent was met by the galling retort that 'the securities of the British government were the best in the world, with perhaps the exception of the United States of America ... and could always be turned into cash at a moment's notice'. After Brennan and McElligott had withdrawn, Henry Guinness, speaking with the Governor's traditional authority as the committee's chairman, said that he wanted 'to hear directly from himself the President's views' and this was agreed.[82] It is a moot point whether he knew in advance what Cosgrave might say, but thought his colleagues must hear it for themselves.

The IBSC deputation met Cosgrave, who was accompanied by Brennan and McElligott, next day.[83] Guinness opened the discussion by referring to the March exchanges between the banks and the government and, in particular, to the banks' expectation that any further advances would be secured by British government guarantee. Cosgrave was in militant mood and began by saying that the government could postpone borrowing the money if they held up compensation payments for malicious injury and made immediate army cuts. That the first step 'would create an immediate outcry, both here and across the water' could scarcely be disputed by a deputation whose leader, Guinness, was himself due compensation. To make further army cuts when the army was already being reduced by 500 men a week was still more daunting and, as Cosgrave bleakly observed, 'would be to withdraw the protection which the army afforded to the Irish banks generally, and to let the country drift back into a state of lawlessness'. He also warned that his government could introduce 'emergency legislation to raise the money by taking the currency of the country into their own hands'. They had no wish to do so, 'but they must have the money and were not going to be caught napping'. They would not seek a British guarantee: if they did, they felt 'destruction would once more commence throughout the country' and, if they had a British guarantee, 'they would not require the assistance of the banks'.

The bankers promptly raised their own spectres in response, most notably the danger of a concerted run, but Cosgrave gave an assurance that if 'there were organised attacks upon the banks as a reprisal for having assisted the finances of the government, they would be prepared to deal with the situation very drastically'. He said that 'if a run were started it would be for purely political reasons, so as to embarrass the government, and not owing to any suggestion that the banks had weakened their resources by lending the money now required by the government'. Although Cosgrave admitted that rumours had reached the government from the south of Ireland that the tactics of their republican opponents 'had changed, and they were devoting their attention now to what they called "business methods"', he and his officials denied that there was any real likelihood of a run. McElligott 'thought there was no more reason to expect a run under existing conditions than in "Black and Tan" times'; Brennan pointed out that there had been no run when the advance of £2,225,000 had been made to the government in March and an additional advance of £7 million would not lead to a run now that the civil war was over.

But the deputation were concerned not merely with this immediate advance but also with the terms of the loan the government intended to launch after the election. Cosgrave resisted pressure to seek a British guarantee if his party won the election. He promised only 'that an application for such a guarantee would not be ruled out', but made it clear that he thought 'the political reasons against such a course ... too big to be overcome'.

The deputation had obtained none of the assurances they had hoped for when, at the end of the interview, they talked privately at Government Buildings. Some, notably the Provincial Bank's representatives, opposed any further advances without a British guarantee. Guinness then intervened, saying that 'the Bank of Ireland would be prepared to assist the government if the other banks were also prepared to assist'; he also suggested that, rather than look for a British guarantee,

> the government would resort to any and every method to compel the banks to advance the monies they required . . . [He] thought it would be most dangerous if any action on the part of the banks caused this question to be brought officially before the Dáil; the banks would be pilloried as holding up the government of the country for selfish purposes.

Guinness's intervention was decisive, although the deputation 'generally thought' that the government would not carry out their threats, 'it was not exactly "bluff", but the expression of the strong opinion of men in desperate need of immediate funds'. That the deputation could not convincingly dispute that the need *was* desperate explains their reluctant agreement to recommend the advance of the £7 million subject to the post-election appeal for a public loan being supported by British guarantee.

A compromise was reached following a further meeting, on 18 June, between Cosgrave and Brennan and a deputation of Guinness, Jameson and J.X. Murphy — all, it should be noted, directors of the Bank of Ireland. Cosgrave said he 'would raise no objection' to the banks exploring the possibility of a British guarantee with the treasury

> on the clear understanding . . . that neither he nor the Irish government should be brought into the transaction. He considered it vital that he should be able to stand up in the new Dáil and say that he had at no time, on behalf of the government, approached the British government with any request for money or guarantees.

In return the banks agreed to advance £3 million to tide the government over until after the election on condition that they would not, in the meantime, launch any public appeal for a loan.[84]

The government duly won their election in August with what one minister over-optimistically described as 'very great' effects on banking opinion[85]— and, on 7 November, Guinness and Jameson met Ernest Blythe, the newly-appointed Minister for Finance. Blythe was looking for the banks' support for the first national loan: it was proposed to issue £10 million of redeemable stocks at 95 per cent and he sought the banks' assurance that they would take up to £4 million in the event of the loan not being fully subscribed; he also wanted the banks to recommend the loan to their depositors. This last posed little difficulty: Guinness, while loftily insisting that the banks could do nothing which would 'render them liable to an action at law in the event of their depositors losing money as a consequence of their bankers' advice', suggested that the prospectuses for the loan could be let lie on the counters of the Bank's public offices. But early agreement on the substantive issue was again thwarted by the matter of the British guarantee which Blythe, like Cosgrave, pronounced politically unacceptable. Blythe went to remarkable lengths, however, to persuade Guinness and Jameson of the impeccable conservatism of his financial policy. The government, he said, intended to balance its budget within a few years and had already decided to cut national teachers' salaries and old age pensions. Enquiries were being made 'as to the possibility of doing away with national health insurance and labour exchanges, neither of which seemed necessary in the Free State'. Further army cuts were planned and the government 'had no intention of interfering with the currency and they realised that the backing of England was necessary for their note issues'.

But not even this extraordinarily orthodox financial testament swayed the more timid spirits of the IBSC, notwithstanding Guinness's telling them that Montagu Norman, the Governor of the Bank of England, had told himself and Jameson that he thought it 'essential . . . that the Irish banks should support the Free State financially in so far as they can do so without any injury to their own stability'. It took another meeting with Blythe and Brennan followed by further private discussion among the deputation in the government's council chamber before the banks finally agreed to take up to £4 million if the target of £10 million was not reached[86]. That they were never called upon to do so, since the loan had been oversubscribed by £200,000 when it closed on 7 December, vindicates Niemeyer's pre-election assessment of the government's financial position: 'there is nothing to despair about in their situation — but they have everything to learn and all their bankers are rabbits'. Niemeyer's advice to Brennan 'to make a point of seeing a leading Irish banker (not a committee of bankers which is entirely useless) two or three times a week' and the fact that he 'indirectly encouraged the Bank of Ireland to give him these private consultations'[87] may explain why Henry Guinness was markedly more positive in the November negotiations than his colleagues on the IBSC. It certainly explains Guinness's reaction to the proposal made by the Royal and Provincial Banks (within a week of the first national loan having been over-subscribed) that a sub-committee should be formed to conduct negotiations for any future government loans:

> while the Bank of Ireland welcomed the proposal . . . it must be remembered that the Bank of Ireland stood in peculiar relations to the government as they had been appointed their financial agents. As a consequence of this relationship there must naturally be intimate conversations between the government and the Governor of the Bank of Ireland.[88]

It may explain, too, why the endeavours of the other banks, led by the National Bank, to get a share of government business as a *quid pro quo* for having contributed to government borrowing in 1923 came to nothing. A succession of letters from the secretary of the IBSC on the instructions of the sub-committee (appointed in March 1924 and composed of one representative each from the Bank of Ireland, Hibernian, Munster and Leinster, Royal and National Banks) to the Department of Finance between December 1923 and March 1925 asking 'what steps, if any, had been taken to provide for the allocation of some portion of the government's banking accounts to the Irish banks other than the Bank of Ireland' were frustrated by that classic Finance tactic of simply not replying.[89]

The banks' reluctance to accommodate the government in 1923 left something of a sour taste in Cosgrave's mouth and the Governor informed his colleagues in March 1924 'that a person in intimate touch' with the President had confided in him that Cosgrave felt 'there was a good deal of profiteering on the part of the Irish banks' and thought their rates 'considerably in excess of the rates charged by English bankers'. But Cosgrave's views may have been jaundiced by the contemporaneous decision of the IBSC to reject a Cumann na nGaedheal request to make a contribution towards defraying their 1923 election expenses by sending a 'courteous letter' expressing the unanimous opinion that the Irish banks 'neither jointly nor severally, should be asked to contribute to party funds'. A further request a year later met with the same reply.[90]

The Bank of Ireland's response to many such appeals reveal occasional relics of the Bank's imperial past: contrast for instance, the Court's order of 3 April 1924 to send a donation of £52 10s. 0d. to Professor J.B. Whelehan's appeal for the relief of distress in Connemara with the order three months later that a donation of £100 be sent to Queen Victoria's Jubilee Institute for Nurses in Ireland.[91] But such episodes cannot disguise the fact that firm ties were forged between Bank and government in 1923 which were never again so arduously tested in the more stable years ahead.

The Banking Commission of 1926 provided no such test. Blythe's intention, as Minister for Finance, was that the commission should only deal with matters consequent upon independence and obtain information which would better enable him to answer Dáil questions. So the ubiquitous Andrew Jameson reported to the IBSC on 22 December 1925 that Blythe 'only wished the commission to deal with the necessary business, he did not wish the commission to deal with the dangerous questions, e.g. [sic] such questions as would set up a visible rate of exchange'. Jameson's response to Blythe's invitation to chair the commission was equally instructive:

> He knew quite well why the government wished him to act ... he had the reputation of being an old-fashioned conservative, and he could understand that they would like it to appear that any recommendations which the Commission might make would have his support as chairman.[92]

Jameson accepted a place on the commission, although not as chairman, and joined forces with McElligott in a minority report which expressed 'unqualified disagreement' with the proposal that the government accounts should be distributed among the different banks. They also opposed the majority proposals that the Currency Commission, whose establishment was envisaged in the Banking Commission's reports, should be made responsible for investing government funds and keeping a register of government stock.

They resisted, in short, the proposal that functions enacted by the Bank of Ireland as the government's financial agent would be better entrusted to the Currency Commission which would thus assume 'rather more of the character and standing of a central bank'.[93] The final report, however, evaded the issue of whether or not a central bank should be established for reasons succintly summarised by Maurice Moynihan:

> that the commercial banks were strongly represented on the commission; that the Bank of Ireland had long enjoyed the prestige and profit of being the government's bank and was not then (or until many years later) in a mood to surrender its privileged position without a struggle; that agreement among the banks on proposals for a distribution of government business among them was not to be expected; and that, presumably, there was no disposition to welcome the intrusion on the Irish banking scene of a stranger in the form of a central institution with powers of supervision and control.

Blythe, in a comment in the Dáil during his speech on the Currency Bill, 1927, in keeping with his undertaking to Jameson in 1925, referred to 'the disturbance that

Plate 24

Brian King
Celtic Knot 1979
Stainless steel
80 × 212 × 45 cms

Plate 25

Gene Lambert
Rocking Horse 1981
Oil on canvas
80 × 86 cms

would have been involved in the setting up of a central bank in opposition to the wishes of the existing institutions'.[94]

That the governments of 1922-32 anathematised 'disturbance' explains the tranquillity which characterised their relations with the Bank of Ireland once the civil war had been won. That the Currency Commission's first meeting, on 23 September 1927, was held at the Bank of Ireland which, in February 1928, agreed to sell 15,000 square feet of its premises fronting on Foster Place to the Currency Commission and that those premises were the commissions's headquarters until 1969 appropriately symbolised the unchanging order.[95]

A concern not unduly to disturb the *status quo* is also evident in the approach to the Bank's statutory position after independence. Under the Irish Free State constitution the laws in force in the United Kingdom were adopted by the new state unless altered or repealed by the Dáil and this applied to the Bank's charter of 1783 as granted and governed by various British statutes. The question of the Bank's 'position and relationship . . . to the Free State on the one hand, and to the British parliament and British treasury on the other hand', if and when their charter was confirmed by the Dáil, had preoccupied the Bank's directors since October 1923, when Henry Guinness first raised the matter with the Governor of the Bank of England, Montagu Norman.[96] But the matter lay dormant until the Irish government included a provision in the 1927 Currency Act that the Bank's charter, 'so far as the Free State is concerned, will not be affected by the repayment of the debt (of £2.5 millions) owed to the Bank by the British government'. This provision, the treasury concluded,

> was not inserted in a spirit of benevolence to the Bank but . . . [because] the Free State government, in their financial embarrassments, have some idea of getting the Bank to ask for the repayment of the government debt with a view to the money being re-lent by the Bank, on the same terms, to the Free State government.[97]

These fears that the government would exert 'great political pressure' to demand repayment of the debt had indeed been expressed by the Governor, Captain Ronald Nutting, in an interview at the treasury, when he explained that the Bank 'for its part had no desire to alter the existing arrangements'.[98] The issues were spelt out by Otto Niemeyer, who had moved from the treasury to the Bank of England, to a former treasury colleague with whom he had arranged Nutting's interview. Nutting, Niemeyer was satisfied,

> does not at all wish to have this debt repaid. On the contrary he regards it as securing to the Bank of Ireland your continuing countenance. *If* and when, therefore, the Irish government make such a request to you I am quite sure the Bank of Ireland would be delighted to see it turned down though they would probably not at that moment dare to say. How far Nutting would tell you of this I do not know, but I am sure this is his real attitude and I think you should know it.[99]

But Merrion Street, no more than College Green or Whitehall, sought change at the cost of confrontation, and it proved a false alarm.

Change in the Bank's statutory position was encompassed in the Bank of Ireland Act, 1929. This was a private bill, effectively sponsored by the Bank but approved by the government; its principal object was to ensure that the control and administration of the Bank would remain with citizens of the state where the Governor, Deputy Governor and at least three-quarters of the directors must be henceforth domiciled and resident. The design, in short, was to 'ensure that the Bank would continue to carry on business as an independent Irish institution, without in any way being dictated to or influenced by any other interest'.[100]

The Bank and De Valera's Ireland

The 1932 change of government, when Eamon de Valera's Fianna Fáil entered into sixteen years in office which more than spans the rest of the period with which this essay is concerned, never seriously challenged the now harmonious relationship between government and Bank. I have written elsewhere of the strength of continuity linking government financial policy of the twenties with the thirties — of the fact, for example, that the financial articles of the 1937 constitution were substantially modelled on those in the 1922 constitution.[101] Constitutional revolutionary de Valera may have been, fiscal or socio-economic revolutionary he most assuredly was not. He no more wanted to alienate the banking community than he wanted to alienate the public service.

That the government was conscious of the sensitivities of the Bank of Ireland in particular became immediately apparent following a meeting between an IBSC deputation, headed by the Governor, Sir Lingard Goulding, and the new Minister for Finance, Sean MacEntee, on 19 May 1932, when anxiety was expressed about the effect of the government's budget proposals upon banking interests.[102] One proposal touched the Bank of Ireland, and the Bank of Ireland alone, directly: namely that it lose its exemption from corporation profits tax confirmed by a High Court decision of March 1925 on the grounds that its stockholders' liability was unlimited by the 1782 act under which the Bank's charter had been issued.[103] A cabinet meeting the very next day decided that the Minister for Finance should examine 'the advisability of introducing legislation to place the Bank of Ireland, if the Governors [sic] so desire, in the same position as the other banks in respect of stockholders' liability'; and a note sent some days later by the secretary to the government to the private secretary to the Minister for Finance — 'to prevent the matter being overlooked' — underscores the government's sense of urgency lest it get ensnared in the red tape traditionally festooning the administrative machinery of the Department of Finance.[104] In vain: two years passed before, following a meeting between Goulding and MacEntee on 30 May 1934 and the submission next day by the Bank of a draft bill and accompanying memorandum, any real progress was made. But delay should not be equated with ill will. The Minister for Finance pronounced the private bill equitable and recommended that it receive government support; the government so decided on 16 November 1934 and the bill was duly enacted on 20 June 1935.[105]

The Bank were doubtless similarly reassured by other episodes, such as Goulding's interview with MacEntee in November 1932 when they agreed 'that to sever the connection between the Saorstat pound and sterling would be a most undesirable, and probably disastrous, step to take'.[106] This is not, of course, to argue that ministers and bankers always saw eye to eye but, when differences did occur, government pressure for change was more moderate than extreme. The 1933 discussions of bank loans to a farming community for whom the 'economic war' had compounded the effects of world-wide recession was a case in point.

Farmers' loans had in fact formed the subject of an 'unofficial conversation' between the Governor, H. J. Millar, and McElligott, who had succeeded Brennan as Secretary of the Department of Finance in 1927 before de Valera came to power. McElligott had then asked about the loans (made to farmers to buy land or for other purposes during or shortly after the First World War) which had 'assumed the nature of "frozen loans"' as the economic climate deteriorated. McElligott stressed that all he wanted was information so that he could assess the dimensions of the problem and whether or not the borrowers' position 'was righting itself gradually'. More significantly he

> emphasised that his enquiry was a purely unofficial one of which the government was not aware, and that there was no intention on the part of the government of interfering in the matter in any way, either in the interests of borrowers or banks.[107]

That McElligott — once described by a senior treasury official as possessing that rare combination of the wisdom of the serpent and the mildness of the dove[108] — and other senior Finance officials with whom the Bank had established close ties, retained practical charge of financial administration despite the advent of de Valera's more interventionist government cannot but have been a considerable consolation to Goulding and his colleagues. Moreover, Lord Glenavy, appointed to the Court of Directors in 1932 and who became Governor in 1945, had been Secretary of Industry and Commerce (and an intimate of McElligott's) until he succeeded to his father's peerage in 1931. It may also be safely surmised that the Bank's directors were fully aware of McElligott's antipathy for the policies which, in his *private* judgment, had led to an unnecessary and damaging economic war.

That de Valera was accompanied only by McElligott must, then, have been of some comfort to Goulding and T. F. Hennessy (Secretary to the IBSC) when they met him in Leinster House, fresh from his second electoral triumph, to discuss farmers' loans. De Valera referred to the growing agitation about the loans and to the feeling that 'in cases where money had been advanced for the purchase of land during the period of inflation the banks should not expect to get their full pound of flesh'. But he also used McElligott's 1931 terminology about wanting 'to know the dimensions of the problem' and stressed that the government was concerned that 'organised movements ... to resist attempts at eviction ... should not go too far'. He said too

> that the government was in much the same position as the banks in respect of the land purchase annuities, and they were anxious that there should be no resistance to paying debts ... He would like to be able to say that in case of misfortune the banks would not be unduly harsh.

De Valera concluded by describing his government as 'anxious to understand the position of the banks' and asked if the Governor could supply aggregate figures showing 'what the banks had done and were doing'. The government

> felt that if any part of the field of credit was not being covered by existing institutions it might become necessary to find some way of covering that field; they had no desire to enter into banking, and their attitude towards the banks was one of co-operation rather than rivalry.[109]

Goulding thought that de Valera's attitude 'was altogether friendly and courteous, and that he appeared to be activated by a real desire to appreciate the position of the banks'. He pressed his banking colleagues to co-operate as fully as possible in providing the statistics required.[110]

That de Valera was a moderate seeking to contain his own extremists emerges from the events leading to the establishment of the Banking Commission of 1934-8. The Governor, still Lingard Goulding, was first apprised of the government's intentions when he was summoned on a Saturday by telephone to Government Buildings where he met de Valera alone. De Valera handed him the draft terms of reference and a tentative list of the commission's personnel. It was a measure of the Bank's influence that when the IBSC assembled in special session to discuss the matter on 13 April, Goulding told them that

> the list of personnel had been modified by the removal of several names [one of which may have been J. M. Keynes whose name appeared on an early list of foreign experts] to which he had taken exception. In the Governor's view the President considered a commission should sit and report, but he did not think any alteration in the system was necessary, he was being subjected to pressure from a large section of his party which he would probably be unable to resist.

The IBSC took the view that the moment was most inopportune for such a move; reference was made to 'the number of experiments that are taking place in Europe and America both in banking and currency' and the opinion expressed that the 'foreign experts' whom the government proposed to appoint 'would probably be predisposed to recommending the establishment of a central bank'. The advisability of refusing to participate in the commission was countered by the argument that 'if the banks declined to take part the commission might bring in a report which would . . . let the banks' case go by default.[111]

But de Valera was reluctant to yield further when he saw Goulding again on 16 April. He did, however, point out that it was hardly possible that the commission could meet before the end of July or report for at least twelve months thereafter, by which time 'he thought the international situation would have developed sufficiently to guide the commission'.[112] The cabinet subsequently decided[113] to increase the banks' nominees from two to three and reduce the foreign experts from three to two; and to invite a representative of commercial interests, J.C.M. Eason, which the banks had also sought; otherwise the composition of the commission remained unchanged, as also did the terms of reference: namely,

> to examine and report on the system in Saorstat Eireann of currency, banking, credit, public borrowing and lending, and the pledging of state credit on behalf of agriculture, industry and the social services, and to consider and report what changes, if any, are necessary or desirable to promote the social and economic welfare of the community and the interests of agriculture and industry.

But the IBSC — together with the Currency Commission which made similar representations[114] — made one further significant gain in getting the government to withdraw their initial memorandum raising certain specific and highly sensitive points for the commission's 'early consideration'. These points were three:

(a) The regulation of currency and credit in the Saorstat.

(b) The advisability of establishing a central bank and the functions and constitution thereof.

(c) The steps which may be necessary or desirable to safeguard the trade, currency and credit of Saorstat Eireann against the possible ill-effects of variations in the exchange values of sterling and other currencies.

While the government justified its retreat with reference to the opinion of Joseph Brennan, chairman of the Currency Commission and already the designated chairman of the proposed banking commission, 'that these matters would, in any event, arise under the terms of reference', the fact remained that the commission was effectively relieved of the obligation to give specific answers to what the Bank of Ireland above all other banks perceived as questions explicitly antagonistic to its interests.

But although the IBSC showed signs of bowing to the inevitable by agreeing on how banking representatives would be nominated — one by the Bank of Ireland (Lord Glenavy); one by the banks incorporated outside the state — the National, Provincial, Northern and Ulster (Michael J. Cooke, chairman of the National Bank); and one by the other banks — Hibernian, Munster and Leinster, and Royal (James M. Sweetman, a director of the Royal Bank)[115] — they made a final effort to persuade the government of the error of its ways. This took the form of a proposal, initiated by the representatives of the Munster and Leinster Bank, that a deputation from the IBSC should meet the Ministers for Finance (Sean MacEntee) and Industry and Commerce (Sean Lemass) as well as de Valera, despite (or perhaps because of) the fact that Goulding had drawn up a letter in advance which implicitly if reluctantly acquiesced in the establishment of the commission.[116] And it seems reasonable to assume that the move may have been prompted, at least in part, by the resentment of the other banks at the Bank of Ireland's primacy as reflected in de Valera's having dealt directly and solely with the Governor of the Bank of Ireland.

Such an interpretation is borne out both by the fact that, exceptionally, chairmen of *all* the other banks (other than the Provincial) attended the meeting arranged with de Valera and his ministers on 10 May and by Goulding's opening remarks to the effect that, as 'he had expressed his own views and those of the Standing Committee as a body' in his recent interviews with de Valera, 'on the present occasion it would probably suffice if the President and ministers could hear some further representations which the individual banks wished to make'. Goulding thus effectively dissociated himself from the proceedings to which he made virtually no further contribution. The 'further representations' of his colleagues focused almost exclusively on the 'disturbing effect . . . on the public mind' of the commissions's appointment and the 'grave danger of uneasiness with the possibility of a run'. But suggestions that 'ever since the change had taken place in the economic policy of the country depositers had become uneasy', and that 'prior to the budget statement there was an extreme degree of uneasiness in the minds of the people' from the chairmen of banks with their headquarters in London and Belfast respectively were scarcely calculated to appeal to government ministers. De Valera was adamant:

> the feeling of nervousness which had been referred to would have to be faced in any event . . . He felt there had been a good deal of scares in advance of the budget which may have been responsible for some of the withdrawals which had been mentioned. As to the holding of the inquiry the mind of the Executive Council had been pretty well made up, and while the views of the banks were deserving of

the greatest possible consideration, he felt that if the government could count on the co-operation of the banks there was not likely to be any anxiety. One of the reasons for the inquiry was the unfortunate position of the Free State as regards sterling which could be changed by the British government without reference to the Free State government. This question must be examined for the country's safety. An increasing demand for the inquiry arose from certain quarters, and the government were convinced that a thorough examination of the whole subject would satisfy this demand and would reveal the fallacies in some of the propaganda which was going on. From every angle the government considered it was wise that the inquiry should be instituted now, and with the co-operation of the banks there was not much to be feared in the long run. The banks might take it that the government were going ahead with the proposal.[117]

And go ahead they did, leaving the banks, as Goulding clearly realised more quickly than his colleagues, no alternative but to co-operate in the interests of stability. The wilder apprehensions of Goulding's colleagues were in any event misplaced. A commission chaired by Joseph Brennan, former Secretary of the Department of Finance and then chairman of the Currency Commission, and including the then Secretary (McElligott) and an assistant secretary (Sean Moynihan) to say nothing of Lord Glenavy, his fellow-bankers and other conservatives, was scarcely a recipe for radical change. The majority report, presented in March 1938, was essentially 'a recommendation to leave things as they were':[118] the Bank of Ireland's position as government banker should be left undisturbed; the link between the Irish pound and sterling should be maintained at the existing parity. The contagion of financial heterodoxy was safely contained in the quarantine of minority reports which were rendered even less effective than usual when the five more liberal commissioners produced three different reports between them.[119]

One recommendation of the majority report had major implications for the Bank of Ireland: namely that the Currency Commission should be reconstituted as a central bank. Although Lord Glenavy, supported by James Sweetman of the Royal Bank, produced an addendum arguing that the proposal was inconsistent with the majority report's opinion 'that nothing whatever is wrong with the system in Saorstat Eireann'[120] — which in turn bore out the findings of the report privately commissioned by the IBSC from Geoffrey Crowther in 1932* — the 1938 recommendation in favour of a central bank can hardly have surprised bankers who, in 1934, had concluded that it was the reason behind the proposed commission of inquiry.[121]

But by 1938 war was looming in Europe. The Munich crisis of September 1938 occasioned the first conference of the banks, in collaboration with the Currency Commission, and at the request of the Minister for Finance, on the implications of a war in which Britain was involved but in which Ireland (described as 'Eire' throughout the relevant IBSC memorandum) would remain neutral. They decided that there need be no undue disturbance in ordinary banking business provided that:

(a) The banks are in a position to meet all reasonable demands of their customers for circulation.

---

* 'the argument may be summarised by saying that if a central bank were set up in an amicable atmosphere, if it were conducted by competent and prudent bankers, and if its profits went to those who provided its resources (that is, largely, the banks) it would probably do little or no harm beyond complicating the structure, and increasing the expense of administration of Irish banking. But by the same token it would do little good.'

Plate 26

Lord Glenavy

(b) Interest rates in Eire are maintained at the same levels as in Northern Ireland.
(c) Effective control over imports is instituted by Eire government.[122]

December 1938 saw the Court of Directors considering air raid precautions, a list of which was approved in April 1939; and in mid June 1939, the Court noted a request from the Department of Industry and Commerce that the banks facilitate the accumulation of reserves of essential supplies.[123] A week later an IBSC deputation (all four of whom were from the Bank of Ireland) received McElligott and John Leydon (then Secretary of Industry and Commerce but soon to become Secretary of the new Department of Supplies) at College Green to discuss the impending crisis. War, said

McElligott, 'was inevitable sooner or later' and the government expected the banks 'to grant special accommodation to creditworthy customers for the specific purpose of accumulating reserves'. He made no suggestion 'as to how [the] banks were to be recouped for loss of interest, or loss in exchange' and offered no government guarantee since a guarantee to the banks would involve a guarantee to importers. He anticipated 'a public outcry' against the banks if they looked for guarantees and suggested they should regard any such losses 'as their contribution towards the precautionary measures'. He asked the banks to place £5 million at the disposal of the exchequer for the purchase of foreign exchange.[124] The banks' concern to be indemnified against loss was the subject of correspondence with the Department of Finance throughout July and August in which McElligott reiterated

> that these concerns, which occupy in some respects a privileged position in the community, should undertake the risks incidental to the accumulation of reserves in advance of an emergency . . . This country being now a separate political and economic entity, a situation exists radically different from that which obtained in 1914. This country should be prepared, if need arises, to conduct foreign trade on its own account, and for this purpose the chief requisite would be a supply of foreign credit.[125]

But the banks stood firm and McElligott eventually gave way, accepting the banks' offer to place £3 million at the disposal of the exchequer and dropping the issue of accumulating reserves of foreign exchange.[126]

McElligott's retreat may have been prompted by the outcome of a visit by the Bank's deputy governor, Sir John Keane, to the Bank of England to inquire 'about the availability of its London funds in the event of hostilities'. He also wanted to know whether in the event of those funds being exhausted, the Bank of England would make a loan against security. The Governor of the Bank of England, Montagu Norman, said 'no':

> The Bank of England looked upon Eire as a dominion, and if they accommodated the Bank of Ireland in a crisis, there would be no reason why they should withhold similar assistance from other dominions — the Bank was not prepared to concede this principal [*sic*]. Mr Norman stressed the view that the banks 'whose centre of gravity was in Eire' should look to their own treasury or the Currency Commission to help them over difficult periods. Sir John pointed out that the position in Eire did not admit of a solution in that way, as the treasury came to the Bank of Ireland when it was short of funds, and the Currency Commission was not a lender of last resort. Mr Norman then urged that as Eire was a separate political entity it should have a Central Bank of its own.[127]

War was declared within a week and the Irish banks immediately agreed, as they had done in the First World War, 'to co-operate with each other in every reasonable way' and 'that no bank would make use of the situation to the disadvantage of another bank'.[128] One immediate and, given Irish neutrality, highly sensitive problem was the provision to be made for bank staff wishing to enlist in the British forces and when, on 21 September, the salary and pension arrangements for such staff were approved, it was agreed

> that no circular dealing with the matter should be issued by any of the banks, and

Plate 27

Cash office ceiling, College Green

Plate 28

Colin Middleton
Leitrim Hills 1971
Oil on board
100 × 100 mm
Signed bottom right with a monogram 'CM'
Exhibited at the Irish Exhibition of Living Art, Dublin 1971

that if any official enquired as to the conditions to be given to the members of staff going on active service, he should be informed verbally, but should not be shown anything in writing.[129]

De Valera adverted to the subject some months later when he asked if it were true that the banks 'were granting less favourable terms' to staff who joined the Irish army. Sir John Keane acknowledged

> that at the outset of the recruiting campaign for local forces questions arose as to service here being 'active service'; it had since been decided by the banks that the same terms as allowed to volunteers for British forces should be accorded those joining the forces of Eire.[130]

This was one of a series of frank exchanges between government and banking representatives when France was falling in June 1940 and when Irish anti-invasion preparations were at their height.[131] These meetings were initiated at the suggestion of Sir John Keane, who, although he did not become Governor until 1941, was already much more prominent than his predecessor, H.A. Henry (about whom Joseph Hone's biographical notes on the Bank's directors are singularly silent).[132] Keane assured de Valera 'that the banks realised their responsibility to help the government in the present situation', although he jibbed at government borrowing to relieve unemployment — 'a problem which constituted "a danger in our midst"', according to de Valera.[133] The overall impression, however, is of close co-operation arising out of a mutually perceived identity of interests between government and banks.

Neutrality has rightly been described as the ultimate expression of Irish sovereignty and it provides the context in which the government finally proceeded with its plans to establish a central bank. The decision was taken in principle by the cabinet on 10 October 1939, but it was only on 11 July 1941 that McElligott called on Sir John Keane and gave him twenty-five proof copies of the Central Bank Bill.[134] The origins of, and debate on, the Central Bank Bill have been the subject of recent and comprehensive treatment elsewhere.[135] Here it suffices simply to point out that the banks, and the Bank of Ireland in particular, yielded gracefully. Their reasoning was well summarised in the opening paragraph of a memorandum drawn up by T. F. Hennessy, the secretary of the IBSC. Given that the bill 'leaves no doubt' as to the government's intention to establish a central bank in consequence of the majority report of the Banking Commission, there appeared

> to be no course open to the banks other than to accept the situation, and concentrate their efforts towards securing such amendments, modifications or alterations in the bill as they consider necessary to ensure that the Central Bank will be established on foundations which will merit public confidence and create the minimum amount of disturbance to the banking and economic system.[136]

Although the government accepted some minor amendments, the principal features to which the banks took exception (such as the preponderance of non-banking directors and the power to regulate the foreign investments of individual banks) remained unaltered — the more peripheral objection that 'the title "Central Bank of Ireland", with a chairman styled the "Governor", seems unfortunate from the viewpoint of the Bank of Ireland, and may lead to confusion'[137] is also worth passing mention. But the exchanges were conciliatory, with Sir John Keane stressing that 'it was the desire of the banks to co-operate in every way' and the new Minister for Finance, Sean T. O'Kelly, reassuring the bankers that 'his own personal predilection was towards no revolutionary changes in financial matters.'[138]

The establishment of the Central Bank, foreshadowed as far back as McElligott's minority Banking Commission report in 1927 and again when the second Banking Commission was established in 1934, was no revolutionary change and was not perceived as such by the Bank of Ireland, which rather recognised it had the support of such traditional conservatives as Montagu Norman and McElligott. 'I spoke to Sir John Keane, the Governor of the Bank of Ireland, a little time ago about the bill', reported a British official in Dublin to a treasury colleague in Whitehall shortly after it was introduced in the Dáil in March 1942; 'he seemed then to be content with it and to be reconciled to the prospect of losing the government account, which the Bank of Ireland has hitherto kept'.[139] But then reconciliation to the loss of the inappropriate in a state now more than ever obsessed with the marks of sovereignty was always the key to the Bank's survival and success in independent Ireland.

Plate 29

Detail of La Touche Venus and Cupid ceiling

References

1   'Memorandum relating to head office premises of the Bank of Ireland in Dublin', 3 May 1920, AOP.
2   Governor (N. J. Synnott) to Sir Hamar Greenwood, 12 May 1920, AOP.
3   TCOD, xliii/447, 452-4 and 11 May 1916.
4   Ibid., xliii/5, 18-20.
5   See Hall, pp. 314-21 for a fuller account.
6   TCOD, xliii/262, 2 Sept. 1915.
7   Colvill *et al.* to Sir John Bradbury, 18 Aug. 1916 — attached to TCOD, xliii/545.
8   See Hall, pp. 326-7.
9   See exchange of letters of 25 and 31 Aug. 1917 (Board Papers, 'gold holdings for export 1915-17').
10 See Hall, pp. 283-94.
11 Minutes of evidence of the twenty-sixth meeting of the Committee on Currency and Foreign Exchanges, 22 July 1919, AOP. Two copies of the relevant issue of *Nationality* (16 Nov. 1918) are preserved in AOP.
12 See TCOD, xlv/437-40.
13 Cf. Hall, pp. 331-2.
14 TCOD, xlvi/9-12; see especially B.P. Blackett of the treasury to Governor, 18 Feb. 1920.
15 Draft letter to the treasury, 16 Feb. 1920, Board papers, excess note issue, 1919-20.
16 Cf. Fanning, pp. 11-13.
17 Memorandum of interview of 4 June 1920, AOP.
18 Anderson to the Governor, 31 Aug. 1920, Governor's correspondence, 1920-24.
19 As note 17.
20 TCOD, xlv/162-4.
21 Ibid., xlvi/30, 37, 56, 166.
22 Cairnes to Anderson, 23 Oct. 1920, Governor's correspondence, 1920-4.
23 Ibid., N. J. Synnott to R. G. Hawtrey, 22 Mar. 1920.
24 See the Governor to Greenwood, 12 May 1920, AOP.
25 As note 1 above.
26 Law agent to R.H. MacRory, 12 Apr. 1920, Law agent's papers, Government of Ireland Bill 1920.
27 As note 17.
28 Memorandum of interview of 18 June 1920, AOP.
29 See e.g., Fanning, pp. 77-8, 96, 122-5 and 291-2.
30 Cf. Patrick Buckland, *Irish Unionism 1: The Anglo-Irish and the new Ireland 1885-1922*, Dublin 1972, p. xix.
31 Memorandum of deputation to London, 5-6 July 1920, AOP.
32 Ibid.
33 See Governor to Walter Long, 4 Nov. 1920 and to George Dunn, 10 Nov. 1920, Governor's correspondence, 1920-24; also TCOD, xlvi/190, for 18 Nov. 1920 where it is confirmed that the Bank's preferred wording had been inserted in the bill.
34 IBSC minute book, 1/1f-1b, 9 Dec. 1913. I am indebted to the Irish Banks' Standing Committee for permission to consult their early minutes for 1922-4; all later IBSC references are from Bank of Ireland archives. IBSC references are identifiable as 'IBSC minute book'.
35 Hall, p. 319
36 IBSC minute book, 1/5-7.
37 Ibid., 1/9.
38 Memorandum issued by the Bank of Ireland *et al.*, 4 July 1919, Board papers, unmarked envelope "A".
39 TCOD, xlv/538.
40 IBSC minute book, 1/17.
41 See TCOD, xlv/563-4, where the draft agreement is reproduced in full.
42 Memorandum on, and prepared by, the IBSC, 30 Jan. 1940, for the Commission on Vocational Organisation, IBSC minutes, 1940, p. 3 (6B).

43 IBSC minute book, 1/21-3; also TCOD, xlvi/61-3

44 As note 42.

45 IBSC minute book, 1/26; 20 Apr. 1920.

46 Ibid., 1/67; 14 Dec. 1921.

47 SPO, G1/1/3, 10; also S. 9.

48 Ibid., also TCOD, xlvi/366.

49 SPO, G1/1/21.

50 Ibid., G1/1/3.

51 Ibid., G1/1/15.

52 Ibid., G1/1/12.

53 SPO, S. 1193.

54 See 'Interview at the treasury with Sir Basil Blackett, KCB and Mr O. Niemeyer', 1 Feb. 1922, AOP.

55 Cf. Fanning, especially pp. 122-30.

56 See 'Interview between the Governor and Professor T. Smiddy of University College, Cork', 15 Feb. 1922, AOP.

57 See 'Visit of the Governor, Mr W. P. Cairnes and the Rt Hon. Andrew Jameson to London, 13-15 July 1921', and related papers, AOP.

58 See TCOD, xlvi/409, 420-21.

59 Ibid., 441.

60 Ibid., 452.

61 Ibid., 458.

62 Cf. Fanning, pp. 131-3.

63 Guinness to Jameson, 13 June 1922, AOP.

64 'Interview at the treasury between the Governor, the Rt Hon. Andrew Jameson and Sir Basil P. Blackett', 16 June 1922, AOP.

65 See Fanning, p. 132.

66 As note 64.

67 PRO, T. 163/14/5.

68 'Transfer Office — memorandum of an interview between the Governor . . . accompanied by the First Auditor, and the President', 3 Nov. 1922, AOP.

69 Memorandum of Cosgrave's interview with a deputation representing the Bank of Ireland 'and the Southern Irish joint-stock banks', the Incorporated Law Society, the Dublin Stock Exchange and Chamber of Commerce, 21 Nov. 1922, AOP.

70 Keith Middlemas, ed., *Thomas Jones: Whitehall diary, III, Ireland 1918-25*, Oxford 1971, p. 216.

71 See Sir Ronald Waterhouse (Bonar Law's private secretary) to the *Evening Standard*, 12 Dec. 1923, Baldwin papers, 101/177.

72 Middlemas, ed., loc. cit.

73 See Lord Birkenhead's character sketch of Healy, *Sunday Times*, 27 July 1924.

74 IBSC minute book, 1/103-4.

75 See Fanning, pp. 133 and 645 (n. 28) for further details.

76 Cf. ibid., pp. 80-98.

77 IBSC minute book, 1/109-10.

78 Ormsby-Gore's memorandum of his conversation with Jameson, 27 April 1923, PRO, T. 176/12.

79 See Donal O'Sullivan, *The Irish Free State and its Senate*, London 1940, pp. 99-108.

80 Niemeyer's memorandum to Chancellor of the Exchequer, 9 May 1923, PRO, T. 176/12.

81 Ibid., Niemeyer to Lionel Curtis, 9 July 1923.

82 IBSC minute book, 1/120-24.

83 'Advances to the Government of the Irish Free State', memorandum of the interview of 14 June 1923, AOP.

84 IBSC minute book, 1/130-34; cf. TCOD, xlvi/572.

85 Cf. Fanning, p. 94.

86 IBSC minute book, IBSC 1/145-51; cf. TCOD, xlvi/623.

87 Cf. Fanning, p. 96.

88 IBSC minute book, 1/160, 12 Dec. 1923.

89   Ibid., 1/161, 165-6, 179-80, 191.
90   Ibid., 1/167-9, 193.
91   TCOD, xlvii/9, 47.
92   IBSC minute-book, 2/15.
93   See Maurice Moynihan, *Currency and central banking in Ireland 1922-60*, Dublin 1975, pp. 60-61.
94   Ibid., pp. 69-70.
95   Ibid., pp. 112-18; also TCOD, xlvii/571.
96   PRO, T. 160/195.
97   Ibid., :F.W.L-R' to 'Gwyer', 6 Oct. 1927.
98   Ibid., note of the interview of 4 Oct. 1927.
99   Ibid., Niemeyer to Sir Richard Hopkins, 3 Oct. 1927.
100   See Hall, pp. 362-5 for a fuller account.
101   See Fanning, chs 6-7 and pp. 630-31.
102   IBSC minutes (1932-3), pp. 50-53.
103   See Hall, pp. 365-6.
104   SPO, S. 2259.
105   SPO, S. 6808.
106   See Goulding to MacEntee, 10 Nov. 1932, IBSC minutes (1932-3), p. 134.
107   Circular letter from T. F. Hennessy, 28 Apr. 1931, IBSC minutes (1931), p. 34.
108   E. Rowe Dutton — cf. Fanning, p. 379.
109   Memorandum of interview at Leinster House, 31 Mar. 1933, IBSC minutes (1932-3), pp. 180-83.
110   Ibid., p. 179 — circular letter from T. F. Hennessy, 7 Apr. 1933.
111   Ibid. (1934-5), pp. 17-18. Cf. Fanning, pp. 373-4 for the point about Keynes.
112   Ibid., p. 26.
113   Ibid., (Secretary of the President's Dept. to Goulding, 4 May 1924); cf. Fanning, pp. 373-4.
114   Moynihan, *Currency and central banking*, p. 203.
115   IBSC minutes for 8 May and 13 July 1934, pp. 24-5 and 46-7.
116   Ibid., p. 26A.
117   Memorandum of interview at Government Buildings, 10 May 1934, ibid., pp. 28-30.
118   James Meenan, *The Irish economy since 1922*, Liverpool 1970, p. 222.
119   Cf. Fanning, pp. 358-63.
120   Moynihan, op. cit., pp. 214-17.
121   See above, p. 84.
122   IBSC minutes (May-Dec. 1938), pp. 49A-B.
123   TCOD, 1/706, 744, 762, 776B, 790B.
124   IBSC minutes (1939), pp. 58A-B.
125   Ibid., p. 63A.
126   Ibid., p. 76.
127   TCOD, 1/822-3; 31 Aug. 1939.
128   IBSC minutes (1939), p. 80.
129   TCOD, 1/836-7.
130   IBSC minutes (1940), 48A/2-3.
131   Cf. Fanning, ch. 8, for a fuller account.
132   Cf. Hall, p. 492.
133   IBSC minutes (1940), pp. 46-54.
134   Ibid. (1941), p. 70.
135   See Fanning, pp. 364-74 and Moynihan, *Currency and central banking in Ireland*, ch. 14.
136   IBSC minutes (Jan-Sept. 1941), p. 84.
137   Ibid.
138   Memorandum of conference with the Minister for Finance, 30 Sept. 1941, IBSC minutes (Oct. 1941—June 1942) p. 1A.
139   Norman Archer to N. E. Costar, 27 March 1942, PRO, T160/1066/F10881/09.

Plate 30   Daniel O'Connell, bronze sculpture by Andrew O'Connor

The Bank and the Visual Arts

Edward McParland

FOR any large institution — bank, or church, or dynasty — patronage of the arts is a serious matter. This is clearly so in the case of the expensive, enduring and public art of architecture. Buildings are important as advertisements. In competitive circumstances they are weapons. And they are open affirmations of how the patron wishes to be seen by the rest of the world. With painting and sculpture the same is true, though the scope is more limited. Portraiture, in oil or marble, can honour dignitaries of the institution, and enhance a sense of tradition. It can provide icons, as we know from the frequency with which branches of the National Bank were, in the past, furnished with portraits of Daniel O'Connell. Further, though the patronage of architects, painters and sculptors is sometimes disinterested, their works remain assets. And whether these works are primarily advertisements, or assets, or artefacts, they are subject to changes of taste, or of liturgy, or of regime: modern Irish bankers, inheriting from their predecessors full-length statues of George III, face problems similar to those faced by modern ecclesiastics inheriting statues of St Philomena.

The Bank of Ireland has a long tradition of enlightened patronage of the visual arts. In architecture this ranges from their early commission (unexecuted) to John Soane for splendid new headquarters in Dublin, to the conversion (directed by Francis Johnston) of the parliament house into a bank, and its subsequent maintenance and restoration, to the building of their present head office in Baggot Street, designed by Ronald Tallon. This building set new standards in the design and execution of major new blocks of offices in central Dublin, and gave rise to the establishment by the Bank of the major collection in the country of works of contemporary Irish painters and sculptors.

For the first twenty years of its life the Bank stimulated some interesting architectural schemes, but built little. There was newspaper gossip in 1782 that the architect Samuel Sproule had been commissioned to convert the arsenal in Dublin Castle 'for the purpose of a National Bank'.[1] This came to nothing, and in the following year Sproule was asked to make the necessary repairs and alterations to the first premises taken by the Bank. This was at the corner of Mary's Abbey and Boot Lane, between Capel Street and the Four Courts (*Plate* 5, page 13).

Sproule was prominent but undistinguished. He was involved in the development of Merrion Square; he provided designs for the Wide Streets Commissioners; he designed the Newry White Linen Hall; and Francis Johnston seems to have worked in his office. By 1786 he had been succeeded at the Bank by Whitmore Davis, so it is no doubt to the early 1780s that we can date Sproule's surviving engravings of unexecuted designs for a new bank (*Plates* 31 and 32): an erased, but not quite illegible signature on *Plate* 31 may be interpreted as Sproule's. The Bank of England, so often at this stage a point of reference for its Irish counterpart, is invoked in the façade, which follows fairly closely George Sampson's Threadneedle Street façade of the 1730s. The design, though tricked out with some currently fashionable motifs, is provincial. If executed, such a building would have been an embarrassment to the Bank. Within a few years it would have been too small, and would not have been amenable to easy enlargement: in 1784 (about the time this design was made) Bank staff totalled twenty-four, apart from Governor, Deputy Governor and fifteen directors; in 1792 this had risen to sixty-three; by 1802 the number was 130.

There are no indications on these engravings of where Sproule's Bank was to be built. If it was to be on the Mary's Abbey site, this would, in a few years time, have caused further embarrassment. As we shall see, this was no time to be investing in property in the neighbourhood of Capel Street.

Sproule's plan shows few of the precautions taken by Francis Johnston in his later designs for the conversion of the parliament house. There is little vaulting (which would have been an obvious fire precaution), and there is profuse glazing. Johnston's Bank, with its windowless walls, had to be much more easily defensible than this.

By 1786 the architect Whitmore Davis, who designed Green Street court house and who was the surveyor of the Paving Board, was being employed on minor works at Mary's Abbey. As with the employment of Sproule, the choice of Davis as architect shows no discrimination on the Bank's part. Davis, too, was a busy second-rate architect, a protégé of the La Touche family to which connection, no doubt, he owed his appointment. Having been censured by the Bank in 1788 for lack of attention to his responsibilities, he was sacked in 1791 and replaced by the obscure Thomas Brown. In

Plate 31   *Plate 32*

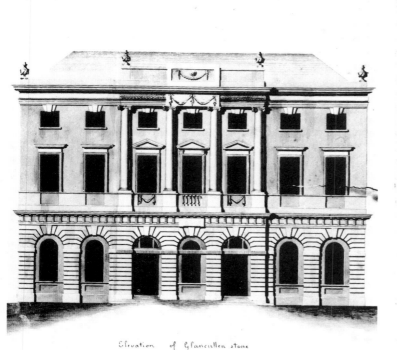

Elevation of Glencullen stone

Plan of first floor

Plate 33

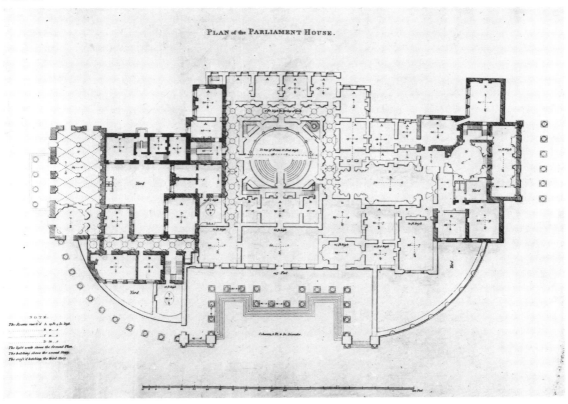

PLAN of the PARLIAMENT HOUSE.

a period when James Gandon was active in Dublin along with other architects of ability such as Thomas Cooley, Thomas Ivory, Thomas Penrose and Richard Johnston, the Bank's choice of second-rate architects is notable.

There had been a rumour in 1784 that Powerscourt House in South William Street had been bought by the Bank as its new headquarters.[2] By 1791 the site of the old Custom House at Essex (i.e. Capel Street) Bridge was in consideration, and two plans survive in the Bank showing proposals for the siting there of the new premises (*Plates* 35 and 36). No accompanying elevations or further details are known.

It is interesting to observe the Bank directors at this time looking around for a suitable site for their headquarters. The neighbourhood of Parliament Street was an obvious choice, being close to the old city and to the established mercantile centre and Royal Exchange. A new street to be known as Bank Street, forming an axis between the new Bank and a gate to Dublin Castle, would add consequence to the building which was by this stage, to judge from these plans, conceived on monumental lines. The proposal ignored the fact, however, that with James Gandon's new Custom House far downstream, a new bridge (Carlisle, now O'Connell Bridge) was in progress and would be opened in 1795. With the proposed opening of Westmoreland Street southwards from this bridge to College Green, and with the linking of this bridge via the new Sackville Street to the road to the north, a completely new thoroughfare was to be formed which would dramatically alter the shape of the city. The centre of gravity would then no longer lie along the line of Capel Street and Essex Bridge (until

1795 the last bridge before the sea), to Parliament Street and the Castle, but would be shifted far to the east, that is to the neighbourhood of Carlisle Bridge where effectively it still lies. In May 1798 the directors still conservatively favoured the old Custom House site, but within twelve months the inevitable pattern of city development made clear to them the advantages of a more easterly site. With two great new avenues proposed (i.e. Westmoreland and D'Olier Streets), radiating southwards from Carlisle Bridge, the Bank opened negotiations with the Wide Streets Commissioners for the vast triangular site between these new streets and what is now College Street (though it is designated Bank Street in the map of 1799 of *Plate* 37).

One cannot help wondering what James Gandon, then the leading architect in Dublin, would have made of this dramatic site, what monument he would have devised as culmination of the plan which had been maturing for over fifty years for the easterly development of the city. There is no record of his having been consulted, and instead John Soane, the architect of the Bank of England, was instructed to prepare plans. For the first time a major architect set about planning offices for the Bank of Ireland. In recognition of the added dignity which this would give to the new avenues, the surveyor of the Wide Streets Commissioners was instructed to prepare fresh designs for the buildings then proposed for the other side of Westmoreland Street.[3]

Soane's drawings (*Plates* 34 and 38), preserved in Sir John Soane's Museum, show him working on two closely related schemes late in 1799. In both, he planned to fill only part of the triangular site available to him. Curiously, he devised no grand northern façade to terminate vistas along Sackville Street and across the new bridge. And clearly he regarded the façades along Westmoreland and D'Olier Streets as subordinate. He reserved the principal architectural show for the façade along

Plate 34

Plate 35

Plate 36

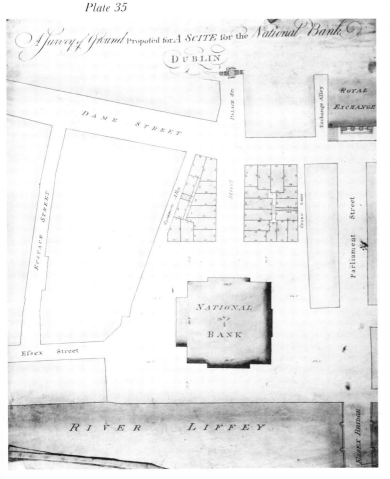

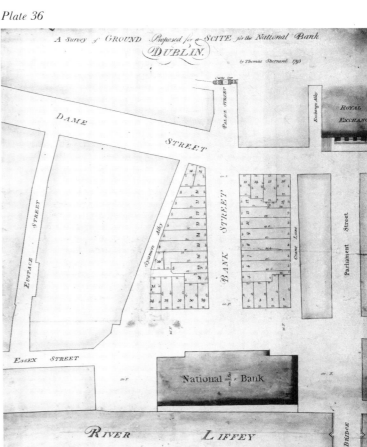

College Street. This front, of about 300 feet, was a long one, and difficult to unify without boredom. His designs have their moments: the Westmoreland Street façade of *Plate 34* would have looked well across from Gandon's House of Lords portico, and the repetition of tall tripartite windows was effective (like Sproule, he was untroubled by fears that windows would be a threat to security). But the succession of disjoint porticoes across the façade was uneasy and arbitrary. Indoors the enormous cash office and principal staircase halls would have been austerely impressive, but his surviving sections promise fewer spatial excitements than were to be found in the interiors he was designing in these years for the Bank of England.

By late in 1801, however, the directors of the Bank were discussing a still more exciting project. Perhaps the Bank could occupy the parliament house in College Green which had been made redundant by the Act of Union of 1800. On 27 March 1802 the lord lieutenant, Lord Hardwicke, signified to the Bank his approval of their offer of £40,000 for the building, and as he considered that 'it may be thought necessary and desirable to make certain alterations in the exterior of the building as well with a view to security as external ornament', he asked that plans should be submitted for his approval before being executed.[4]

A competition was announced for which architects were invited to submit designs for the conversion of the building into a bank. The premiums were awarded as

101

Plate 37

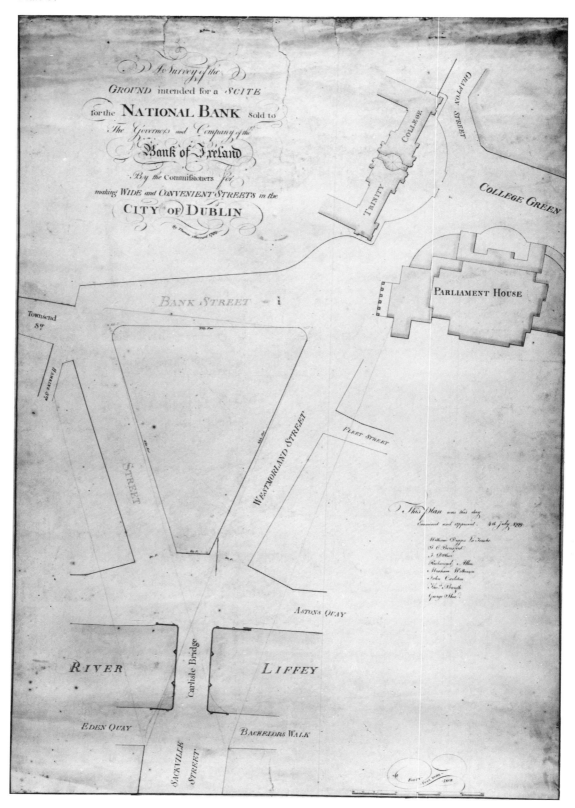

Plate 38

follows: first prize of 200 guineas to the pseudonymous competitor, T.V., now known to have been Gandon's partner Henry Aaron Baker;[5] second prize of 150 guineas to John Foulston of Plymouth, and third prize of 120 guineas to Joseph Woods of London. The Bank had, previous to their announcement, appointed Francis Johnston — who may have entered the competition but whose entry has not been identified — as architect to design and execute the conversion.

In the late 1720s Edward Lovett Pearce had designed the parliament house to serve precise demands of the Lords and Commons. The octagonal Commons chamber (rebuilt by Vincent Waldré after a fire of 1792) occupied the centre of the plan, while the Lords chamber lay to the east. Later additions had failed to make the exterior symmetrical (*Plate 33*): a free-standing colonnade of the 1780s swept back in a curve from Pearce's forecourt to Foster Place, while on the other side James Gandon's more severe screen wall curved back to join up with his House of Lords portico. Now was the time, it was felt, to achieve external symmetry. But how? With two curved colonnades? With two severe curved screen walls?

Other problems to be faced concerned the degree of reverence due to Pearce's building and its eighteenth-century extensions. With terrifying objectivity, Charles Abbot, the chief secretary, had earlier outlined various possibilities for the building.[6] It could, he said, be sold to the Bank, or it might become the stamp office, or the registry of deeds. Or it could be demolished: he had had the site and materials valued at £41,000. (Hence, perhaps, the sum agreed with the Bank.) Now, happily, that demolition was ruled out, how were architects and the Bank to treat the great interiors?

On this point Abbot was persistent: there should be a private agreement with the Bank 'that the two chambers of parliament shall be effectually converted to such uses as shall preclude their being again used upon any contingency as public debating rooms'.[7] The implications of this were clear. The chief secretary's inflexible view, had it been carried into effect, would have meant that there should be no large rooms in the Bank. Such a stipulation was clearly impractical. In his communication to the Bank quoted above, confirming his approval of the purchase, the lord lieutenant made no reference to it. And it was ignored by the Bank from the start. The specification of necessary accommodation which was circulated to competing architects by the Bank recommended that the House of Lords be left unchanged.[8] Henry Aaron Baker, the winner of

103

the competition, candidly proclaimed in his *Necessary observations, addressed to the governors and directors of the Bank of Ireland, relative to the plans proposed for that building*, which was published in Dublin in 1803, before adjudication of premiums, that his 'first intention ... [was] to retain entire those rooms of the present building, which were thought of too much importance to deface — namely, the Lords and Commons ...' And in the executed work, Francis Johnston preserved the House of Lords intact. If the Commons chamber went, it was not to satisfy Abbot, who seems to have been alone in urging, and getting, the Bank's agreement to this confidential condition of sale. Nor was it — as Lecky says — for fear that 'disquieting ghosts might still haunt the scenes that were consecrated by so many memories'. It was because the Bank wanted, as specified in its competition brief, its large cash office to be close to the public street.

The competition of 1802-3 marked a watershed in Irish architecture, as was appropriate for an event which resulted in the obliteration of the House of Commons. Gandon, who had dominated Irish architecture since 1780, had begun his final building, the King's Inns, in 1800 and was soon to retire from practice. His influence on the competition designs was marked. His partner Henry Aaron Baker proposed a dome on the lines suggested earlier for the parliament house by Gandon. And from the *Observations, &c. on appropriating the parliament house to the Bank of Ireland* (Dublin 1803) we learn that competitor number 20 took his pavilions from those of Gandon's Custom House, number 9 his cash office from the long room of the Custom House, and number 14 the centre of his north front from Gandon's Nottingham County Hall. At the same time, new men like Richard Morrison and Francis Johnston were launching careers which marked a return in Irish architecture to professional dominance by native architects. Established attitudes towards architectural style were about to be upset by the revelations of the Greek revival. The nature of patronage, too, was changing, with much greater emphasis now being placed on public work in provincial towns and cities than had been common in the eighteenth century. Even the notion of settling the choice of architect by competition indicated a shift from the attitudes of the previous twenty years. Then, James Gandon's monopoly of major public commissions was so justifiably complete that competitions, quite common before his arrival, became unusual. It is not recorded that he entered the Bank competition. By 1803 the tight control by the clique which had brought him to Ireland and had relentlessly advanced him in the previous twenty years was broken. Powerful among this pre-Union clique had been Frederick Trench, Sackville Hamilton and Andrew Caldwell: these three were now asked by the Bank to advise in selecting the winner of the competition. But power was no longer theirs. They failed to agree among themselves, and the Bank proceeded independently to award the premiums.

A number of designs submitted in the competition survive in the Bank archives. Two dreary elevations, one signed G.X.W. (*Plate* 39), the other 'W.W. London' (*Plate* 41) show the western colonnade duplicated on the east, and the area of Pearce's fore-court closed off with a screen wall. Two entries of Richard Morrison's survive, and Henry Aaron Baker's well-known principal elevation is now joined by his plans, section and other elevations which have recently come to light. It is interesting to compare Baker's winning designs with the unplaced Morrison ones, and to compare all of these with Francis Johnston's early and executed designs.

Baker proposed isolating the building, giving it four important façades arranged on a rectilinear plan which obliterated the curved screens of the older building (*Plate*

40). He retained the Commons chamber as his cash office, thereby ignoring the competition brief that the cash office should be near the street. Part of the Lords chamber became his court of proprietors. He retained Pearce's forecourt, extending it on either side by straight colonnades in a manner which, while it enhanced the columnar excitements of this front, would unfortunately have distracted attention from Pearce's great centrepiece (*Plate* 42). His plan is disappointing. Morrison is much more confident in his arrangement of circulation and formal vistas (*Plates* 45 and 46); and within the perimeter of Baker's façades the arrangement of yards and buildings is incoherent and uneconomical: his great section (*Plate* 44) cuts through astonishingly little habitable internal space. His proposed new north façade (*Plate* 43) is of interest for his suggestion of how the old parliament house should address itself to the new developments of the city as implied by Carlisle Bridge, but is, in itself, more pompous than grand.

The greatest value of his newly discovered section may be noted here, though it refers more to the history of the parliament house than to that of the Bank. It shows details of the House of Commons, as rebuilt by Vincent Waldré after the fire of 1792. No other representation of Waldré's Commons is known.

Morrison's designs (*Plates* 45-48), though unsure in the details of scale (his domes look very weak in contrast with Baker's), and though overburdened with sculptural decoration, are finer in plan. He should — where Pearce's forecourt was concerned — have left well enough alone, but indoors he spared Pearce's corridor and House of Lords, and knitted Gandon's Lords lobbies more worthily into the general circulation than did Baker. His open courts are more economically disposed, and his cash office is more easily accessible from the street, through Pearce's vestibules which he intended to preserve, at least in plan. Morrison had been paid by the Bank in 1802 for a plan — still surviving in the Bank — of John Soane's Bank of England. It would be interesting to know how far his internal treatment and decoration would have reflected the influence of Soane: one would like to know more about the note ledger office of his first design (*Plate* 45: the tripartite space south of Gandon's circular Lords lobby). Perhaps, as on the exterior, the demands of the old parliament house circumscribed his tendency to borrow from Soane.

It is remarkable, particularly in view of the close similarity of his plans to Francis Johnston's executed work, that Morrison remained unplaced in the competition. His disappointment must have been aggravated by other failures in these years when he was eclipsed in Dublin by Francis Johnston's success with public commissions. No doubt this was the reason for Morrison's energetic cultivation of a provincial practice on which he eventually established his reputation.

Johnston achieved external symmetry with minimal alterations (*Plate* 50). The curved freestanding colonnade on the west became (like the screen wall on the east) a curved screen wall with an engaged order of Ionic columns. This led to the unGandonesque solecism of an Ionic order leading to the Corinthian portico of the House of Lords (*Plate* 51). This intimate juxtaposition of orders, according to *The Life of James Gandon,* by James Gandon junior and Thomas J. Mulvany, suggested 'such critical censures as the merest tyro could inflict, but which the professor of experience would never indulge in'.[9] This sounds extravagant, particularly in the context of today's insensitivity to the classical discipline in architecture. But Gandon must have been deeply shocked at Johnston's sad expedient. He must have felt that, in more ways

Plate 39

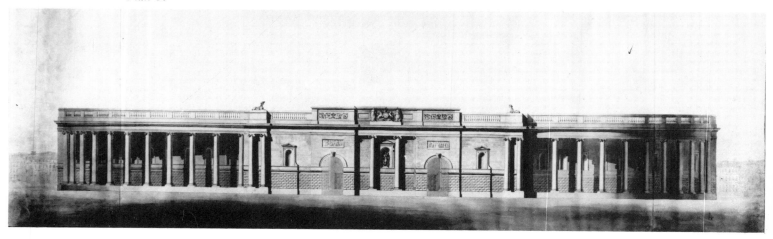

Plate 40

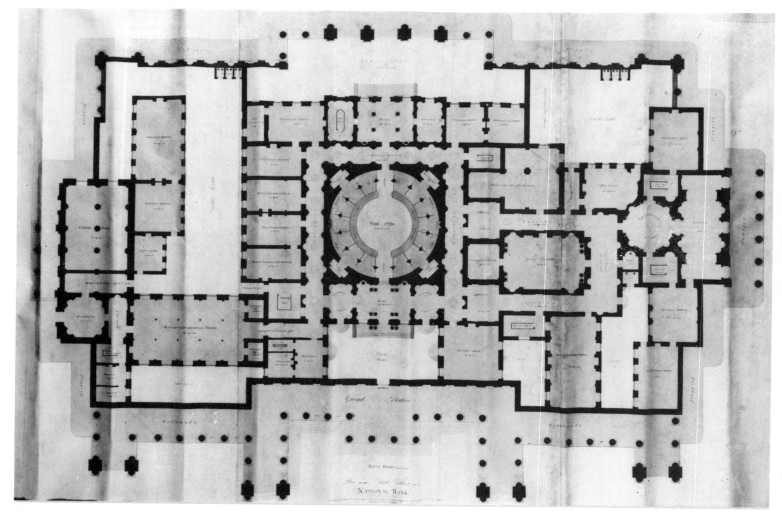

Plate 41

Plate 42

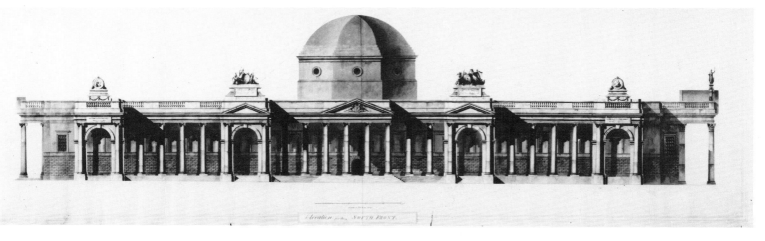

Plate 43

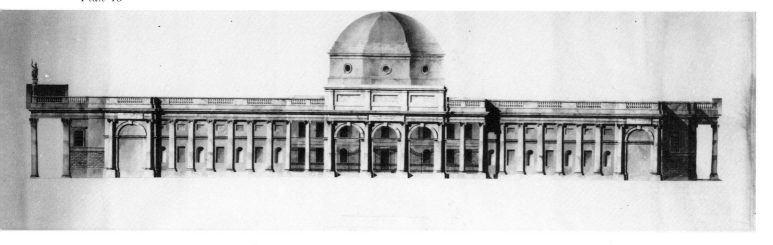

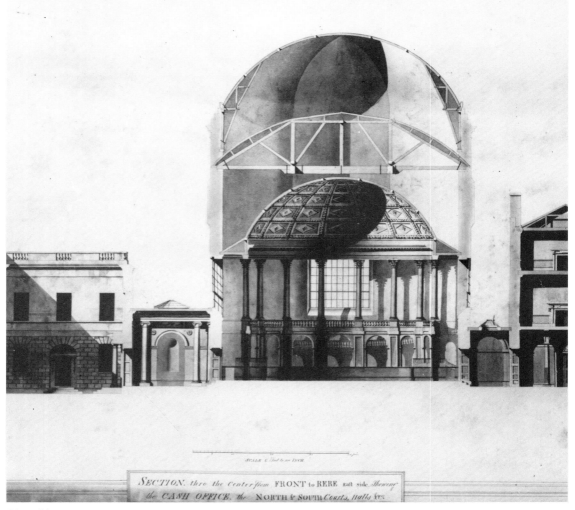

Plate 44

than one, the conversion of the parliament house and of his own work there marked the end of an era.

Happily, the satirists were busy:

> With bursting anguish yon proud Fane [the parliament house] I eyed
> Where Erin's independence grew and died;
> Yet there let wealth accumulate her store,
> For there the dross reign'd paramount before.
> Proud colonade! and scarce in Europe match'd,
> How are thy ruins to be maim'd and patch'd?
> 'Twere well, if spreading correspondent wings,
> A nobler phoenix from the ashes springs;
> But concord flies, where many wou'd control,
> One mind alone can form a perfect whole;
> Yet some vain fool, pretending to the spark,
> Of heavenly genius, groping in the dark,
> Ionic and Corinthian structure scans,
> And melts in one a dozen varying plans.
> (Anon., *The Metropolis*, second edition. Dublin 1805).

That Johnston kept Soane's Bank of England in mind when planning his interiors is clear from his board room (*Plate* 52) and Governor's room, which are taken from Soane's Governor's room. This indebtedness is further revealed in his personal ledger and discount offices (also on the site of the old Commons chamber). It is clear, too, from

108

Plate 45

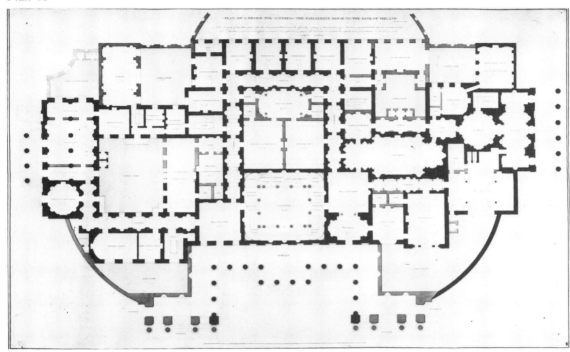

Plate 46

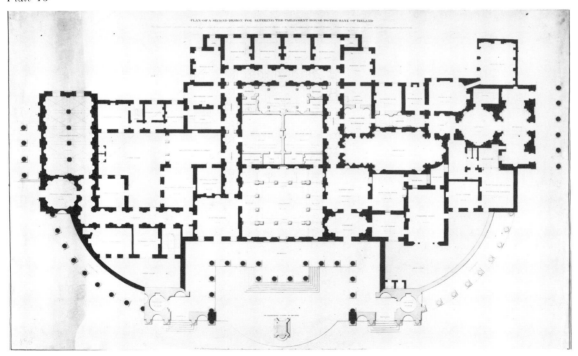

his suggestion to the Court that the walls of the cash office be lined with Bath stone, since 'the new offices of the Bank of England are finishing in this manner and I should wish to have it in my power to make our principal office as handsome as any of theirs.'[10]

Plate 47

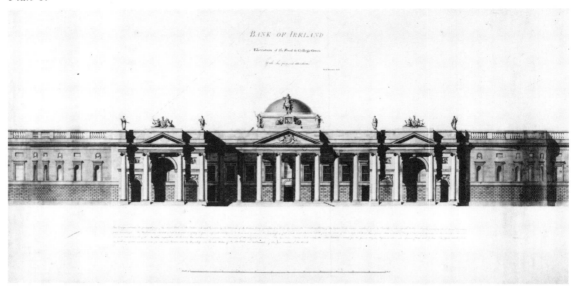

Plate 48

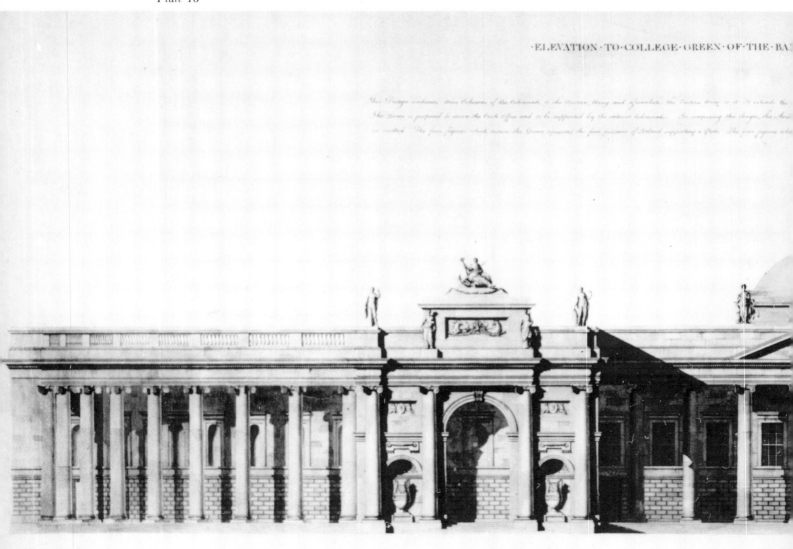

The cash office (*Plate* 53) is a splendid room, and is the first of a long and distinguished line of Irish banking halls. No earlier bank interior in Ireland can have been the model. Gandon's Custom House long room served a remotely similar function as public office. It may have inspired the arrangement of counters and desks confined to the pedestal zone of an order which articulates the entire space, though this was also the solution of George Sampson's hall in the Bank of England. Johnston, however, broke notably new ground in the structure of his ceiling (*Plate* 54). A flat area of great richness and considerable span (48′ x 30′) floats above a brilliantly glazed clerestory or lantern. The delicate vertical members of this lantern rise — above a void — from the outer rim of a deep cantilevered cove. (Morrison had proposed a similar rectangular lantern for his cash office.)

To judge from an early plan attributable to Johnston (*Plate* 49) he originally proposed free-standing colonnades surrounding the cash office, an arrangement closer to Gandon's Custom House long room than was executed. In March 1805 he was permitted to enlarge his original plan for the office to the detriment of neighbouring spaces (*Plate* 50): Pearce's apsed east vestibule was lost, and the enlarged cash office jutted out awkwardly beyond the line of the east corridor so that a fine internal vista was lost. The counter and desk arrangement of *Plate* 49 would have more effectively reinforced the architectural logic of Johnston's articulation of the cash office than does the present arrangement. The space behind the counters then corresponded to the

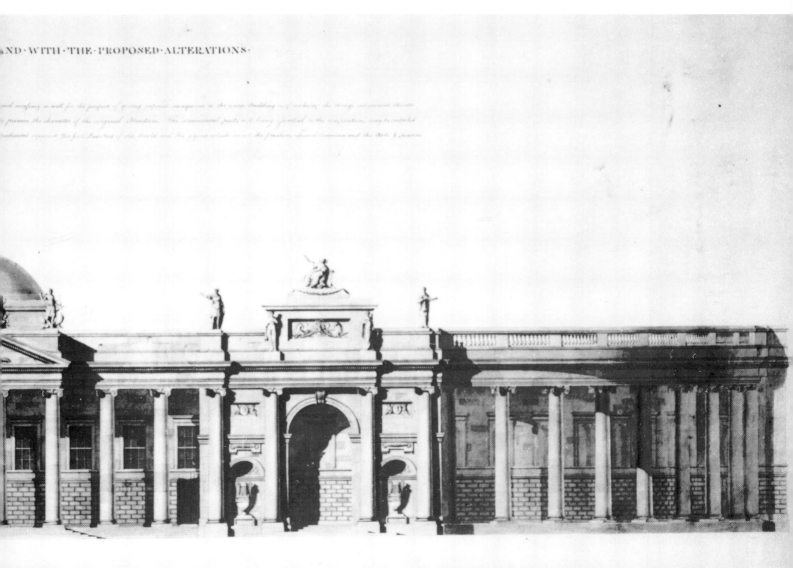

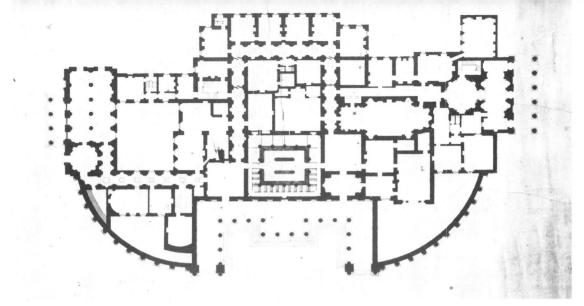

Plate 49

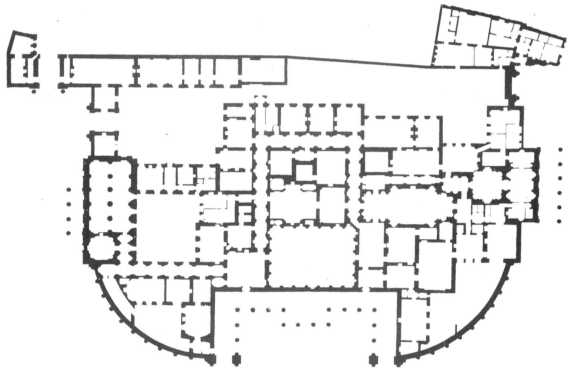

Plate 50

cove above, while its partitions emphasised the network of lines which, rising from ground level through the Ionic order, was continued to its final resolution, above the beams of the cove and the piers of the lantern, in the intersecting patterns of the flat ceiling. In proposing colours for this room, Johnston made explicit his understanding of the articulation as a network of lines: 'my plan would be to carry the Portland teint throughout, on all the *principal* parts, that is, those directly over and bearing on the columns, which I call the framing of the room, and the Bath stone teint on the subservient parts, as the pannels [*sic*] and grounds'.[11]

So successful, internally, is his cash office ceiling that we can be pleased that Johnston rejected the idea of a dome. Externally the results of this decision are less satisfactory. The building outside fares perfectly well without a dome, but suffers in

112

Plate 51

some views from the conspicuous superstructure of Johnston's cash office lantern rising above Pearce's pediment and attic.

The decoration of the cash office was subject to the insistent geometry of the architecture. The plasterwork was executed by the firm of Charles Thorp. Its deep relief, the balance between its geometry and the lively naturalism of its details, and its structural suggestiveness represent a remarkable departure from the more taut and stylised decoration fashionable in the late eighteenth century. Still more remarkable is Johnston's west hall (*Plate* 55), where the horizontal rustication, continuous Greek fret, idealised Vitruvian scroll and coffered barrel vault are — while rooted in a knowledge of antiquity — remarkably independent of Gandonian neo-classicism. Consciously or otherwise, Johnston's design here is sympathetic to the robust taste of Edward Lovett Pearce.

In a number of ways the alteration of the parliament house was part of a marked shift in taste and patronage as well as in politics. And even in the choice of sculptor for the external enrichments of the Bank the old guard had to yield. As sculptor to Gandon for the Custom House and Four Courts and for the portico of the House of Lords, Edward Smyth had produced work of a quality not yet adequately recognised outside Ireland. Curran tells the story of how, despite Johnston's early anxiety that Smyth should be responsible for the new statues for Pearce's south pediment, he eventually recommended to the Bank that Smyth be employed merely to execute the designs of John Flaxman. The trophy of arms over the Foster Place gateway was executed by Thomas Kirk.

The altered building was opened for banking business in 1808, though minor work continued for a number of years. The cost of the alterations, to 1811, was

Plate 52

Plate 53

Cash office, College Green

£115,297.11s.7½d.[12] It is estimated that the total cost of Thomas Cooley's and James Gandon's Four Courts between 1776 and 1802 had been £114,000; the cost of Francis Johnston's new General Post Office, begun in 1814, was to be £115,000. It is a tribute to the discretion of the Bank's directors that, for exactly the same sum, they did not demand more ostentation: they ended up with a building which, from the outside, looked much the same as the one they had started with.

In the early years the directors commissioned work from a number of important artists other than Flaxman. In 1808 it was agreed to commission a portrait of John Foster, then Chancellor of the Irish Exchequer, 'by one of the first Artists in London (of his own choice)'.[13] Foster nominated Thomas Lawrence. In 1813 John Bacon was paid £1,500 for a statue of George III, which is now on loan to the Irish Georgian Society. Peter Turnerelli provided busts of Wellington and George III which survive in the House of Lords (for some mysterious reason Thomas Kirk was paid £27.6s.0d. in 1823 'for re-carving the bust of George the 3rd & c').[14] For transparencies — probably ephemeral decorations of the Bank during the royal vist of that year — Thomas J. Mulvany was paid over £200 in 1821, and it was agreed in the following year to order busts of George IV and Nelson from Kirk; these, too, survive in the House of Lords. Curiously, no great portrait collection of Bank worthies ever grew up. In more recent times an important ceiling from the La Touche Bank in Castle Street which was about to be demolished was installed in the directors' luncheon room, and various objects connected with the old parliament house have returned to College Green, among these the mace of the House of Commons and the chandelier which now hangs in the House of Lords.

John Soane fared badly at the Bank of England, where in this century, his interiors were destroyed by the bank. There is every reason to believe that had his Dublin building been erected, it would have been treated more reverently by directors who, from the start, respected and maintained the work of Pearce, Gandon and Johnston. Inevitably there have been changes, the saddest of which was the reconstruction of some of Pearce's basement vaults in the 1940s. One eighteenth-century critic had gone so far as to consider the vaults to be among the finest features of the parliament house.[15] Otherwise much care has been devoted to maintaining the building worthily, in recognition of its importance as one of the country's greatest monuments. In 1971 a programme of cleaning and restoration of the external stone-work was begun, work which was completed in 1982. Not only was the stonework cleaned (the granite by grit-blasting, the Portland stone by washing) but the decayed stonework was recarved: a high proportion of the visible external stonework of the building today is new. In the patient thoroughness of execution, and in the fastidious and scholarly care taken with classical detail, this work has set new standards in architectural restoration in Ireland.

Architecturally, the Bank rested on its College Green laurels for the rest of the nineteenth century. By 1900 sixty-one branches (excluding sub-offices) had been established throughout the country, but few of these were of notable architectural quality. In a century of high competence among Irish architects it is disappointing to see the Bank of Ireland surrendering to other banks the lead it had established at the parliament house. If the directors had continued to keep an eye on the Bank of England, they would have been impressed by the seriousness with which the design of branch buildings was tackled by Soane's successor Charles Robert Cockerell, who erected superb offices in the 1840s in Bristol, Liverpool and Manchester. David Bryce

Plate 54

Plate 55

— familiar to commercial Dublin in the 1850s and 1860s with his offices for the Dublin Standard Assurance Co. (now the Northern Bank in O'Connell Street) and for other companies in College Green and Dame Street — designed banks in Scotland which are among the most distinguished classical buildings of the second half of the nineteenth century in Britain. And if, among Irish architects, Benjamin Woodward or J.J.

118

McCarthy could not be expected to surrender their attachment to Ruskin and Pugin in favour of the classicism desired by the Bank, there were many competent, and some brilliant, men to whom the Bank might well have turned. John Skipton Mulvany, Charles Lanyon, William G. Murray, or Thomas Drew, would each have been a worthy choice, and indeed all — except Mulvany — designed excellent offices for other Irish banks.

One could speculate that, complacent with the architectural dominance assured by its College Green building, the Bank disdained the kind of competitiveness whipped up by the *Irish Builder*'s comment on Armagh in 1868: 'The Belfast and the Northern Banks have both expended large sums in beautifying the town, and we do not see why the Provincial should be content with its present mean office'.[16] Perhaps architectural reticence, if not humility, was part of the tact with which, as Dr McDonagh has pointed out, the Bank judiciously maintained its supremacy. And other points he makes may be relevant here too. A reluctance to innovate, and the superior buoyancy of competitors' profits in the 1860s and 1870s, are consistent with the relative dullness of some nineteenth-century Bank of Ireland branches. Dullness may have been taken to indicate commendable thrift. But the real answer is probably more prosaic: the Bank was undiscerning in its choice of architect, and its attachment to a single firm made more difficult to attain that variety which enlivened the branch architecture of other banks.

Francis Johnston died in 1829; by the end of that year eleven branches of the Bank had been opened. The extent of Johnston's responsibilities after the completion of work on the parliament house is not clear. Curran seems to be mistaken in attributing to him the design of the Newry branch, for which the building contract was signed only in 1833 with the firm of Duff and Jackson; and in the year before Johnston's death 'John Jones, Architect' was paid for building a branch in Clonmel. (The Newry branch is to the same design — with plan reversed — as the Wexford branch [*Plate* 56], for which Joseph McDaniel's proposal for building was accepted on 24 January 1832.) In 1829 George Halpin, engineer of the Ballast Board and designer of lighthouses, was appointed to inspect and survey the state of branches throughout the country. He seems to be the one designated as bank architect in the minutes of the meeting of the Court of Directors on 22 November 1831, but he had no monopoly in the design of branches: he designed the Dundalk branch in 1845, but the Cork branch in the South Mall (*Plate* 57) was the work of Thomas Deane whose proposal to erect the building was accepted on 9 October 1838. With the appointment of Sandham Symes as bank architect in 1854 a new chapter of branch building opened. This chapter was a long one, as members of the firm of Millar and Symes remained architects to the Bank for the next 100 years.

That Symes was no Charles Robert Cockerell is clear. To make up for this, maybe, he borrowed frequently from Cockerell in his windows and corner entrances. But his great model was the Palazzo Farnese in Rome: classical, but without orders (except as frames for windows or doors), this provided a formula for buildings of three storeys, with emphatic cornice, quoins and continuous sills. The model was a flexible one: the number of bays, and even of storeys, was variable, and it could accommodate itself with as much dignity to the undecorated facades of Mountmellick as to the florid ones of Kilkenny (*Plate* 59). And it was a model favoured by other banks: Lanyon produced a stylish version in Belfast for the Belfast Bank, Bryce invoked it in Edinburgh in his Western Bank and Union Bank.

In both the major cities of Belfast and Cork the Bank of Ireland was architecturally outclassed (*Plates* 57, 58), in Belfast by Lanyon's Belfast Bank and Northern Bank and by James Hamilton's Ulster Bank (all, admittedly, head offices, not branches), and in Cork by William G. Murray's Provincial branch and by Thomas and Kearns Deane's Savings Bank. The Cork and Belfast branches, however, were still too good to be demolished in that busy decade, the 1960s. It was at this time, too, that some branch interiors were radically altered. The parallels with ecclesiastical renovation are close. It was as if a bankers' equivalent of a Vatican Council had decreed deep mahogany counters to be as suspect as altar rails. The bank clerk was to be no longer a hierophant, he was to be a friend. Friendliness was not to be inhibited by carved woodwork and polychrome tiles, it was to be engendered by artificial laminates. And so some branches lost their Victorian fittings. But, as in other areas, the optimistic expansiveness of the 1960s has given way to more cautious attitudes; it is now accepted that prudence and economy (quite apart from artistic piety) recommend a conservative rather than a radical approach in the treatment of older branches.

In the early twentieth century things livened up in branch building. The Palazzo Farnese was forgotten and Millar and Symes — with great versatility and considerable virtuosity — introduced a new range of styles into their repertoire. And other firms of architects were occasionally employed. There was Queen Anne for the Queen's Bridge branch in Belfast (*Plate* 60), and Art Deco for Larne (*Plate* 61). Terenure went Romanesque. And in 1930 A.G.C. Millar designed an agent's house for Kanturk with a smattering of the Bauhaus (*Plate* 64). In fact, its flat roof, glazed corners and white walls are so many stylistic tricks, like the Queen Anne oriels, or the Romanesque arches; its plan is completely traditional. The modern movement had a great future in Bank of Ireland architecture, but this was not the start of it.

The triumphant recognition of the modern movement came in the erection of the new head office in Dublin. Accepting the limitations of the College Green site, and accepting the responsibility of leaving substantially intact the altered parliament house, it was decided to accommodate the expanding headquarters in a new building on a new site not far from the centre of the city. In 1968 a site in Baggot Street was purchased on which excavations for an office building of two blocks (*Plate* 65) had already begun. The architect for this scheme, Ronald Tallon of Michael Scott and Partners, now Scott Tallon Walker, was retained by the Bank. He was instructed to make no radical departure from the two-block scheme already initiated, at least in terms of scale and composition of the first two blocks required by the Bank, but to modify it by using superior building materials and by providing superior services (such as air-conditioning) within. At an early stage the Bank planned to erect a third block along Baggot Street, on the site of earlier buildings then existing and just visible on the left of the drawing of *Plate* 65. Thus, where Johnston had to alter an earlier building, Tallon's design for the Bank was also circumscribed, this time by an earlier scheme of his own. And while Tallon's Bank was to be uncompromisingly modern, it was to be — in materials, finish and presence — a worthy successor to the earlier head office.

Tallon's first scheme for three blocks was modified somewhat in execution. Originally the two blocks in front were to be of equal dimensions but placed at right angles to each other, so that one block had a long facade on Baggot Street, the other a short one. With the completion of the tall rear block and of the lower block with the short

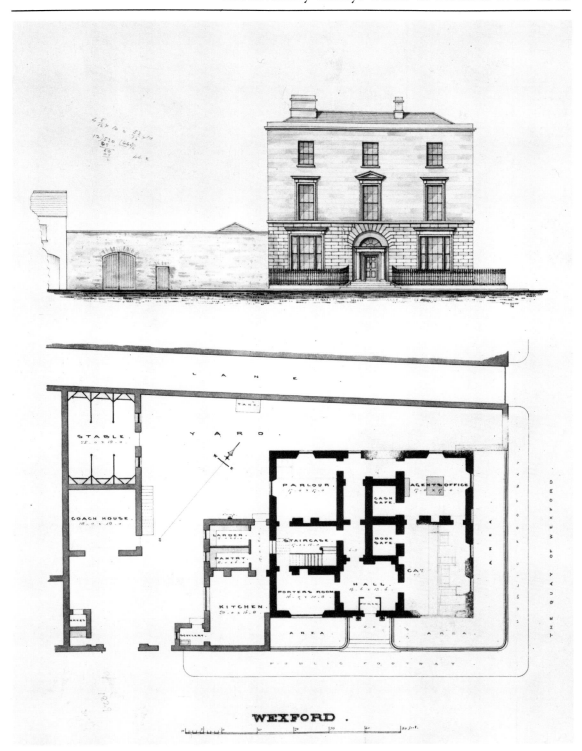

Plate 56

street façade, it was decided to alter the dimensions of the third block, by increasing the floor area but reducing the height by one storey. More of the site was thus covered by building, but the advantages of the change were clear. There was now a higher proportion of open office space to central core within the third block, and the variety of height in the three blocks enhanced the composition. Even the façades to Baggot Street were enlivened by the juxtaposition of a long relatively low building with a narrow taller one (*Plate* 66).

121

Plate 57

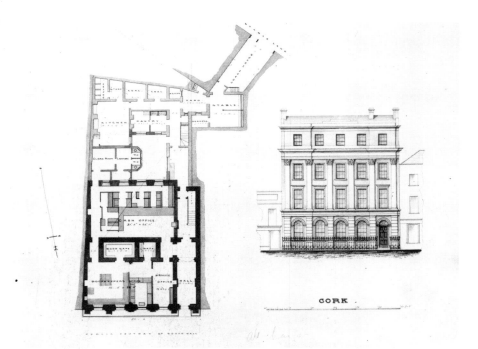

CORK.

Plate 58

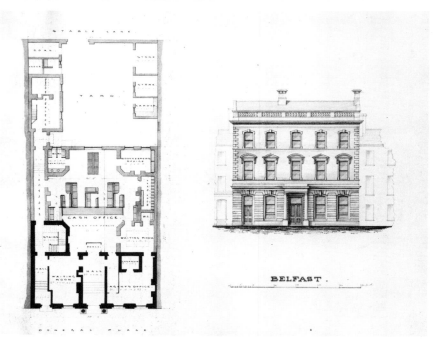

BELFAST.

Plate 59

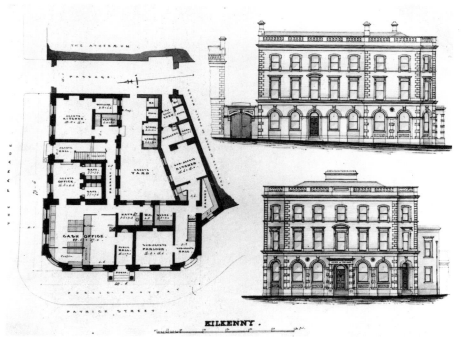

KILKENNY.

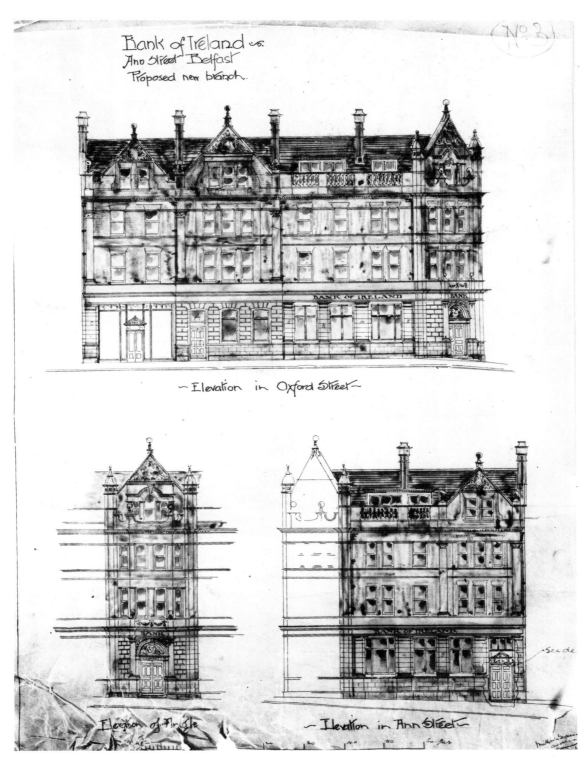

Bank of Ireland
Ann Street Belfast
Proposed new branch.

~ Elevation in Oxford Street ~

~ Elevation of Tingle ~

~ Elevation in Ann Street ~

Plate 60

Judgment of the building must take into account its relationship to the architecture of Mies van der Rohe: van der Rohe's Seagram Building in New York, built in the 1950s, is justifiably the most frequently cited parallel with — and prototype for — the Baggot Street building.

One of the most important components in the office tradition of the firm of Scott Tallon Walker has been the 'Miesian'. In some ways the Baggot Street building marked the culmination in Tallon's work of this exacting and classical approach to architecture, an approach which Tallon himself would claim to have modified somewhat in his subsequent work. Reticence of articulation, precision of detail, the reliance on fine — often luxurious — natural materials, the pursuit of refined propor-

123

Plate 61

tion, modular planning with a fondness for rectilinear rather than curved patterns, the careful relationship of one block of a composition to another (with much attention paid to the open spaces between): such generalised principles as these were, in Baggot Street, given still more specifically Miesian expression in the elevation details, and in the arrangement of interior space.

In some ways the Baggot Street office is better than the Seagram Building (*Plates* 66-71). Its forecourt may be relatively cramped, but the relationship of its three blocks to each other is more simply (and, therefore, more effectively) presented than is the massing of the different components of the Seagram Building which — in side views — is occasionally incoherent. Further, being under the control of a single owner there is a uniformity of furnishing and internal treatment throughout the three blocks which greatly enhances the artistic coherence of the whole. The interiors on all upper floors are consistently more interesting than those of the Seagram Building (and other skyscrapers by van der Rohe). Ample ceiling heights, the uniform use of fine materials and the generous provision of natural light are partly responsible for the success of the interiors. Even more important, however, is the variety and freely-flowing nature of the space. Instead of a strict division between corridors and individual offices, more interesting arrangements of space are made possible by the varied use of walls which, rather than forming closed boxes of separate rooms, act as separating screens in open and lightsome spaces (*Plates* 70 and 71). Paradoxically, such special excitements,

124

Plate 62

Theo McNab
Room 4/2 1975
Oil on canvas
197 × 122 cms

Plate 63

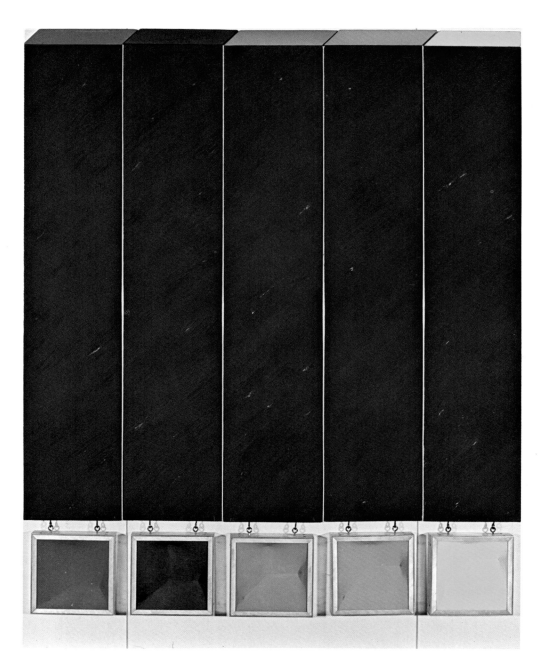

Roy Johnston
Quintet 1971
PVA on cotton duck
1.680 x 1.370 mm
Signed: Roy Johnston '71
Exhibited at the 'Young Irish Artists' Exhibition, Galway 1971 and
Edinburgh 1972, in association with Rosc '71

Plate 64

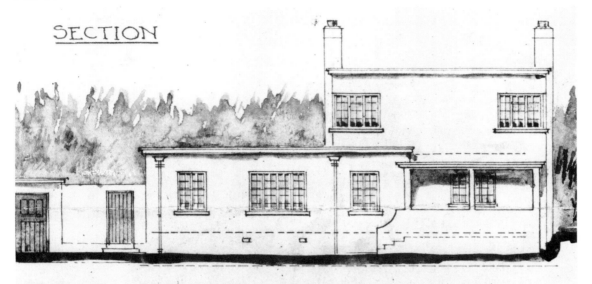

Plate 65

pioneered by Mies van der Rohe in, for example, his Barcelona Pavilion of 1929, were denied him by the exigencies of office skyscraper design.

Judged by such demanding standards, however, as the masterpieces of van der Rohe in New York and Chicago, head office is seen to have shortcomings. The memory of the sublime magnitude of the Parthenon always mitigates the pleasure we derive from a small garden temple, however fine. Similarly, so specific are the allusions of head office to vastly larger buildings that expectations of grandeur are raised which are not adequately fulfilled (and which should not be fulfilled in the heart of Georgian Dublin). The solemn ground-floor voids of the Seagram Building, bounded by plain expanses of travertine, or granite, or glass, and punctuated by great bronze columns, are more grand than the corresponding spaces in head office where the outer glass wall is uncomfortably close to the central granite core. Further, the logic with which van der Rohe unites interior and exterior is less relentlessly pursued in Dublin. Tallon's internal columns, for instance, are not clad in bronze as are his external ones, so the more classical pretensions of a unified system of vertical support are surrendered. And in the Seagram vestibule the mosaic ceiling is seen to be a continuation of the ceiling of the external colonnade, separated from it only by a slim bronze member and a plane of glass. This establishes a unity of interior and exterior which is reinforced not only in the bronze cladding of the columns both inside and out, but also in the continuation as floor inside the vestibule of the granite paving outside. In Dublin, the sheen and modular texture of the Seagram mosaic are lost in the white rendering of the colonnade ceiling, and the vestibule ceiling is lowered to accommodate air conditioning. Finally, uneven weathering, patination and cleaning have at least temporarily deprived the building of the rich lustre of the Seagram Building.

That the building sustains searching criticism is a measure of its quality. To Lance Wright in the *Architectural Review* 'it is almost certainly the purest example of the style [of Mies van der Rohe] in Europe's off-shore islands and . . . is probably one of the most sensitive uses of the style anywhere . . . it is a pleasure to see an adequate amount of money so beautifully spent'.[17]

Plate 66

In an important part of the Georgian city which had received rough handling from other neighbouring buildings there is something of the velvet glove about head office. There is no doubt either of its elegance, or of its forceful presence in an area of smaller eighteenth- and nineteenth-century domestic buildings. The demolition of part of Baggot Street to accommodate the third block was regrettable, however necessary it was for the completion of the Bank's design. Yet the architect's claim that the whole head office composition is now sensitively related to the Georgian neighbourhood which survives is entirely justified, not by the banality of façade pastiche but by the inherent quality of the building and its careful grouping of masses. The enormous main block is far withdrawn from the street line, while the two lower blocks in front mediate between their immediate Georgian neighbours and the tall block behind (*Plate* 66).

Head office makes its point architecturally, but with a reticence which is paralleled in Francis Johnston's self-abnegating exteriors in College Green; paralleled, too, in the nineteenth-century branch buildings, where the avoidance of Victorian flamboyance saved the unimaginative Symes from serious lapses of taste. Happily this well-bred reticence is relieved in the Baggot Street office by paintings and sculptures which are disposed throughout the building and which constitute the major collection of Irish art of the 1970s.

That architecture may rely on painting and sculpture in achieving its full effect is a venerable tradition. And because head office eschews the purely architectural over-

Plate 67

statement of the Brutalist tradition, in favour of more neutral expression, it offers an ideal setting for the dashing and often extrovert work of contemporary artists. Whatever is reticent — even anonymous — about the ground-floor vestibule of the main block in head office is spectacularly enlivened by Patrick Scott's great Aubusson tapestry, *Blaze.* Internal axes are given brilliant focal points. Sensuous undulations of light and colour, as in Alexandra Wejchert's *Flowing relief,* enhance the rectilinear discipline of the architectural frame. The interlocking office spaces and passages — themselves defined by planes of natural materials — granite, oak or wool — are three-dimensionally enlivened by the changing perspectives of paintings and sculptures (*Plate* 71).

Works to be included in the collection were selected initially by Ronald Tallon, some of whose other buildings — such as the Carroll factory in Dundalk and the Science Building in University College, Galway — are given dramatic emphasis by the use of external sculpture. The Court, having agreed to establish a collection of contemporary Irish art, set aside £100,000 in 1971 for the purpose. By late 1972 over £50,000 had been spent, largely at public exhibitions. Purchasing slowed down immediately after 1972: only one of the works in head office (a tapestry by Louis le Brocquy, *Men of Connaught*) was bought in 1973. Since 1974, the collection has continued to grow, very largely under the guidance of Neil Monahan who, in addition, has advised on purchases of paintings and prints for branches.

The nucleus of this collection, therefore, was formed by the architect of the buildings in which it is housed. This nucleus was assembled in a very short period in the early 1970s, dictated as much by what was then available at exhibitions as by any wish to build up a comprehensive collection of contemporary Irish art. Some artists were commissioned, among them Tim Goulding, Alexandra Wejchert and Michael Farrell and, though very few works executed before 1969 were bought, Patrick Scott's *Autumnal Landscape* and Camille Souter's *The West,* both of 1964, joined the collection. Non-Irish artists represented at this early stage included Victor Vasarely, Derek Hirst and Robert Indiana.

Tallon's collection has the coherence and limitations of a personal selection: the Bank's generosity in establishing a budget for purchasing works of art, and the spirit shown that these be the works of contemporary rather than of more traditionally established figures, were matched by the freedom given to Tallon to purchase without reference — except in the most expensive cases — to the directors of the Bank. Consequently the collection as it stood in 1973 revealed Tallon's sympathy with the linear precision, chromatic liveliness, abstract interests, and international — often American — affiliations of Irish artists, many of whom had been inspired by the Rosc exhibitions held in Dublin in 1967 and 1971. The landscapes of Norah McGuinness and T. P. Flanagan, therefore, or the early painterly works of Patrick Scott and Camille Souter, stand apart from the more cosmopolitan works — more typical of the early collection — of William Scott, Cecil King, Anne Madden, Michael Farrell, and the later Patrick Scott. In precisely the same way in sculpture, a work such as Oisín Kelly's *Marchers,* with its narrative theme and plastic modelling, stands apart from the works of Alexandra Wejchert, Gianfranco Pardi, Brian King, Gerda Frömel, John Burke and Michael Bulfin and their clean-surfaced, hard-edged, precision-tooled forms and inorganic associations.

As successor to Tallon in building up the collection, Neil Monahan has added to it the interest of greater comprehensiveness and diversity, while maintaining its

Plate 68

emphasis on contemporary works of Irish artists. He has added works by artists already represented, and has continued to buy occasional foreign works, by Dali, Kokoschka, Miró and Henry Moore. The most expensive painting bought for the collection, Jack Yeats's *Eileen Aroon*, came in 1977, bought specifically for the directors' suite (a retreat, maybe, from the rigours of the *avant-garde* conscientiously encouraged elsewhere in the building, in favour of more established Irish modernism?). Further, Monahan has introduced artists not represented earlier: Nano Reid, Brian Bourke, Patrick Collins, Gerard Dillon, and others whose representational work belongs to a more recognisably continuous tradition of Irish painting than does the work of other Irish post-Rosc artists.

There was a time when Bank of Ireland branches were distinguishable from Hibernian and National ones by the Paul Henry prints: the National had prints of Daniel O'Connell, while the Hibernian had views of its College Green head office. And while difficult questions of balance between Hard Edge and Pop were being answered in Baggot Street, an assistant manager was writing to head office complaining that his new branch 'has a very bare appearance': appropriate to the interests and business of his clients, he craved some racing prints. While there is no policy at the moment of dispersing works from the head office collection to branches throughout the country, Monahan has purchased contemporary prints and paintings for this purpose. Further, it is increasingly common for paintings in the head office

Plate 69

Plate 70

Plate 71

collection to travel from Baggot Street for temporary exhibition in Ireland and abroad. This is an inevitable consequence of the importance of the collection, which exceeds that of any public or private collection of contemporary Irish art in the country.

The collection in head office (and its published catalogue) is the tangible side of a more extensive patronage of the visual arts. Having itself won an award in 1978 in the European Museum of the Year scheme, the Bank agreed to sponsor one of the scheme's prizes for temporary exhibitions. It sponsored an exhibition of Irish painting and sculpture of the 1980s, 'The Delighted Eye', as part of the Sense of Ireland Exhibition in 1980. Further, 8,000 square feet of the ground-floor vestibule of the main block of the Baggot Street building are given over to the public display of temporary exhibitions. In purely architectural terms this exacts a high price. The controlled austerity of a Miesian vestibule can be too demanding, and too aloof, for all but the most strategically placed (and selected) works of art. Temporary — sometimes amateur — pieces, with the storage and display problems they create, can give a homeliness to the space which detracts from its grandeur. Perhaps such purist considerations are, in the long run, unimportant in contrast with the hospitality and encouragement offered to exhibitors in head office.

In any review of the last two hundred years, the high points of the Bank's artistic patronage remain the purchase of the parliament house, the competition for its conversion (and its subsequent maintenance and restoration), the erection of the Baggot Street head office, and the building up of the collection of modern Irish works of art. Establishing itself in College Green helped to consolidate the easterly development of the city, and almost certainly influenced the subsequent development of College Green and Dame Street as a bankers' enclave. The competition occurred at a moment of change in both style and patronage in Irish architecture, a change which was influenced by (and which might almost be symbolised by) the Bank's initiative. Johnston rose magnificently to the occasion and, however much he may have melted into one 'a dozen varying plans' familiar to him from the submissions of the competitors, his cash office established a norm for bank design in Ireland for the rest of the nineteenth century.

There was a steady generosity to fine architects — to Soane who to judge from his designs was instructed to plan on the grandest scale, to Johnston and to Tallon. And there seems to have been no demand, while spending large sums, for mere ostentation. If this reticence shades off at one extreme into dullness, it is expressed at the other in the classicism of Baggot Street, and in the prudent restoration of the College Green building: a few weeks with a sand-blaster would have produced an effect visually indistinguishable — to a large part of the population — from the present fruits of eleven years of fastidious craftsmanship. And this restoration was only part of the acknowledgment by the Bank of its responsibilities to the past. Johnston's conversion preserved much of Pearce's masterpiece, which remained largely undisturbed by 150 years of growing demands on head office accommodation. In a city where the interiors of buildings are still virtually unprotected by any conservation law, this is a triumph for piety, not legislation. Finally, while there has been, in the Bank's artistic patronage, an emphasis on the encouragement of Irish artists, this has not been doctrinaire: Vasarely and Miró join Flaxman and Bacon to serve as points of comparison and reference for their Irish colleagues.

134

Plate 72

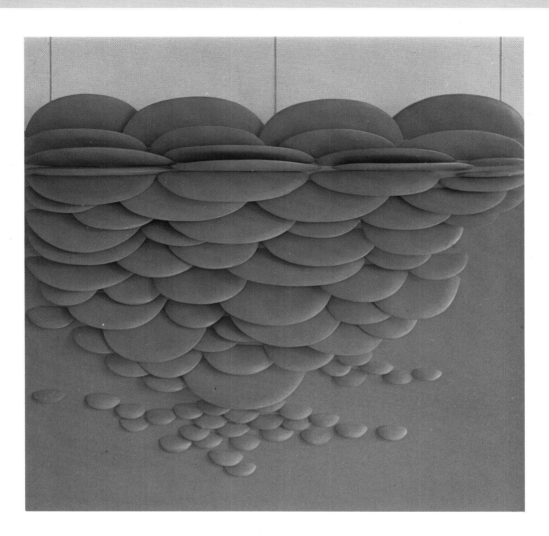

Alexandra Wejchert
Red Relief 1972
Commissioned work
Acrylic painted timber relief
1.550 x 1.800 mm
Signed: Alexandra Wejchert 72

Plate 73

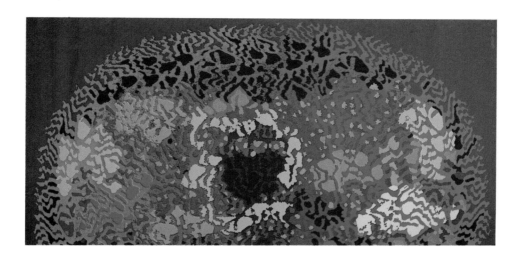

Patrick Scott
Eroica 1979
Aubusson tapestry
305 × 610 cms

The record may be uneven: Sproule and Davis in the eighteenth century, Halpin and Symes in the nineteenth, could not establish or sustain for the Bank the architectural supremacy which passed occasionally to other hands. The record is, however, notable and, in its balance of the conservative and the radical, as in its influence on the arts in Ireland over two centuries, unique.

References

(References in the text and notes to Curran are to C. P. Curran, 'The architecture of the Bank of Ireland' in F. G. Hall, *The Bank of Ireland 1783-1946*, Dublin and Oxford 1949.)

1   *Freeman's Journal*, 10-12 December 1782.
2   *Freeman's Journal*, 11-13 May 1784.
3   City Hall, Dublin, Wide Streets Commissioners' minutes, 22 July 1799.
4   TCOD, iv/73, 10 Apr. 1802.
5   *Dublin Journal*, 28 June 1803.
6   PRO 30/9/114 ff. 34-7.
7   This stipulation is discussed in William E. H. Lecky, *A history of Ireland in the eighteenth century*, London 1892, v, p.418, and in Curran, pp.457-8; the documents they quote from are PRO 30/9/114 ff. 34-7: PRO 30/9/113 ff. 130-33 (see too, PRO 30/9/118 ff. 143-4), and in the British Library, Add MS 35712, ff. 73-4; see too Charles Abbot, Lord Colchester, ed., *The diary and correspondence of Charles Abbot*, London 1861, iii, p. 283.
8   There is a copy of the brief (or of part of it) in Sir John Soane's Museum, London (LXXII, 4).
9   James Gandon junior and Thomas J. Mulvany, *The life of James Gandon*, Dublin 1846, pp. 85-6.
10   TCOD, iv/287, 9 Oct. 1804
11   Ibid., v/218, 1 Sept. 1807.
12   Ibid., vi/196, 8 Oct. 1811.
13   Ibid., v/330, 384-5, 19 July 1808, 21 Feb. 1809.
14   Ibid., viii/289, 21 Jan. 1823.
15   *Freeman's Journal*, 7-10 January 1769.
16   *Irish Builder*, 15 October 1868, p.259.
17   Lance Wright, 'Banker's acropolis', *The Architectural Review*, cliii, no. 912 (February 1973), pp. 96-7.

List of Illustrations

All prints and drawings illustrated are, unless otherwise stated, in the Bank archives, architectural drawings collection.

All photographs are by David Davison of Pieterse Davison International Ltd, with the following exceptions:

Plates 34, 38	Godfrey New Photographics Ltd
Plates 67, 68, 70	John Donat Photography
Plate 50	Photographic Centre, Trinity College Dublin

Plate 74

This untitled abstract sculpture in sheet steel by John
Burke stands outside the Baggot Street head office

The Changing Economic Environment*

Dermot McAleese

THE discussion of this chapter focuses on four interrelated issues: first, the inter-action between the banking system and the economic environment; second, the main changes in the Irish economy since the Second World War; third, the impact of economic change on monetary and exchange rate policies; finally, the prospects for the Irish economy in the eighties.

While this essay deals more with the banking system as a whole than with the Bank of Ireland *per se*, the Bank constitutes so significant a part of that system that events affecting the whole must inevitably have significant consequences for the part. For this reason, economic developments whether they take the form of inflation or balance of payments problems, unemployment or industrial growth, in so far as they have a direct impact on the banking system, will also affect the Bank's level of activity and profitability. Hence, an examination of past and prospective developments in the economy and resultant changes in policies relating to the banking system is a useful element in the assessment of the Bank's progress in recent years.

The Banking System and the Economy

The primary economic function of commercial banks is to hold deposits and to honour cheques drawn upon them — in short to provide the economy with the largest component of the money supply. People and businesses need money in order to tide them over the timing differences between the flows of expenditure and income and to reduce the risk of becoming illiquid. Businessmen also hold balances to improve the efficiency of other financial transactions and are willing to pay in terms of interest forgone for this efficiency.

Economic growth generates an increase in the demand for money. As income increases, so does the value of transactions in and out of individual and corporate bank accounts and consequently the desire to hold larger average money balances. There is, in fact, a certain statistical regularity in the relationship. Defining money as currency held by the public plus current and deposit accounts of the licensed banks, econometric analysis of the Irish monetary system suggests that each 1 per cent increase in real income will normally be associated with a 1.4 per cent increase in the demand for money. Since bank deposits constitute 90 per cent of the money supply, this positive relation between economic growth and money demand is good news for the banking system.

Not all banks will benefit equally from economic growth, partly because of differences in efficiency between banks, and partly because growth will affect different categories of banking in different ways. As customers get richer, they accumulate

---

I am indebted to Professor W. J. L. Ryan and Mr Patrick Carey for comments on a previous draft and to David Mooney for research assistance. The usual disclaimer applies.

larger liquid balances and become more sensitive to the interest forgone by holding money in currency or current account deposits as opposed to higher-yielding but less liquid deposit account balances. A further impetus to transfer to higher-yielding deposits is given by inflation which raises nominal interest rates and accentuates the cost of holding non-interest-bearing currency and current accounts. These factors help to explain the rapid change in the structure of the Irish financial system in recent years. Resources have shifted from current accounts to interest-bearing deposit accounts and from the associated banks to the non-associated banks and the building societies. The non-associated banks now account for 31 per cent of bank deposits compared with 16 per cent in 1971, while building society deposits have grown at nearly twice the rate of bank deposits during the decade. Domestic institutional influences relating to the operation of the credit guidelines, liquidity ratios, and disclosure and taxation of deposit interest have also played a rôle in supporting this trend.

If banks benefit from growth and have an interest in sustaining it, they also suffer in times of economic stagnation. As customers become more cautious and less optimistic about the future, they borrow less. Paradoxically, however, the onset of recession tends to be accompanied by an increase in demand for the 'output' of banks rather than by a decline. Customers unable to repay their loans on schedule want more credit, not less. The banks' viability is threatened not so much because people do not want to borrow but because they need to borrow, or have already borrowed, more than they are capable of repaying. Bad debts provision begins to increase and a certain dubiety develops about the quality of many bank assets. The exposure of banks to the risk of bad debts has been highlighted in recent years by the forced rescheduling of the loans advanced to the Mexican and Polish governments and by the less publicised special arrangements on behalf of what the IMF describes as 'low income developing countries' whose external debt is now well in excess of twice the value of their exports.[1] Within a country, the same pattern of events is evident as bad debts provision becomes a heavier charge on profits, and loans are renegotiated in response to the mounting financial difficulties of personal and corporate borrowers.

The degree of price stability is another aspect of the environment which has a substantial impact on the banking system. Money being the raw material of bankers, it is not surprising that they should be concerned in a special way with developments in the real value of money. Rising prices have been eroding its real value for decades but more rapidly than ever during the last decade.

Inflation is a matter of concern to bankers for a number of reasons. Rising prices are inevitably accompanied by increases in interest rates which in turn have implications for the structure of bank assets and liabilities. Reference has already been made to the shift from current accounts to deposit accounts. Inflation also has a bearing on exchange rates — purchasing power parity theory states that an inflation rate in excess of that prevailing in trading countries must lead to a depreciation in the exchange rate — and banks have to be alert to these effects in determining their portfolio and advising customers. At a more mundane level, inflation can also have significant implications for bank profits, although the extent to which this is the case is still a matter of some controversy. There is also disagreement about how profits should be defined in an inflationary situation. That such disagreement is not an academic exercise is illustrated by the £80 million gap between the £121 million profits earned by the AIB and the Bank of Ireland groups in 1981-2 on a historical cost basis and the mere £41 million profits earned by calculating them according to current cost conventions.

Inflation has other, potentially more dangerous, destablilising effects. It distorts patterns of investment and can undermine competitiveness with adverse consequences for economic growth. By undermining the function of money, inflation involves transactions costs which can cumulatively amount to a significant sum. Inflation also engenders insecurity and obsessive concern with the distribution of income which in turn fuels more inflation. The resultant strains on society, if unchecked, can lead to difficulties for the democratic process, with excessive power accruing to factions and lobbyists.[2] At the same time, the process of checking inflation, once it has been unleashed, entails substantial economic costs also, as recent experience in Western Europe and the United States has all too painfully shown. Policies which give priority to the objective of reducing inflation have a tendency to be deflationary. This is particularly true of monetarist policies. As Goodhart observed, the difficulty with these policies is that the degree of deflation required in any given context to secure a reduction in inflation is uncertain:

> deflation is extremely painful and unpopular and in an uncertain world it is never clear how much deflation will actually be required, or over what time span, to achieve some given desired deceleration in inflation.[3]

Perhaps all that can firmly be concluded is that banks, no less than the entire economy, function best in the context of consistent policies and stable institutions; an environment in which depositors feel confident as to the stability and redeemability of their deposits and borrowers are not encouraged into reckless spending by the prospect of being able to repay their loans in depreciated currency.

So far our discussion has considered how economic growth and inflation affect the banking system. To leave the matter there would be to give an unbalanced impression. For the relationship between the economic environment and financial institutions is two-way. A smoothly functioning organisation of banks, money and credit has long been regarded as an essential lubricant of economic growth — something which may not make growth happen but without which economic growth cannot be sustained. Historians of the Industrial Revolution, for example, have identified the existence of a developed banking system as one of Britain's major advantages in entering the era of modern growth. If that was true then, how much more vital a rôle money plays in our present, vastly more specialised and inter-dependent society.

In the first instance, banks have made important contributions to creating new and more economical forms of money. The progression from gold to bank notes and from bank notes to bank deposits reflects this continuing search. Even during the past twenty years, continuous innovations have been introduced in the chequing system which helps to increase the 'moneyness' of bank balances. New forms of money are being created — for example credit cards which in many respects perform the function of money as a means of exchange. The essential gain to society from all these activities arises through avoidance of the inconvenience and difficulty of barter (which requires for its consummation what is technically known as the double coincidence of wants) at minimum cost.

Banks also act as intermediaries between savers and spenders.[4] In this respect, they compete with many other institutions in the financial sector, such as the building societies, insurance companies, the Industrial Credit Corporation (ICC) and the Agricultural Credit Corporation (ACC). Like these, the banks also act as a conduit for channelling savings into domestic uses. In mid-1982, loans to the private sector by the licensed banks totalled £5,900 million. These loans percolated to all sections of the economy. Sixty per cent of the total is divided equally between agriculture, manufacturing and personal lending (which includes the familiar personal bank overdraft and house mortgage and bridging loans). A further 27 per cent is absorbed by transport and distribution and the remaining 13 per cent goes to miscellaneous sources.

Apart from periodic exhortations to the banks to discriminate in favour of 'productive' as opposed to 'unproductive' lending, the Central Bank has generally left it to the banks to decide how these vast sums are allocated. True, in recent years, explicit guidelines have been set for personal lending (other than housing) but the amounts involved add up to just slightly above 10 per cent of advances by licensed banks. Even here, the authorities confine themselves to stipulating the amount to be lent within this category. To whom the banks lend is considered very much their own business.

The allocation of credit confers significant power on the banks. It involves decision-taking at a number of levels from branch manager up to board level. The predominant determinants of the allocation of advances are first the prudential motive — will the creditor be able to repay the loan? — incorporating the overriding obligation of a bank to safeguard its depositors' money and secondly, subject to this constraint, the desire to make profits which in turn implies the necessity of assuming risk. One such risk takes the form of trading short-term liabilities (deposits) against longer-term assets (loans) and the other involves the establishment of a probability distribution of success in its loan profile ('failure' representing bad debts and/or delayed repayments of debts). Risk-taking is an essential element in banking. The higher-risk loan carries the higher interest charge and hence is the more profitable, if serviced on schedule. The bank must take a balanced view of the conflicting dictates of profit and safety in order to achieve an optimal solution.

The economic calculus outlined above does little to impress those who see the banks as owners of one of the commanding heights of the economy. Calls for nationalisation have been heard in Ireland as elsewhere. The case has been made that the banks favour the rich, an assertion summarised in the old adage that 'if you need a hundred pounds you call the bank, if you need a million, they call you'.[5] Undoubtedly, there is something in this argument. Economies of scale make large loans a more attractive proposition, other things being equal, than small loans, and for this reason, banks may appear to differentiate between their more substantial and smaller customers. Another instance of this differentiation occurs in the interest rate structure of the banks, which favours large depositors over small depositors. In August 1982, for example, the associated banks offered 10 per cent on deposits under £5,000, $13\frac{1}{2}$ per cent on deposits between £5,000 and £25,000 and $16\frac{1}{2}$ per cent on deposits over £25,000. In part this gradation reflects economies of scale; in part, the more intensely competitive market for large deposits. The point is that technical considerations such as the higher cost of administering small accounts would point to higher deposit rates and lower lending rates for the large transactor even in a nationalised banking system.

Proponents of nationalisation might accept these points without necessarily conceding the case. Their objection to the present system centres on the concentration

Plate 75

Baggot Street exterior, daylight

Plate 76

Robert Ballagh
Two People with an Adolph Gottlieb 1972
Acrylic on canvas
2.400 x 1.220 mm
Signed on reverse

Robert Ballagh
Woman with a Giuseppe Capogrossi 1972
Acrylic on canvas
2.440 x 1.220 mm
Signed on reverse

of power at board level, with the question being raised as to the appropriateness of a small group of individuals, some of whom may occupy strategic positions in the economy and may be at once board members and major customers of the banks, determining the allocation of bank advances. The power of a bank's board can, however, easily be exaggerated. The proportion of new advances which require board approval in a large associated bank nowadays is unlikely to exceed 20 per cent. Decisions on these matters are being increasingly delegated to branch, regional and area level. Nationalisation is unlikely *per se* to make much difference to the behaviour of banks unless it is accompanied by very specific guidelines on the allocation of credit. Strict adherence to such guidelines might in turn lead to inefficiencies and would certainly undermine the profitability of banks. The alternative of nationalisation would not so much dilute the power of the banks as confer it on a different set of people and one might well ask whether there may be more effective ways of securing a more even distribution of wealth and income than through nationalisation of the banks.

Another more general line of argument is that a nationalised banking system would give priority to socially productive loans which a profit-maximising private bank might turn down. Instances of market failure can be multiplied in which the private return to a project, say to a voluntary body trying to keep open a swimming pool, may be less than the return calculated on the basis of social costs and benefits. The possibility of divergence between private and social returns does not, of course, constitute a case for nationalisation. It must be shown that this would be the least-cost method of correcting the cause of market failure, a stricter criterion. There is much empirical support for the view that problems of this nature should be tackled at source — by means of a subsidy to the swimming pool in the above example — rather than by indirect means.

This has also been the view of successive Irish governments. Where special credit needs are apparent, special facilities are offered — the ACC and ICC are examples in point, as are the interest-free loans and grants offered to industry by the IDA. In addition, a whole range of measures have been taken to control the banks. Since 1971 the Central Bank is empowered to grant or revoke bank licences. Its credit guidelines set specific limits to the amount of credit individual banks can extend. Its approval must be obtained for changes in bank interest rates and bank charges and it takes a view on the 'appropriate' rate of return to capital employed in banking. The Central Bank also dispenses a considerable amount of 'jawbone control', that is, control by moral persuasion. Public intervention has extended even to the enactment of special legislation to control bank officials' remuneration. Although Irish banks are in private ownership, the notion that they are in consequence free to do as they like is quite at variance with reality.

The public accountability of banks is further reinforced through the system of liquidity ratios. The primary liquidity ratio refers to the relationship between the banks' cash and deposits with the Central Bank on the one hand, and its current and time deposits and net external liabilities on the other. Apart from satisfying a prudential need, funds lodged in the Central Bank also provide an indirect source of finance to the government. The banking system holds over £600 million in primary liquidity on hand and with the Central Bank, equivalent to 10 per cent of its resources. Since the rate paid on these deposits is about 3 per cent below market rates, this may imply a degree of hidden taxation.[6] The banks are obliged to hold a further 15 to 25 per cent (for non-associated banks and associated banks respectively) of their resources in

147

government paper to satisfy the secondary liquidity ratio. This ensures that a significant proportion of any increase in bank lending automatically accrues to the government. The total amount outstanding under this heading amounts to almost £1,400 million. The exchequer is in the position of obtaining an automatic annual injection of over £200 million on this account, a safe and secure source of finance which does not have to be purchased on the open market. Of course, interest is paid on this debt, and very high interest in recent years, but there is an element of implicit subsidisation of government here, as in the case of primary liquidity. With no secondary liquidity ratios, the banks would certainly continue to invest in government paper but the proportion of their assets held this way would fluctuate in line with market conditions and the demand for private sector advances and the government might well end up having to pay more to ensure adequate take-up of its issues.

In view of the emphasis placed on the banking system's contribution to the economy, it may seem strange that the Republic has been able to survive a number of bank strikes over the last decade, an occurrence which until recently was unheard of elsewhere in developed economies.[7] The most recent prolonged stoppage lasted from 28 June to 6 September 1976 and involved closure to the public of the main clearing banks, which then accounted for more than two-thirds of bank resources and which had a network of some 670 branches. Following a detailed survey of the effects of this dispute, the Central Bank came to the conclusion not markedly different to that reached on the basis of studies of previous stoppages:

> The strike caused considerable inconvenience to the general public and the business and farming communities. It necessitated the diversion of time and resources into seeking and arranging alternative financial services and, in the case of businesses, to managing their financial positions and arranging for payment of employees. Retail sales were depressed early in the strike but improved in August and September. Sales of property were also affected adversely and it is likely that some investment plans were postponed. Trade figures suggest that foreign trade was largely unaffected. However, had the strike been more prolonged, its adverse economic effects would have become considerable.[8]

Inconvenience, postponement of investment but no effect on foreign trade: this may appear a rather mild consequence of the paralysis of a major part of the financial sector. It is instructive of how this sector works to review the reasons for the Central Bank's conclusion.

First, a large proportion of the associated banks' functions were undertaken by the non-associated banks and, to a lesser extent, by building societies and other financial institutions. Two weeks had elapsed between the announcement of strike notice and closure which had given the public time to make transfers from the associated banks to their accounts elsewhere. The high degree of substitutability between the services offered by different parts of the banking system was underlined.

Second, the absence of exchange controls between Ireland and the UK at that time meant that substitute facilities were also offered by Northern Ireland and British banks.

Third, the 'moneyness' of cheques drawn on associated bank accounts was preserved to some degree in that they were still widely accepted by public houses, shops, supermarkets, building societies and companies.[9] As the strike developed, however, the acceptability of cheques lessened. The notion of preserving goodwill and future custom was then counterbalanced by the interest losses on the traders' growing stock of uncashable cheques. Had the strike continued longer, serious liquidity difficulties would have appeared on this account.

Fourth, Central Bank notes were used to substitute for bank deposits. The note issue rose by £78 million between mid May and mid June, an increase of 25 per cent over the initial level, and sterling notes were retained in circulation rather than repatriated through the associated banks. This is further evidence of the extreme fungibility of money, a quality which underlies the difficulties experienced by the authorities in attempting to control any single part of a highly interrelated financial system.

The question posed earlier as to how the economy managed to survive without banks needs to be rephrased. The bank strike did not close all banks: the country continued to have access to banking services of the non-associated banks and banks in the United Kingdom and to the support services of other elements in the financial sector. In addition, the Central Bank and government departments assisted matters by injecting a large increase in bank notes into the system. Finally, cheques themselves took on something of the character of money through widespread acceptance and endorsement. But this happened only because the strike was not expected to last indefinitely.

Irish experience of bank strikes does not call for revision of the earlier proposition that a modern economy cannot survive without a banking system. Rather it points to the high degree of substitutability between different parts of the financial sector. The importance of minimising the economy's vulnerability to possible future interruptions, through development of alternative banking and financial institutions outside the associated banks and through maintenance of close links with the UK banks, is something which the authorities doubtless must keep in mind in framing banking policy. It is also worth noting that the break in the link with sterling and the post-EMS imposition of exchange controls between the UK and Ireland will have the effect of reducing that degree of access to the UK market which helped to mitigate the effects of previous bank closures.

The Changing Structure of the Irish Economy

Asked to contribute an outsider's view of the Irish economy, Professor Michael Fogarty of the Policy Studies Institute, London, remarked that whereas just after the Famine the national income per head in Ireland was at the level one can observe today in India, by the time the World Bank came to draw up its world development indicators in 1978, Ireland had qualified into the top group of industrial market economies.[10] Our concern here is with the last twenty-five years or so of this development. It was during this period that Ireland really changed its status from a predominantly agricultural to a predominantly industrial society.

Irish GNP *per capita* at the end of the seventies was $4,210, equal to two-thirds of the UK level and less than half the average for industrial market economies. The adult literacy rate was 98 per cent and life expectancy at birth was seventy-three years, the same as in Britain and only marginally below the United States' seventy-four years. Living standards, as measured by GNP *per capita*, had almost doubled since 1960. The proportion of the labour force working in agriculture was 19 per cent compared with 36 per cent two decades earlier. With declining numbers in agriculture came a dramatic increase in the proportion of the population living in urban areas, particularly in the Dublin conurbation and the eastern regions of the country. The population of the Republic has now reached almost 3.5 million, a level unsurpassed since 1871.

In explaining these developments, emphasis must first be placed on the favourable world economic climate. The post-war period was one of unprecedented growth, extending throughout the OECD and sustained with only minor recessions until 1974. Never before had the Western world experienced such a prolonged period of uninterrupted growth. Global prosperity and full employment conditions in the OECD labour markets helped the Irish economy in two ways. First, a liberal international trading order developed which was particularly favourable to foreign investment and conducive to exports. Second, the tight labour markets of the UK meant that opportunities were available for emigration from Ireland, which enabled the country to escape the adverse consequences of a rate of natural increase well in excess of that of continental Europe.

But the encouraging external conditions explain only part of the story. Notwithstanding the rising tide of prosperity in Europe and the USA, living standards increased by only 12 per cent in Ireland during the period 1949-56 compared with an OECD average increase of 35 per cent and a UK increase of 19 per cent. Clearly, rapid growth in the developed world was not in itself a sufficient condition for an Irish economic recovery. Throughout the fifties, moreover, Ireland experienced emigration on a scale which went well beyond the point of beneficent release of population pressure. At a rate of 40,000 persons annually, the efflux of young people was resulting in an absolute decline in the Republic's population. Indeed it was the perceived failure of the Irish economy to respond to the opportunities offered by the growing prosperity abroad which led to fundamental reappraisal of economic policy in the course of the 1950s, culminating in the White Paper on *Economic development* and the *Programme for economic expansion,* both published in 1958.[11]

These documents charted a new economic strategy around three basic themes. One was a commitment to a more competitive outward-looking development pattern for Irish industry and agriculture. Emphasis was placed on the need to export and on the desirability of attracting foreign industry to supplement indigenous efforts. Another was the explicit recognition given to Ireland's agricultural potential and to the necessity of improving agricultural export performance based on better utilisation of pasture and development of food processing industries. A third element was the insistence on the need for a change in the pattern of public investment from non-productive social outlets to directly productive projects which would be helpful to, in modern terminology, the exposed traded sector of the economy.

A forecast growth rate of 2 per cent per annum was announced, the term 'forecast' being deliberately preferred to 'target' as indicating what might reasonably be expected to be achieved by adoption of the new strategy. A contemporary reader would be struck by the extent to which what would now be called 'a supply-side approach' was endorsed. Emphasis was placed on getting policies right and letting the profit motive and the private sector, guided where necessary by state action, get on with their work thereafter. As McCarthy percipiently observed:

The section in *Economic Development* dealing with financial and monetary policy is ten pages long, while the best part of 200 pages deal with supply-side questions. This seems to me to be about the correct ratio.[12]

In a contrasting vein, Kennedy and Dowling in their comprehensive study emphasise the rôle of sustained demand expansion.[13] The part played by government in stimulating this demand was singled out for particular commendation. Reinforcing the point, they criticise the contraction of government expenditure in the mid-fifties as an over-cautious response to the balance-of-payments difficulties of that time. (In the light of what might charitably be called the 'under-cautious' response of later governments to much greater balance-of-payments deficits, future historians may issue a kinder verdict on that aspect of policy.) It must, however, be remembered that an expansionary stance in fiscal policy was highly compatible with the ethos of the sixties. This was the decade of development, adopted as such by the United Nations and the OECD. It was a time when a collective commitment by the OECD to a target increase of 50 per cent in living standards could be announced without appearing either presumptuous or ridiculous. A readiness to use monetary and fiscal policy to stretch demand to full employment levels was part and parcel of government policy in most European countries. An OECD report on growth experience of the 1950s, published just a few years after *Economic development*, accurately reflects the thinking at that time:

> The most general pre-condition for rapid economic growth is existence of an adequate and sustained pressure of demand on the productive resources of the economy. Where this condition is fulfilled, there develop generally optimistic and dynamic attitudes among entrepreneurs and workers. In turn, the record suggests that the existence of such confident expectations about the possibility of disposing of additional output produces in the event rapid increases in productivity through their effects on investment, innovation and mobility.[14]

Irish fiscal policy was certainly 'supportive' of growth during the sixties in terms of expansion in aggregate demand. Public expenditure increased from 33 per cent to 43 per cent of GNP during the decade. Public consumption of goods and services rose by 3.9 per cent annually on average and, notwithstanding the strictures on non-productive outlays, social expenditure escalated in line with total expenditure. In fact, over the period as a whole, expenditure under the social headings of health, education and welfare increased from 13 per cent of total public expenditure in 1960 to 19 per cent in 1970. Moreover, this expenditure was launched from a base-level social infrastructure which had, in the words of the First Programme, given the country 'an infrastructure of housing, hospitals, communications, etc. which is equal (in some respects, perhaps, superior) to that of comparable countries'.[15] Strange though it may seem to contemporary readers, some of the emphasis on the need for productive investment arose from the belief that investment for social needs would no longer be necessary and that some alternative use of the resources thereby released would have to be found.

Although the growth of the public sector was strongly in evidence during the sixties, it must be said that its rate of expansion pales into insignificance compared with later experience. A staggering rise took place in the ratio of total public expenditure to GNP in the period 1971-80 — from 43 per cent to 63 per cent. Another point of contrast with the earlier period is the large proportion of the increased expenditure in recent years financed by foreign borrowing; prior to 1973, foreign borrowing was negligible. Around this time, the principle of balanced current budgets was abandoned with, in retrospect, the most unfortunate consequences. It is also likely, although this is difficult to substantiate, that public sector outlays were better controlled and more efficiently spent than in the seventies. A government intending to concentrate on productive investment started out in a frame of mind conducive to asking the right questions and setting the right criteria.

Government policy played a crucial rôle in setting the scene for expansion and in laying the supportive base on which expansion could take place. The main priority was to strengthen the nation's psychological frame of mind — a factor which Dr Whitaker was to emphasise again and again in his writings: the psychological factor, the release of a dynamic, the importance of sustaining an atmosphere of enterprise and progress. This was achieved through the then novel initiative of publishing a programme for expansion. A further objective was to establish a commercial policy designed to push Ireland towards a position where export markets could be developed and which would attract foreign investors. This was achieved through the progressive dismantling of tariff barriers, through the securing of improved access to the markets of the UK and Europe (the Anglo-Irish Free Trade Area and the EEC) and through fiscal incentives to exporters and manufacturing investors both foreign and domestic. The third objective, to reallocate government expenditure towards more immediately productive purposes, proved more difficult to attain. A qualified success is all that could be claimed under this heading on the grounds that the public sector was restrained relative to later excesses and was probably more productively allocated.

Economic performance abroad and sound policies at home were not, of course, the only factors at work in explaining Ireland's post-1958 growth. Social and psychological forces underpinned and in turn gained strength from economic change in accordance with what Professor Gunnar Myrdal once described as 'the cumulative and circular pattern of causation' so often observed in the process of development. Kennedy and Dowling identify some of these forces:

> the emergence to responsible positions of a new post-independence generation, placing greater emphasis on solving unemployment and emigration than on ending partition or restoring the Irish language; the assumption of a greater rôle in international affairs . . . and the sense of pride and purpose derived therefrom; and the influence of key personalities in dissipating the cynicism, born of apparent failures, about Ireland's economic prospects and in arousing enthusiasm for economic growth as a prerequisite to the achievement of more fundamental national goals.[16]

It is the old story, as true in economics as in other areas of life, that nothing succeeds like success.

The growth process which got firmly under way at the end of the fifties lasted until the oil crisis of 1973-4. Perhaps the most notable change it brought about was the reversal in demographic trends. The Irish population, having declined with few interruptions since the Famine, at first stabilised and then started to increase in the early sixties. A decline in population of 0.5 per cent per annum in the period 1949-61 was transformed into an average annual growth of 0.7 per cent during the period 1961-73, which rose still further to 1.5 per cent in the late seventies. In the relatively short space of thirty years, perceptions of the Irish demographic problem have changed from lamentations over the adverse economic and social effects of the Irish diaspora to an uneasy presentiment about the consequences of a rate of population growth closer to that of a less developed country than an advanced European nation.

During the fifties, the decline in population was viewed as a factor retarding economic advance, because of the decline in aggregate demand associated with it. A growing population held out the possibility of a vibrant demand for locally produced goods (food, clothing) and for the investment in building needed to house it. Land was regarded as an abundant factor which could supply food as required, hearkening back to what Professor Louis Cullen has called 'the naive and almost medieval belief of Irishmen that their environment was naturally fertile'.[17] The existence of an under-utilised infrastructure implied that population growth would place no unduly heavy strain on the public capital programme and through it on the public finances. Looking back it is clear that this latter expectation was indeed close to the mark. The social investment of the fifties made it possible to accommodate the rising population of the sixties with minimum stress. It was not until the mid-seventies that the necessity for a massive re-investment in infrastructure became apparent.

No less evident a feature of the economy's transformation has been the increased importance of foreign trade in the economy. The standard index of openness is the ratio of exports to gross national product. This ratio was 25 per cent in 1960. Since then, it has doubled to 51 per cent. A rise of similar proportions occurred in the imports/GDP ratio during the same period. The higher degree of openness of the economy was associated with rapid absolute growth rates of exports, particularly manufactured exports, and also 'invisibles' such as tourism. Without this impressive export performance, growth would have been constrained by balance-of-payments pressures. To a large extent, Ireland's post-war development was export-propelled.

In explaining export growth, account must again be taken of the encouraging international environment measured in terms of economic growth and of the movement towards trade liberalisation. To turn these opportunities into practical achievement, however, required domestic policy measures which focused on exports and provided incentives to encourage businessmen and farmers to pay greater attention to export markets. These measures were gradually implemented from the mid-fifties onwards, with export profits tax relief schemes, programmes to encourage export-oriented foreign investment, the seeking of membership of the EEC in 1961, unilateral tariff reductions in 1963 and 1964, the conclusion of the Anglo-Irish Free Trade Area (AIFTA) Agreement in 1966 and membership of the EEC in 1973. The progression to an outward-looking perspective was gradual but consistent. The need for a greater export performance was stressed and restressed right through the sixties by politicians and economists.

It is clear in retrospect that the most successful element in the export promotion programme was that relating to manufactured exports; and that the most effective measures affecting manufactured exports concerned the attraction of foreign-owned firms to establish export bases in Ireland. Thus agricultural exports, on which so much had been written, increased at only a slightly faster rate in the sixties than in 1949-61 (6.9 and 6.1 per cent annually respectively). In this instance market access was clearly an important constraint. Irish exports to the continental European market were hampered by the EEC's Common Agricultural Policy and access to the UK market was uncertain and for much of the time unremunerative. Agricultural products tended to be excluded from the more liberal trading climate.

Manufactured exports by contrast did benefit from improved market access. The AIFTA agreement removed some UK tariffs but more importantly gave some (though not total) assurance of continued preference in the UK market to Irish goods. The Dillon and Kennedy GATT tariff rounds also brought a significant reduction in the European Community's common external tariff and the rapid growth of demand in the EEC, combined with full employment, created a climate which was tolerant to imports from outside the Community. The manufactured goods' share of Irish exports rose from 6 per cent in 1950 to 18 per cent in 1961 and 33 per cent in 1968. These goods now account for more than 60 per cent of Irish merchandise exports. The government's firm intention of seeking membership of the European Community, maintained undeviatingly through the sixties, was an important source of assurance to enterprises building up export markets in the EEC at that time.

Although Irish firms made a contribution to this increase in exports, the major input came from overseas firms. The removal of protectionism in the home market was highly effective in improving the efficiency of Irish industry as measured by labour productivity. And this, combined with the more competitive cost-conscious internal environment, was helpful to those firms which were able to export and needed competitively-priced inputs. Considerably less success was experienced in getting indigenous firms both to improve efficiency *and* to branch out into export markets. Perhaps they were too busy simply surviving the shock of free trade. Despite warnings on the necessity to adapt and the significant material aids to carry out the necessary adjustments, many firms procrastinated. Others tried, but found the task of breaking into the export market expensive and difficult. Such success as was achieved was mostly in the UK rather than the continental market.

To explain the 19 per cent growth in manufactured exports in the 1960s, therefore, and the diversification of Irish export markets, the main emphasis must be placed on overseas export-oriented investors. New green-field plants were set up all over the country both in the developed east and the underdeveloped south and west. By 1966, these enterprises accounted for 50 per cent of Irish manufactured exports. These firms brought employment to areas which for generations had become accustomed to emigration. With this employment came demand for local services: leisure activities, professional, construction. For every job created in one of these new firms, another appeared as a result of indirect spin-offs. Unlike their Irish-owned counterparts, the foreign subsidiaries had the advantage of large market organisations with economies of scale which enabled them to penetrate the European market. With that came the diversification of Irish exports. The share of exports absorbed by the UK market fell from 74 per cent in 1961 to 65 per cent in 1971, a trend which continues to the present (40 per cent in 1981).

Success in the export development drive meant that Ireland was able to sustain a growth of 6 per cent annually in industrial output over the period 1961-73. Accompanying this was an expansion of 2 per cent in industrial employment. Service industries (which include the public sector) also grew vigorously by 3.7 per cent annually, compared with 1.6 per cent during the fifties. Agricultural output advanced by 1.7 per cent per annum, a modest growth rate although superior to the 0.9 per cent achieved in the fifties. Thus, helped by agriculture and tourism, a small strategic group of manufacturing firms spearheaded the development effort from which other sectors and firms could progress. A survey by the Irish Export Board covering three-

Plate 77

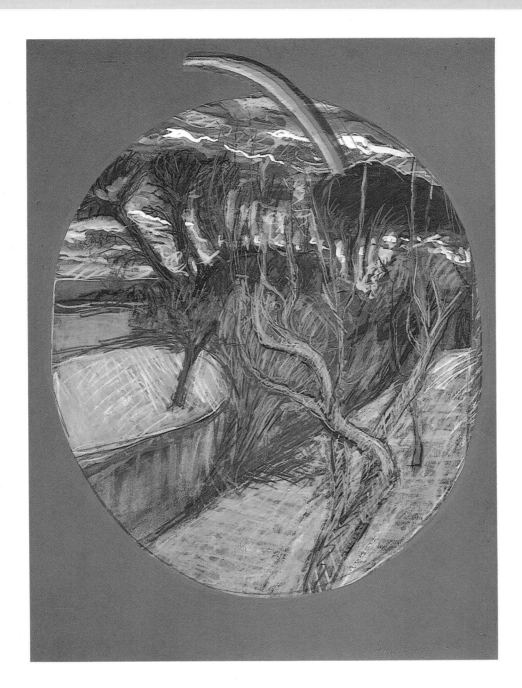

Brian Bourke
Landscape, Early Spring '74
Gouache and pencil on paper
760 × 560 mm
Signed: Brian Bourke '74

Plate 78

Martin Gale
Secret Places 1982
Acrylic
92 × 122 cms

quarters of manufacturing exports showed that a mere fifty-five production units, all of them foreign-owned, accounting for 18 per cent of employment and selling their output directly to affiliated companies, are responsible for 62 per cent of the value of these exports. Another finding was that two-thirds of Irish industrial exports were sold by multinationals which in turn sold 75 per cent of their output abroad.[18]

'The key distinction between the pre- and post-1960 periods has been the large-scale inflow of export-oriented manufacturing subsidiaries of transnational corporations.'[19] In reaching this conclusion, Nolan stresses the need to proceed to an analysis of why 'sourcing' by foreign firms occurred so widely in the 1960s and why Ireland was successful in attracting a disproportionate share of this footloose industry. Developments in production techniques which enabled manufacture to be broken down into a series of separate processes and also developments in managerial techniques and communication are cited in explanation of the 'multinationalisation' of industrial production. Also essential was the climate of free trade, convertibility of currencies and rapid world growth. It then became possible for footloose industrial projects to appear, some of which were willing to locate in small peripheral countries in order to serve external markets. Soundly conceived and consistent domestic policies, backed by stable government and competitively priced labour and implemented by a first-rate industrial promotion agency in the form of the IDA, placed Ireland in a position to obtain a substantial share of this market in footloose projects. Without congenial external conditions, the foreign investment strategy, which surely succeeded beyond the most optimistic expectations of those framing policy in the late fifties, would have been a non-starter. And without the right policies, Ireland would not have exploited these possibilities to the extent that it did.

The main structural changes in the economy therefore have been: (i) the increase in population, (ii) the rising share of industry in national output and employment and the corresponding decline in agriculture, and (iii) the emergence of a large foreign-owned element in Irish manufacturing which is highly export-oriented. These structural changes have been associated with unprecedented prosperity which has percolated to most regions and income groups in the community. The economy has, in the process, also become more vulnerable. Prosperity in a small economy depends on specialisation and specialisation means exports. Although production is small, our share of the market in specialised niches can be high. Ireland is a major producer on a European scale, for example, of tennis balls, hospital disposable products, cream liqueurs and computer-related office equipment. Consequently, a recession in the European market must have a serious impact on Irish sales, almost irrespective of what countervailing action is taken at a domestic level. This vulnerability is enhanced in so far as a large proportion of exports and an even larger share of export *growth* emanates not from indigenous firms but from foreign-owned subsidiaries.

The implications of this higher degree of dependence on foreign trade became apparent in the seventies. The oil-induced recession of 1974-5 brought home the extent to which the economy relied on external sources of energy as well as on external markets for our industrial goods. But the pain associated with intellectual recognition of dependence was to a considerable extent anaesthetised by recourse to foreign borrowing, particularly since 1979. Increasing doses of foreign capital have been resorted to in order to maintain illusions. By late 1981, however, it was becoming increasingly apparent that the need for structural adjustment would have to be faced and that economic actors would have to respond more flexibly to the exigencies of a difficult international situation. This aspect of national development will be discussed in the final section of the chapter.

Monetary Policy and the Exchange Rate

The objective of monetary policy is 'to safeguard the integrity of the currency' and to ensure that 'in what pertains to the control of credit, the constant and predominant aim shall be the welfare of the people as a whole'. The phraseology is that of the Central Bank Act 1942 which established the Central Bank and entrusted it with the implementation of monetary policy. 'Safeguarding the integrity of the currency' means protecting its real purchasing power and the definition of the second function suggests that, in considering different ways of achieving this objective, a broad economy-wide view should be taken.

The events in the real economy outlined in the last section took place against a backdrop of continuing inflation. Between 1953 and 1959, prices rose by 16 per cent. The next decade saw a further increase of 48 per cent. Inflation gained momentum in the seventies with a more than threefold rise in prices between 1969 and 1979. Since then prices have again almost doubled. Viewed against these figures, the integrity of the currency has not so much been safeguarded as re-interpreted. The meaning attached to it gradually changed from 'protection of absolute purchasing power' to 'one for one parity with sterling' in the post-war years. Since 1978, integrity of the currency signifies something quite different again: 'no unilateral devaluation relative to the EMS central parities'. Such an exchange rate target commits the authorities neither to zero inflation, nor to the inflation rate of narrow band EMS countries (since only a *unilateral* change in the Irish parity is ruled out; there is nothing to prevent other EMS partners devaluing or revaluing), nor to a stable effective exchange rate, nor to a fixed real effective exchange rate — in short, a fluid, elusive and not altogether satisfactory definition of integrity!

It is a standard proposition of international economics that an open, trading economy's inflation rate is heavily influenced by its exchange rate regime. Small countries tend to import inflation from their larger trading partners in the context of fixed exchange rates. A country of Ireland's size tied into a one-to-one parity with a country of the size and importance of the UK would, according to the theory of small open economies, be bound to inflate at broadly the same pace as Britain. Empirical fact in this instance conforms convincingly with economic theory. During the twenty-five years from 1953, UK and Irish prices each rose by roughly a factor of four and a half.

For much of the post-war period, however, inflation was comparatively mild and so the main concern of the Irish authorities was to preserve the sterling link rather than worry about the consequences of the link should British inflation begin to accelerate. Preservation of the sterling link in turn meant keeping the balance-of-payments deficit within reasonable bounds. Measures to achieve this objective were considered to be largely the business of fiscal rather than monetary policy. Because the banks had relatively large holdings of sterling assets and could therefore operate with minimal reliance on the services of the Central Bank, little attempt could be made to enforce an independent monetary and credit policy.[20] The Central Bank did, of course, comment regularly on current economic developments and at various stages in the fifties it engaged in some sharp verbal exchanges with the government. Concern was expressed about the balance of payments, the level of foreign debt (the result of

Marshall Plan loans), the growth of public sector expenditure — familiar themes of the Central Bank, which earned it the sobriquet 'the banshee of Foster Place'. At this time also the important question of the independence of the Central Bank was raised, successfully established and clarified. The independence at issue, however, largely concerned the Central Bank's right to publish criticisms of government policy in the Annual Report, not its independence on monetary policy matters. The Central Bank Act 1942 had left the bank without legal power to control credit. In Dr Moynihan's words, the act 'did not include a single clause that could be invoked by the Central Bank as conferring specific power to restrain the growth of bank credit in the state'.[21] 'Moral suasion' and 'informal consultations' with the banks and the government were the Central Bank's only effective weapons. It may be added that governments in the fifties showed evidence of being more sensitive to Central Bank strictures than later governments which have tended to tolerate and on occasion even endorse the Central Bank's animadversions without any perceptible impact on the conduct of public sector finances.

From the mid sixties onwards, however, prompted by the quickening pace of inflation, the Central Bank began to assume a more active rôle. The commercial banks were encouraged to lodge their external assets with the Central Bank, a process which was virtually completed in 1970. Credit guidelines, liquidity ratios and advice on the level of capital inflows to the non-associated banks were also introduced in an effort to control the volume of bank lending to the private domestic sector. The Central Bank Act 1971 strengthened the position of the Central Bank by transferring to it the powers of licensing and supervision of the commercial banks, by authorising the imposition of liquidity ratios and by securing the transfer of the exchequer account from the Bank of Ireland to the Central Bank. Its present array of instruments for managing liquidity therefore consists of the short-term facility (by which the Central Bank comes in as lender of last resort for short-run credit), foreign exchange swaps (by which the Central Bank lends Irish pounds in exchange for foreign currency), quotations for term deposits, variations in the prime liquidity ratio and variations in interest rates on government securities.

These separate measures taken together laid the foundations for a more effective control of the supply of credit. That they were not sufficient is evident from comparison of actual bank credit with advised expansion. In three of the six years from 1966 to 1972, actual exceeded advised credit levels by a factor of 50 per cent. The Central Bank opted for a more flexible system of control through liquidity ratios before reverting again in 1977 to credit guidelines. Since February 1979, a much closer correspondence between private sector credit guidelines and actual outcome has become evident. Guidelines of 18 per cent, 13 per cent and 15 per cent in the three years to 1981-2 compare with outcomes of 19 per cent, 13.4 per cent and 15.6 per cent.[22] This performance reflects both the enhanced powers of the Central Bank in dealing with the banks and a more realistic approach on the part of the authorities to what monetary policy can reasonably be expected to achieve.

The limitations of the authorities up to the time of the EMS were summarised by Professor Gibson:

> as long as the fixed exchange rate (with sterling) and freedom of movement of funds is strictly adhered to, attempts by the Central Bank to pursue monetary and credit policies (including interest rate policy) substantially different from those in Britain are bound to fail.[23]

159

Monetary policy could have a marginal impact on total credit and perhaps also on its allocation between different uses (i.e. personal vs corporate; 'productive' vs 'non-productive'). The ultimate constraint on domestic policy was the escape hatch to the London market: if Irish credit policy attempted to be restrictive, borrowers were able to get all the loans they wanted in London with no exchange-rate risk; if Irish policy were less restrictive than the UK, lenders transferred their cash from Dublin to more lucrative cross-channel outlets. The consequences, acknowledged by the Central Bank, was that 'Irish interest rates were determined effectively by UK rates'.[24] Money supply was, in technical terms, endogenous (not capable of control by the authorities). All the authorities could do was to influence the composition of the money base as between domestic assets and official reserves of foreign exchange. Tight credit attracted capital inflows and increased reserves; and easier credit led to loss of reserves.

Dependence on British monetary policy (in the formulation of which the Irish authorities were naturally not consulted) and its corollary, the high 'imported' rate of inflation from the UK, were much discussed in academic and official circles during the seventies. This in turn led to renewed debate about the desirability of maintaining one-to-one parity with sterling. The link with sterling had, of course, come under fire on a number of occasions since 1922. Immediately after independence, fears were expressed about the deflationary effects of an overvalued pound on the Irish economy following sterling's return to the gold standard. (A separate Irish pound was not established until 1928, six years after independence.) Later, in 1931, when Britain left the gold standard a collapse of sterling was feared and the Minister for Finance at that time made it clear that should such a collapse occur, Ireland would have to break the sterling parity. The wisdom of letting the Irish pound devalue in line with the British pound was debated in 1949 and again in 1967. In each case the balance of advantage was judged to rest with maintenance of the *status quo*. When the issue arose again in the seventies, the vital difference was the existence of an alternative exchange rate regime, the European Monetary System (EMS), which would, it was expected, include the UK as well as the other member countries of the EEC and which promised adjustment assistance in the event of a tougher exchange rate regime causing dislocation.

An EMS including the UK promised to provide two advantages of overwhelming importance: a stronger and less inflationary currency regime, and exchange rate stability with currencies accounting for 75 per cent of Irish trade. In the event, the UK decided against participating in the EMS. The Governor of the Central Bank explained the choice facing Ireland in the following terms:

> an EMS which included the UK was attractive — though not necessarily painless. The real problem emerged when it became clear that the UK might not join. To put it bluntly, the issue turned on whether, granted that it would be right to join if the UK did, would it be right not to join if the UK didn't? The decision to join without the UK was not an easy one. Factors which weighed in the balance included the alternatives open to us, the inappropriateness of an indefinite prolongation of the sterling link, the benefits in terms of a reduction in inflation to be obtained from adherence to a hard currency regime, a commitment to a major Community initiative, the extent to which the new system differed from the old and, of course, Community support in the form of resource transfers.[25]

The new exchange rate arrangements promised exchange rate stability covering only 25 per cent of Irish trade instead of the 75 per cent coverage which would have materialised had the UK joined.

The one-to-one parity with sterling was broken in March 1979. The sterling/pound rate fluctuated considerably during the following twelve months around a declining trend. The last quarter of 1980 saw a significant rise in sterling which continued into 1981. The Irish pound fell to 74p. sterling in mid-February 1981 and it has remained substantially below parity with sterling since then. By mid-1982, the Irish pound was worth 80p. sterling. Far from providing the economy with a stable effective exchange rate, membership of the EMS has been associated with a cumulative effective exchange rate decline of 14 per cent.[26]

It was the unexpected strength of sterling, not weakness of the Irish pound within the EMS band, which precipitated the latter's effective devaluation. As sterling strengthened, Irish import prices increased, giving a further impetus to the inflationary spiral already in motion as a result of the increase in oil prices. Inflation and earnings per employee continued to rise at over twice the average rate obtaining in the EMS countries, thus causing a severe deterioration in Irish competitiveness relative to the rich markets of Western Europe. The improved competitiveness in the UK market offered little compensation. Had a more determined effort been made to align Irish costs (in particular salary and wage increases) to the level pertaining within the EMS, the adverse effects on domestic prices of a strong pound sterling could have been at least partially offset through a 'crawling peg' revaluation agreed with the EMS partners and designed to keep the effective exchange rate constant. This was not to be. It all goes to show the justice of the many warnings that the EMS would pose problems as well as offering possibilities. By not adopting stronger policies on the incomes front, and despite explicit recognition that strict disciplines would be required to maintain a competitive cost structure, the Irish government left itself highly vulnerable to the inflationary consequences of a stronger pound sterling.

The break in sterling brought with it a substantial increase in the costs of transacting business with the UK. McCarthy estimated these at £5.5 million, equivalent to nearly 1 per cent of GNP per annum, an amount which would rise with inflation and increasing trade volumes.[27] Offsetting these costs, however, were adjustment assistance in the shape of EMS interest subsidies (£44 million, £45 million and £46 million in 1979, 1980 and 1981 respectively) and the gain in seigniorage as sterling bank notes were withdrawn from circulation and replaced by Irish notes. An additional cost of EMS entry arose from the introduction of exchange controls between Ireland and the UK in December 1978. The application of these controls imposes a clerical and reporting cost on banks and business even where the transactions are permitted. Where they are not permitted, as McCarthy observed, 'the loss takes the form of the costs of portfolio disequilibrium for the law-abiding or of the resources devoted to evasion for the felonious'.[28]

The imposition of exchange controls and the fluctuating sterling exchange rate have modified but have certainly not destroyed the link between Irish and UK interest rates. Examination of three-month interest rates over the three-year period to end 1981 shows that Irish rate trends tend to follow international trends, particularly those of the UK and Germany. For brief periods only can a significant divergence be observed. At the end of 1980, for example, large increases in liquidity due to official foreign borrowing depressed Irish interest rates to an exceptional degree; later, in spring 1981, the Irish interest rate had risen to the point where a 3.5 percentage point gap opened between Dublin and London. While interest levels here and abroad continue to differ, the tendency remains for movements upwards or downwards to be synchronised.

A number of powerful economic forces underlie this tendency to convergence. First in importance are what are technically known as 'leads and lags'. Since traders enjoy a certain latitude as regards the timing of payments for exports or imports, the rates of interest prevailing in Ireland and abroad play an important rôle in determining when and how foreign-exchange liabilities will be paid. If Irish interest rates are relatively attractive, payment will be deferred as long as possible, leading to an accretion of funds in Dublin and downward pressure on the interest rate. If Irish rates fall below those abroad, traders have an incentive to accelerate payment of foreign exchange bills in order to earn higher rates of trade discount or substitute external for internal sources of trade credit. This brings about an upward pressure on Irish interest rates as liquidity flows out of the Dublin market. Exchange controls are by and large powerless in face of these leads and lags. A second equilibrating factor is the existence of substantial funds, perhaps as much as £1,000 million, held in Irish banks by non-residents which could prove mobile if interest rates diverged too markedly. Foreign-currency on-lending by Irish banks, an activity which is permitted by the Central Bank for certain types of transactions, is also likely to be affected by interest rate differentials. Fluctuations in intra-company borrowings by Irish subsidiaries of multinationals further add to capital mobility. Taken together, these factors ensure that the Irish interest rate is highly dependent on external influences. The corollary also holds: that 'the scope for significant central bank influence on term interest rates in a small open economy such as Ireland's, operating a quasi-fixed exchange-rate policy, is quite limited'.[29]

From the perspective of monetary policy, therefore, the main consequence of EMS has been to substitute for one policy target, maintenance of the sterling link, another, maintenance of Ireland's central parity with the EMS. In order to achieve this objective, the Central Bank relies on private sector credit guidelines which it is now in a position to enforce with considerable rigour. Taking public sector financial requirements as given, the authorities decide on the level of private sector credit which is consistent with the level of reserves necessary to safeguard the exchange rate target.

In joining the EMS, the expectation was that attachment to a low inflation currency area would entail low inflation in Ireland. This expectation has been disappointed. Price increases averaged 18 per cent in the four years 1979-82, a full eight percentage points above the EEC average. Even in late 1982, the gap between Irish inflation of 18 per cent and Germany's 5 per cent remains dauntingly large. As long as sterling remains outside the EMS exchange rate mechanism, adherence to EMS disciplines offers Ireland no assurance of either a stable effective exchange rate or EMS inflation rates. This has been the lesson of experience rather than the prediction of the more extreme forms of small open economy models. At the same time, the prospect of the Irish authorities moving to a stricter, less inflationary exchange-rate regime appear unpromising in the light of balance of payments deficits which have averaged 11 per cent of GDP in recent years. If Irish inflation is coming down (as now appears likely) this is not because of the EMS currency arrangements, but because inflation in each of Ireland's major trading partners is easing.

The question remains as to whether the monetary authorities should have taken stronger action against inflation. Prior to 1979, the issue was whether Ireland should have broken the sterling link and opted for adherence to a stronger currency union (the European 'snake' for instance) or to a floating regime based on some effective exchange rate target. The Governor of the Central Bank stated that the latter possibility had been under consideration before the EMS initiative was announced. Although some economists urged a move in this direction, the majority view combined dissatisfaction with the *status quo* with misgivings about the superiority of the alternatives. Thus, breaking the sterling link might initially reduce Irish inflation but this left open the question of whether or how soon would Irish costs fall proportionately. If there was to be a long time-lag, competitiveness would suffer and employment would decline, leading to pressures on the exchange rate, accelerated inflation and a contrite return to the *status quo ante* in a worse condition than the economy left it. Throughout the debate, it was assumed that sterling would remain a weak currency, a wrong assumption as it turned out, but one which was universally held in financial circles within and outside Britain during the seventies. Another underlying assumption, and one which subsequent events were to prove all too correct, was that Irish governments would find it difficult to adhere to the stern discipline in fiscal and incomes policy which would have been required by a stronger exchange rate.

Since 1979, credit guidelines of increasing sophistication have been set for the banking system. The Central Bank has had to formulate policies in relation to foreign currency on-lending, on interest rates, and on the definition and scope of the guidelines. Its task has been complicated by the continued growth of financial intermediaries not subject to its control, notably the building societies, the Agricultural Credit Corporation and the Industrial Credit Corporation. By far the greatest difficulties have been presented, however, by the unprecedented expansion of government monetary financing in recent years.

The growth of the public sector has already been alluded to as a feature of development in the sixties and seventies. In recent years, however, it has been transformed from a feature into a major problem. Government expenditure now amounts to more than 60 per cent of GDP compared with 46 per cent in 1977. Much of this increased expenditure has been financed by borrowing: the public sector borrowing requirement having risen from 13 per cent of GNP in 1977 to a projected 1982 level of 22 per cent. Most of the exchequer borrowing in turn has been from foreign sources, 73 per cent in 1982 compared with 22 per cent in 1977. Monetary financing of the borrowing requirement has increased from 44 per cent in 1977 to 83 per cent in 1982. To complete the catalogue, the current budget deficit amounts to 8 per cent of GNP; this deficit can be taken as a crude indicator of the extent to which borrowing is used to finance current needs.

Although it has been assiduous in identifying and pointing out the dangers to the economy of the deterioration in the public finances, the Central Bank has no direct control over fiscal policy. Since public sector credit is determined by the government, the monetary authorities must perforce focus on private sector credit in attempting to control total credit. If total credit needs to be restrained (because, say, an overrun of government expenditure is creating balance of payments pressure), the Central Bank faces the dilemma of imposing all the burden of adjustment on the private sector. The dilemma is further accentuated by general acceptance on the part of government no less than economists that the private sector must be encouraged to grow more rapidly. It is scarcely surprising, therefore, to find the Central Bank being criticised on both flanks, for at once being too lax and too stringent in its private sector guidelines.[30] And no less surprising to find the General Manager of the Central Bank, Mr Bernard Breen, declaring with an understandable note of exasperation that 'the overall stance of monetary policy has been compromised to a large extent by the size of the Exchequer borrowing requirement'.[31]

A related problem is that of deciding on an appropriate balance-of-payments target. The monetary authorities must aim to steer the economy towards a sustainable position on the current account of the balance of payments which, historically, has tended to imply a deficit. If a current deficit is considered compatible with balance-of-payments equilibrium, taking account of the need for development finance in a growing economy with an increasing population, it makes quite a difference how this is financed. A current deficit matched by inflows of private equity capital from abroad is obviously different to one financed by official foreign borrowing since the latter is not self-liquidating in the event of the finance being used unproductively. This suggests that the level of official reserves is only one of many factors which the Central Bank must take into account in assessing the balance of payments position. Official reserves *less* public sector foreign borrowing is perhaps a more relevant concept as advocates of a DCE (domestic credit expansion) approach suggest.

During the 1970s, the Central Bank tended towards the view that the balance-of-payments deficit should be accommodated, provided sufficient foreign borrowing was undertaken to safeguard the level of official reserves. It did so with some reluctance. Latterly a stronger line has been taken and the need for 'a strategy of adjustment' has been called for. The statement on monetary policy 1982 reflects this new perspective:

> The major concern of monetary policy is with the level of the current balance-of-payments deficit and the manner in which this impinges on the external reserves. The Bank has consistently advocated the need to adjust the balance between expenditure and output, so as to correct the current external deficit, and it is strongly of the view that the process of correction which has been initiated should be effectively sustained.[32]

It further adds that monetary policy should not be such as to accommodate any slippage in the projected balance of payments but should rather be fully supportive of any tendency for a lower deficit to emerge. There is evidence therefore of increasing concern with the *net* position in official reserves which would be an essential element of a DCE approach.[33] The DCE approach, however, affords the Central Bank no escape from the dilemma that adherence to a DCE target in the context of continuing growth in monetary financing by the public sector can only result in further pressure on an already depressed private sector.

So much for the rôle of monetary policy in protecting the value of the currency. As earlier noted, macroeconomic decisions on monetary policy occupy only part of the time and constitute only part of the functions of the Central Bank. Its task includes not alone determining the appropriate level of reserves but also ensuring that these reserves are properly managed so as to yield adequate rates of return. The broad trend in interest rate policy must also be supplemented by day-to-day interventions in the money market designed to prevent excessive fluctuations. In achieving this aim, the authorities have recourse to such instruments as the short-term credit facility (in which the Central Bank effectively acts as lender of last resort and thereby sets a floor

Plate 79

Pauline Bewick
Daffodils 1982
Watercolour
79 × 57 cms

Plate 80

George Campbell
Dun Aengus, Inishmore 1969
Oil on canvas
760 x 1.020 mm
Signed: Campbell
Exhibited at the David Hendriks Gallery, Dublin, October 1969

to interest rates), foreign currency 'swaps' (the exchange of domestic funds for foreign exchange 'inflowed' through the banks) and changes in required liquidity ratios. The Central Bank must also look after the production and distribution of bank notes, a vitally important function, largely unsung because so efficiently discharged. Much activity is also engaged in the licensing and supervision of the banking system.

While credit guidelines fulfil a useful macroeconomic function, they suffer the disadvantage of limiting the degree of competition between banks. The guidelines apply to individual banks. The more efficient banks have on occasion complained that the guidelines restrict their scope for expansion. This criticism certainly carries weight and it was one of the major reasons for the abandonment of credit guidelines in the UK in 1971. Given the serious condition of the economy, there is an understandable reluctance to change to a more flexible system of credit control through, say, liquidity ratios, where any advantage to the economy through increased competitive efficiency might be offset by the disadvantage of weaker control of aggregate credit expansion.

The Central Bank has also been involved in the debate over the special bank levies in 1981 and 1982. Although these levies were imposed on a temporary basis in response to the financing needs of successive governments, they raise important issues of principle. The Central Bank is charged with the supervision of the banking system and as such it has a legitimate interest in the continuing financial viability of the system. To ensure viability it is necessary for the banks to make profits, since these provide a direct source of additional capital (only 20 per cent on average are distributed) as well as protecting the banks' capacity to generate additional capital from outside sources. At the same time, the Central Bank is concerned that the banks should not use their oligopoly power to earn excessive profits at the expense of the public and, through its powers of monitoring bank charges, interest rate changes and liquidity ratios, it has considerable power to enforce its views on the banks in this regard. At the time the bank levies were imposed, the Central Bank made it clear that bank profits were not excessive in relation to its criteria. On the contrary, bank profits have been at the bottom of or below the recommended range. The Commission on Taxation, taking a similar view, concluded that there is no case for special levies on banks on the grounds that their tax payments are artificially low in relation to their profits.[34] The logic of the argument suggests, therefore, that the levies, being temporary, should now be withdrawn or that the costs of paying them should be passed on to the customer, in which case the levies can be regarded as an indirect tax.

Prospects for the Eighties
It is clear from the earlier sections that the most exciting and successful period for the 'real' money economy was the period from the late fifties to the early seventies. By contrast, the most significant events in terms of monetary and exchange rate policy occurred in the seventies. For it was during this decade that the battle against inflation was joined in earnest and, in Ireland as elsewhere, the instruments of monetary control and the implications of different exchange rate regimes came to assume a rôle at least equal to that of policies directly affecting real output and employment.

Since the first oil crisis, virtually no improvement has been achieved in income earned on a *per capita* basis in Ireland. Gross National Product (GNP) rose by 3.2 per cent annually between 1973 and 1981 but, after correction for terms of trade and taking account of increasing population, the 'true' GNP *per capita* increase has been estimated at only 0.2 per cent annually.[35] In the context of double-digit inflation, this marginal increase is barely perceptible. Small wonder that, in Dr Whitaker's words, 'the withering of the bloom has enhanced rather than dimmed the bright memory of the 1960s. They have, in retrospect, taken on the aspect of a paradise lost'.[36]

Part of the explanation lies in external circumstances. The oil price increases of 1973-4 and 1979-80 bore heavily on an economy dependent to the tune of 70 per cent of its energy requirements on imported oil. The world economy also suffered. The 150 per cent increase in oil prices in 1979-80 actually imposed a heavier burden on the oil-consuming countries than the 300 per cent rise of 1973-74, primarily because the second increase was from a higher base.[37] The resultant decline in growth meant that external conditions were anything but favourable to expansion of Ireland's traded sector. In addition, emigration prospects worsened as unemployment in the UK rose to unprecedented levels and legislation in the USA barred the market to all except skilled and professional migrants.

Membership of the EEC was a countervailing factor which proved immensely helpful to Ireland's development. The immediate beneficiary of entry was the farming community. Real incomes per head in Irish agriculture rose by 72 per cent between 1970 and 1978 compared with a corresponding income increase of 17 per cent in the EEC. Higher CAP prices, supplemented by an increase in output volumes of some 30 per cent, explain this high income growth.[38] Although there were some setbacks to particular groups of farmers in 1974, the growing prosperity of the rural sector was visible in the number of new farm houses, in the proliferation of cars, the improvement in outhouses and farm machinery and the higher productivity of cattle stocks. Farm incomes collapsed between 1978 and 1980, virtually to their original pre-EEC level, as farmers were squeezed between rising input costs on the one hand and minimal output price increases on the other. Output prices failed to keep pace with inflation partly because of low EEC price review increases and partly because the commitment to EMS meant that Irish inflation rates were no longer being matched by compensatory depreciations of the Irish pound. Some improvement in the farmers' position was recorded in 1981 and 1982 but 1978 real income levels are still some way from being restored.

Although industrial growth in the Western world slowed down in the 1970s, Ireland continued to enjoy considerable success in attracting new industries. Competition for footloose projects was, needless to say, cut-throat during this period. Countries and regions vied with each other in offering incentive packages of escalating generosity to induce external investors to set up in their area. Despite this, the IDA managed to persuade large numbers of overseas plants, about half of them from the United States, to establish in Ireland by offering incentives which were still significantly less than the social benefits likely to accrue from them. The Telesis Report on industrial policy offers an indication of how well Ireland did comparatively. Of a sample of 230 foreign-owned green-field projects located in Ireland, Northern Ireland, Scotland, Wales and Belgium during the years 1978-9, the Republic attracted 185 — roughly 80 per cent of the total.[39] This success reflects well on the IDA. It also illustrates the lesson that good economic policy takes time to take effect. Much of the credit must also be ascribed to the EEC for providing secure access to the European market — virtually a *sine qua non* for enterprises thinking of an Irish location as a platform for exporting to Europe.

External and internal pressures leaned most heavily on indigenous industry during the seventies. Large job losses were recorded in both foreign and indigenous firms. But whereas in the case of foreign firms these losses were compensated by the arrival of new ventures, those in indigenous industry were matched by no offsetting expansions. Rising labour costs and the inflationary environment left Ireland vulnerable to external competition which had intensified as a result of sluggish demand in Europe and from which Ireland's commitment to the EMS allowed no escape through exchange rate depreciation. The figures for import penetration are disturbing even allowing for the fact that some degree of domestic market loss is the inevitable corollary of intra-industry specialisation. Between 1977 and 1981, the share of competing imports in domestic consumption rose from 29 per cent to 38 per cent. Import penetration increased most rapidly in the clothing, footwear and leather industries (from 41 per cent to 57 per cent) and in metals and engineering (from 39 per cent to 51 per cent). Few if any sectors of industry remained unscathed.

The lack of correspondence between the evolution of costs in the Irish private sector and the need for employment generation owes much to the inadequately controlled expansion of the government sector. General government expenditure rose in absolute terms and the average increase in real public consumption rose to 5.8 per cent annually. The public sector's share of GNP exceeded 60 per cent and the country had to finance a public sector borrowing requirement in excess of 20 per cent of GDP in the early eighties. Of these three factors, only the last truly distinguishes Irish experience from the general run of EEC countries. A growing share of government in GNP is a feature of even the German economy where the government expenditure/GDP ratio rose from 37 per cent to 47 per cent in the course of the decade.

Unemployment has for many years been endemic in Ireland. The rate of unemployment has always tended to be higher here than elsewhere in Europe and, even in the best of times, jobs have been scarce relative to the number of applicants. As in other countries, the demand for labour in Ireland has been hit by the recession. Unemployment has risen by more than half since 1979 to a level of 144,000 in April 1982. It is little consolation to note that Ireland's place at the top of the EEC unemployment table has been taken over by Belgium and no less incredibly, for a brief period in 1981-2, by the UK. Such comparisons, however, draw attention to the global character of the unemployment crisis and of the need for international as well as national policy measures to deal with it. Ireland's position is particularly acute for two reasons. First, the rapid growth in population carries with it the threat, not alone of unemployment remaining high, but of its increasing very quickly and markedly unless remedial action is taken. Second, Ireland's unprecedented run of large balance of payments deficits and the corresponding unsustainable rise in foreign debt mean that the government must retrench its expenditure in order to restrain further increases in foreign borrowing. In effect this implies that aggregate public sector demand must be squeezed at exactly the time when the unemployment situation would call for a stimulatory fiscal stance. The dilemma cannot be resolved by a straightforward unilateral application of Keynesian remedies, however constructive a rôle such remedies might play on an internationally co-ordinated basis. In so far as a solution to the unemployment problem exists, it must be found in the context of the needs of a small open economy, reliant for its prosperity on the exposed trading sector, with substantial leakages of expenditure into imports, and with competitiveness in its widest sense a top priority. These features of the economy were brilliantly delineated in *Prelude to Planning*, one of the most influential reports of the National Economic and Social Council.[40] Research on Irish unemployment has taken this economic framework as given and has gone on from there to analyse measures which can be adopted to make the existing labour market work more effectively. Kennedy, for example, makes the point that 'in Ireland the growth of employment is in part *cost-constrained* (e.g. wages too high relative to productivity) or *resource-constrained* (absence of relevant skills, lack of investment of the right kind, insufficient enterprise), rather than purely *demand-constrained*'.[41] Walsh, in a succession of percipient studies over the last decade, has done much to deepen our understanding of the nature of these constraints on the labour market. In a recent study (with Nolan) he concludes that:

> Growth in output will continue to be the most important source of new jobs, leading to a reduction in unemployment. But unemployment can also be reduced by lowering the number of vacancies remaining unfilled at each level of the economy's overall performance. Matching job seekers to vacancies more quickly can be done by a better flow of information between employers and those looking for work, by a greater willingness and larger incentives for job seekers to change residence and/or occupation in order to get a job, by a closer match between the skills possessed by school leavers and those sought by employers, and by a social welfare and income structure that ensures a significant monetary incentive for the unemployed to accept job offers at prevailing wages. *In all these areas, there is substantial room for improvement in the way the Irish labour market operates* [my italics].[42]

As one of the poorest regions of the Community, the case could be made that Ireland requires more investment than other countries; that this necessarily involves additional capital investment by the government and that the foreign borrowing to finance such investment is economically justified.

If investment performs the function it is designed to perform, i.e. raise future private consumption possibilities, then in due course a pay-off could be expected which would result in diminished pressure on the standard of living. But although Irish investment rates bear favourable comparison with those of Japan, they have yielded decidedly un-Japanese rates of GNP growth. There are many reasons for this, some of which relate to the much-publicised inefficiencies of the public sector capital programme, others to the long lapse of time before infrastructural investment begins to bear fruit and others still to the deterioration in the cost position in Irish agriculture and industry relative to foreign competitors. It is not necessary to rehearse the arguments for and against the expansion of public sector expenditure reflected in the high growth of public consumption and the public capital programme. What is certain is that curbs in public expenditure are now inevitable and that Ireland faces the eighties from a basic standard of living twice as high as twenty years ago but with problems no less severe. Whereas at that time businessmen and policy-makers looked forward to the prospect of a booming world economy and a supportive, expansionary fiscal stance, they must now face the less promising prospect of sluggish world growth, threats of protectionism and across-the-board cutbacks in government expenditure.

The monetary authorities have, as we have seen, nailed their sail firmly to the mast of EMS membership. There is a sense in which this approach could be called 'monetarist' since in effect an exchange rate target is being substituted for the money supply target more familiarly associated with Professor Friedman and his disciples. To the extent that a tough monetary and exchange rate policy is complemented by an equally tough line on government expenditure in general and public sector remuneration levels in particular, the menacing adverse effects of monetarism on output and employment will be minimised.

170

The Central Bank is now in a stronger position than ever before to enforce credit guidelines but, as we have seen above, the economic effectiveness of such guidelines can be negatived by fiscal policy which all too often has gone in an opposite direction to monetary policy in the past. There are now definite signs that this is changing. If the necessary measures are taken, the prospects for the recent fall in inflation being maintained in the future are reasonably favourable. In that event, while it may be unduly optimistic to expect paradise to be regained in the 1980s, the country could look forward to a halt in its economic decline and a definite progression to better things.

References

1   IMF *World economic outlook* 1982, table 31, p. 171.

2   For applications of these well-known propositions to Ireland, see D. McAleese and W. J. L. Ryan, ed, *Inflation in Ireland: a contemporary perspective*, Dublin 1982, *passim*.

3.   C.A.E. Goodhart, *Money, information and uncertainty*, London 1975, pp. 216-17.

4   This is a subsidiary function of a bank. Savings in economic terms means abstention from consumption. It is a flow concept and quite distinct from the concept of financial savings. Savers and spenders will both have deposits with their bank!

5   Or the Ogden Nash variant:
          One rule which woe betide the banker who fails to heed it
          Never lend money to anybody unless they don't really need it.

6   'Commission on taxation — recommendations on aspects of taxation of financial institutions', *Irish Banking Review*, September 1982, p. 10. The Commission's methodology could, however, be disputed on this point.

7   The following analysis draws on two excellent surveys by Antoin Murphy and by the Central Bank staff respectively: A. Murphy, 'Money in an economy without banks: the case of Ireland', *Manchester School*, March 1978; 'The economic effects of the bank dispute', *Central Bank of Ireland Quarterly Report*, autumn 1976. The former paper discusses the consequences of the 1970 closure which lasted from May to November 1970.

8   Central Bank, op. cit., p. 20.

9   Murphy, op. cit., lays more stress on this factor in his analysis of the 1970 dispute than commentators on the 1976 dispute have done. Retail shops and public houses accepted large numbers of cheques. As Murphy notes, 'one does not serve drink to someone for years without discovering something of his liquid resources.' Acceptability of cheques in 1976 had diminished partly because of higher interest rates then prevailing and also because the intoxicating atmosphere of the public house may perhaps have led to a somewhat inflated view of the drawer's financial worth in the previous strike.

10   M. P. Fogarty, 'The Irish economy — an outside view', in *The economic and social state of the nation*, Dublin 1982, p. 25.

11   *Economic development*, Dublin 1958; *Programme for economic expansion*, Dublin 1958.

12   C. McCarthy, 'Economic development and economic policy', *Administration*, Summer 1979, p. 208.

13   K. A. Kennedy and B. R. Dowling, *Economic growth in Ireland: the experience since 1947*, Dublin 1975.

14   Organisation for Economic Co-operation and Development (OECD), *Policies for economic growth*, Paris 1962, par. 5, p. 1.

15   *Programme for economic expansion*, par. 7, p. 2.

16   Kennedy and Dowling, op. cit., p. xvi.

17   L. Cullen, 'The Cultural Basis of Modern Irish Nationalism', in R. Mitchison, ed., *The roots of nationalism: studies in Northern Europe*, Edinburgh 1980, p. 94.

18   Speech by Mr Sean Condon, chief executive, Irish Export Board to the Commerce and Economics Society, University College Cork, 26 November 1981.

19   S. Nolan, 'Economic Growth', in J. O'Hagan, ed., *The economy of Ireland: policy and performance*, Dublin 1981, p. 188.

20   N. J. Gibson, 'The Banking System', in N. J. Gibson and J. E. Spencer, eds, *Economic activity in Ireland: a study of two open economies*, Dublin 1977, p. 246.

21   M. Moynihan, *Currency and central banking in Ireland 1922-60*, Dublin 1975, p. 461.

22   P. Bacon, J. Durkan and J. O'Leary, *The Irish economy: policy and performance 1972-1981*, Dublin 1982.

23   Gibson, op. cit. p. 262.

24   T. O'Connell, 'What determines Irish interest rates?', *Irish Banking Review*, June 1982, p. 24.

25   C. H. Murray, 'The European Monetary System: implications for Ireland', *Central Bank of Ireland annual report* 1979, p. 101.

26   B. M. Walsh, 'Ireland's membership of the EMS: expectations, outturn and prospects' in P. J. Drudy and D. McAleese, eds, *Ireland and the European Community*, Cambridge, forthcoming.

27   C. McCarthy, 'EMS and the end of Ireland's sterling link', *Lloyds Bank Review*, April 1980, p. 36.

28   Ibid., p. 36.

29   T. O'Connell, op. cit., p. 21.

30   Bacon, Durkan and O'Leary, for example, argue that the guidelines should have been adjusted downwards in 1979 (op. cit., p. 64); whereas any rise in interest rates designed to reduce demand for credit meets with instant political disapproval.

31   B. J. Breen, 'Some perspectives on Ireland's participation in the EMS', *Central Bank of Ireland Quarterly Bulletin*, winter 1981, p. 57.

32   Central Bank of Ireland, *Annual Report 1982*, p. 13.

33   The extent of the deterioration in the net reserves is indicated by the rise in the official foreign debt/reserves ratio from a fraction well below unity a decade ago to 1.14 in 1977 to 3.29 in 1981. The debt ratio takes no account of the value of the domestic assets which the foreign borrowings were used to finance but analysis of the structure of government expenditure suggests that a significant proportion of the borrowing was for unproductive purposes.

34   *First report of the commission on taxation: direct taxation*, Dublin 1982, p. 389.

35   K. A. Kennedy, 'Poverty and changes in the socio-economic environment in Ireland, 1971-81', paper read to Council for Social Welfare conference on poverty, Kilkenny, 6-8 November 1981.

36   T. K. Whitaker, '*Ireland's development experience*', paper read to the 1982 annual conference of the Development Studies Association, Dublin, 24 September 1982.

37   According to Bank of England estimates, the burden on oil consumers of the oil price increases was $4\frac{1}{2}$ per cent of the GNP in 1979-80 as against $2\frac{1}{2}$ per cent in 1973-4. H. B. Rose, 'The Prospects for World Economic Recovery', *Barclay's Review*, August 1982, p. 45.

38   *Farm incomes: analysis and policy*, National Economic and Social Council, Dublin, July 1982, p. 7.

39   *A review of Irish industrial policy*, National Economic and Social Council, Dublin 1982.

40   *Prelude to planning*, National Economic and Social Council, Dublin, October 1976.

41   K. A. Kennedy, "Employment and unemployment prospects in Ireland", *Irish Banking Review*, September 1980, p.22.

42   B. Walsh and S. Nolan, "Jobs and the workforce", Confederation of Irish Industry, Business Series No. 11, Dublin, August 1981, p. 30.

The Evolution of the Modern Bank

James Meenan

THE work of the Bank between the wars reflected the course of events in the country. The transfer of political authority from London to Dublin carried implications for the business of banking. The new Irish Free State possessed full power to legislate on banking and currency, a right that had been emphatically reserved to the imperial parliament in every proposed measure of home rule. On the other hand, the supremacy of Westminster in these matters remained unaltered so far as Northern Ireland was concerned. The Bank had to adjust itself to the problems of operating under two different jurisdictions.

The economic changes were no less important than the political. The effect of the severe fall in prices in 1920 was to be exacerbated by the great depression. The consequences of the collapse were felt most severely by the farmers who, at least those who lived in the Free State, were to be affected even more severely by the economic dispute with Great Britain between 1932 and 1938. The agricultural price index (based on the average of 1911-13 at 100) rose to 288 in 1920. Thereafter it fell to 132 in 1927. A small recovery to 139 in 1929 was not then considered as any alleviation; yet 1929 was to be the best farming year for a generation to come. By 1935 the index was down to 83. In both parts of the country producers and traders had profited from the period of sharply rising prices. Many of them found themselves over-extended when the price level broke and the great expectations on which they had (usually successfully) based their applications for increased bank credit had vanished beyond recall. There were others who either by good luck or good judgment had avoided over-commitment and were now in possession of war-time savings whose value increased as prices fell.

These changes were reflected in the Bank's balance sheet. On 31 December 1913, discounts and advances stood at £9.6 million and investments at £9.1 million. Both had grown sharply in preceding years which had been almost uniformly prosperous. Wartime inflation brought advances to a peak of £18.8 million at the end of 1921. Thereafter there was a severe contraction and for the rest of the inter-war period advances rose over £15 million only exceptionally. On the other hand investments showed an even greater increase which was to be maintained long after inflation had been ended. At the end of 1921 they totalled £25.2 million. They exceeded £30 million in 1922 and again in 1924. Thereafter their value fell away but they never fell below £20 million, except in the climacteric year of 1931; and in the middle thirties they oscillated around £24 million. This gain was not peculiar to the Bank. It was reflected in varying degree throughout the banking system. This was something new. Throughout the long debates on home rule, there ran the question whether the proposed government in Dublin, even with a very restricted field of action, could possibly pay its way without a substantial subsidy from Westminster. Ironically, the last years of the Union provided the new state with the sinews of financial independence.

Throughout all these economic and political changes the essential features of the Bank's organisation remained largely unaltered. It was still conducted, as it had been since 1783, by the Court and its committees. Decisions affecting the affairs of customers still passed through their hands and were transmitted to those who had to meet those customers face to face. An agent was very much an agent. The title differed from the usage of the other banks, where the title 'manager' was used. It may have appeared somewhat archaic, appropriate to the comparative antiquity of the Bank. In fact it emphasised that there was no delegation of authority or responsibility. No doubt, there were always some agents who notoriously acted on their own initiative but they were the exceptions. Effectively, decisions lay in the hands of the Court, assisted by the General Manager and the chief inspectors. The general managership was itself a comparatively recent innovation. R. J. Buckley was appointed in 1927: until then everything passed through the hands of the Secretary. But the General Manager, like the Secretary before him, remained the mouthpiece of the Court. Essentially the conduct of affairs until long after the Second World War differed little, personalities apart, from what it had been before the First. Even the slow growth of branches, to meet the needs of an expanding city such as Dublin, was halted in the years after 1934.

A couple of remarks might be made about this centralisation. In the first place it was made possible by the slow pace of business in the inter-war years. The central business of banking revolved around the rise and fall of prices, especially of agricultural prices, and their effect on the solvency of customers. These problems were intensified but not in any essential changed by the depression or the economic dispute with Great Britain. A new element was introduced by the establishment of tariff-protected manufactures, especially after 1932, but their operations were still small-scale. They did not force the Bank or the banking system as a whole into new ways of operation. Essentially the Bank, like all Irish banks of the period before the end of the Second World War and indeed later still, was passive, not active. It reacted to change as best it could and indeed with a reasonable amount of success. That it should seek to guide, much less create, these changes was not yet part of its approach to its business.

The point might as easily be put in a less flattering way. For all practical purposes the Irish banks in general, not solely the Bank of Ireland, had come to fulfil the function of savings banks. The relative lack of economic development in the early years of this century, and the slow pace of change in that development, produced this result. The areas in which there was an appreciable rate of turnover of money were few indeed, principally in the cities, Dublin and Cork and (to a much greater extent up to 1920) the area around Belfast. The fortunes of the rest of the community depended on the trend of agricultural prices and the vagaries of the weather. For their part, speaking generally, the farming community placed their savings on deposit in the banking system rather than in shares or (least of all perhaps) in the improvement of their land. As a class, Irish farmers saved but they did not invest. The bank deposit came to be regarded as the emergency chest on which a family might draw for exceptional circumstances, the education of their children, their professional courses, their marriages. When drawn on for such purposes, it had to be replenished without delay. So much so that it was accepted that many farmers in need of assistance from a bank would negotiate advances and pay the interest on them rather than draw on their deposit accounts. In these circumstances it was no wonder that deposits and cash in the banking system grew from £33.3 million in 1890 to £45.9 million in 1910 and to

Plate 81

The Bank's main computer hall at Cabinteely, Co. Dublin

Plate 82

Baggot Street exterior at night

£182.9 million in 1920. In the Bank of Ireland, it may be hazarded, accounts were used more commercially than elsewhere; but they must have reflected this concept of banks as receptacles for savings.

At the same time, the relatively restricted nature of the economy, both agricultural and industrial, meant that the demand for advances did not fluctuate greatly apart from seasonal needs. To take again the returns for the Bank in the years just noticed, discounts and advances were £5.4 million in 1890, £9.2 million in 1910 and £17.9 million in the exceptional circumstances of 1920. Wartime prosperity and the propensity to leave money on deposit meant that the Bank had ample resources to invest while still maintaining adequate liquidity. This distinguished the Bank of Ireland and the entire Irish banking system from what was taken as normal elsewhere. In 1932, for instance, the young Geoffrey Crowther investigated the working of the system at the invitation of the IBSC. He noted that 81.8 per cent of the resources of the Irish banks were held in deposit accounts. The corresponding percentages for England and Wales and for Scotland in that year of acute depression were 47 and 62 per cent respectively. This was a system of savings banks rather than of banking as usually understood. (Later in that decade it emerged that, even after the depression and the Anglo-Irish economic dispute, the banking system owed more to the farmers than the farmers owed it.) In the circumstances of 1932 and for years to come, the Irish banks had no need of a central authority to act as a lender of last resort.

176

That remark leads naturally to a brief mention of an imponderable factor in the conduct of the Bank of Ireland. The establishment of the Central Bank of Ireland still lay in the future. For very many decades before then, the Bank of Ireland had been in an exceptional position. It was the oldest bank in Ireland; it was also the biggest. It had held the government account since its foundation. It was to the Bank of Ireland that the Bank of England and the treasury addressed themselves when matters of common concern arose throughout the nineteenth century and, more frequently, during the First World War. On its side, the Bank of Ireland had exercised a degree of leadership in Ireland: the Governor was always chairman of the IBSC. Not all of this resulted from formal agreement; nor did it work automatically. It did mean that the Bank, especially from the middle of the nineteenth century to the middle of the twentieth, felt itself to be in a special position. It cannot always have been a comfortable position. One has the feeling that at times the Bank must have felt at odds with itself and with the sometimes conflicting responsibilities of a semi-public institution and a profit-making and competitive enterprise.

The outbreak of the Second World War in 1939 set up a chain of events which was to destroy the placid existence that has been summarily described. But we must begin with reference to a matter which arose early in the war years. It was regrettable in the extreme and it was to have lasting results.

In 1917 the bank officials formed the Irish Bank Officials' Association. In December 1919 an agreement between all the Irish banks and the IBOA recognised the right of the IBOA to negotiate on behalf of its members. Provision was made for arbitration in default of agreement. This was not long in coming. The first reference to arbitration in February 1920 concerned minimum scales of salary. The ensuing award noted that all scales were based on the assumption that they would be paid free of income tax.

During the following twenty years, employment in the banks was attractive and greatly sought after. It provided secure employment in a country where that quality was comparatively rare: it gave, especially in rural Ireland, an assured social status. It was also very well paid by the standards of the time. Writing in 1970 Dr Fogarty noted that in the late 1930s staff earnings in the banks were some three to four times as high as those of adult men in industry. To be sure, the absolute standards of pay were not all that high but every comparison favoured the bank official and the receipt of a tax-free salary was an immensely valuable perquisite. In Dr Fogarty's phrase, the bank officials were 'on to a very good thing'.[1]

But they suffered from one great handicap — a persistent and demoralising block in promotion. In 1919, the banks felt themselves bound in honour to take back those officials who had volunteered for war service and were now demobilised. At the same time, taking a sanguine view of post-war prospects, they took on further staff. The deflation of 1920 and the events of the next few years in Ireland frustrated all these hopes. The banks, and their officials, found themselves in a situation in which there were now more people to do the same, or even a contracting, amount of work. In these circumstances, it could take an official twenty to twenty-five years to get as far as being a cashier.

The Banking Commission, which sat between 1934 and 1938, referred cursorily and unfavourably to the manner in which bank salaries were paid. Paragraph 341 of the majority report noted that

> Apart from the obvious objection on civic grounds to indemnifying an important body of citizens against fluctuations of income tax, we are of opinion that it is undesirable that the financial mechanism of the banking system should undergo disturbance from this cause, which should be a personal matter for the officials concerned.

The foregoing passage was not printed in the heavy black type which the Commission reserved for its recommendations. (Oddly enough it did use the heavy type for its advice that bank dividends should be declared in gross terms, that is, subject to deduction of income tax.) It was far from being the most important of its recommendations but ironically it was by a long way the first to be implemented.

When the Commission reported in 1938 the standard rate of income tax stood at 4s. 6d. in the pound, to which it had been reduced in 1935. A shilling was added in 1940. Clearly the banks then felt that further increases were inevitable if the war was prolonged. In this expectation they were quite correct. They feared that the agreement of 1920 would become an insupportable burden. They approached the IBOA with an invitation to review the position which clearly envisaged a major revision of the agreement. Not unexpectedly perhaps, this approach was not successful.

It is clear that in what followed the banks (because of course all the banks were jointly concerned) acted on legal advice which had been carefully considered. It still seems amazing (and harsher adjectives could be, and were then, used) that they did not take equal care to supplement the legal procedure with an approach which would have been generally seen to be as sympathetic and humane as circumstances allowed. In December 1940 a circular in identical terms went out from each bank to its staff. It noted that negotiations with the IBOA, which had been in progress for a number of months, had not resulted in agreement. Accordingly, members of the banks' staff were informed that their contract of service would terminate on 30 June 1941 and that after that date, unless re-engaged, they would be paid whatever pension they were entitled by their service to receive. The circular then set out a revised contract of service which transferred the obligation to pay tax from the bank to the official. In conclusion, the circular informed each official that he or she should sign a formal acceptance of the new contract. If this was not done by 28 February 1941 the official would be deemed not to have accepted re-employment.

The required acceptances were received. There was room for an argument about the revised scales which was settled by arbitration. The banks and the IBOA also reached an agreement for the establishment of a negotiation committee and, in case of failure to agree, of an arbitration board.

The matter ended there, for the moment. Certainly it can be argued that the concession of paying salaries tax-free was far-reaching indeed. It is curious that it did not attract the notice of government, though indeed in 1920 the British government in Ireland had much more urgent matters on its hands. But it is possible to believe that if the agreement had been made, not in 1920 but in some subsequent year, say 1926, the Minister for Finance and the secretary of his department would certainly have had something to say on the matter.

But that was not all the point nor indeed even the real point. Quite apart from the grievance of losing a valuable perquisite, officials felt, then and later, that they had been most brusquely treated and that the banks might well have combined their legalistic approach with a fuller and more co-operative sympathy with the problems which had now been created for them. The tone of the circular, emphasising as it did the contractual relationship between the banks and their officials to the complete exclusion of any other bond, seriously affected the feelings of loyalty and common purpose. It was a most damaging and unnecessary blow to good relations between the banks and their staffs; and it might well be that the damage done in the Bank of Ireland, where tradition had been especially highly prized, was even greater than elsewhere.

The full extent of the damage was not to be perceived until some years later. During the war years salaries everywhere were tightly controlled by emergency powers orders. The difficult task of adjusting them to post-war circumstances provided only too many occasions of conflict. These could not be processed by the Labour Court, as disputes elsewhere in the economy were processed then, because the IBOA refused to appear before it. The result was that the banks were closed on account of disputes at the end of 1950 and again at the end of 1954.

On both occasions the disputes were patched up rather than settled. They were to break out again, and the resultant bank closures were to be much more prolonged, in 1966, in 1970 and most lately in 1976. From every point of view, these conflicts were more damaging than anything that had gone before. The economy was much more active and therefore much more vulnerable. There were now, as there had not been in the fifties, other banking services available; and there was every risk that accounts once lost to the system might not be regained. Foreign trade and investment had both grown greatly but confidence was severely shaken by the spectacle of a country without a banking system. Finally, these events embittered still more relations within the industry. There is a sense in which the matters at issue between the banks and their officials have been very much what might be expected in any business anywhere, pay, promotion, conditions of service and the like. Elsewhere, fortunately, there has not been anything approaching the distrust and resentments which have flourished in the field of banking. What seems even more damaging is the fact that each of the recurrent disputes appears to have ended in relations becoming worse than they were, instead of placing them on a reasonable basis. There seems to be much truth in the remarks made by the Governor to the General Court of the Bank in February 1967 that

> the predominant reason probably lay in the long history of unsatisfactory relations in banking . . . There seemed to have been a belief that Boards of Directors still thought in the manner of nineteenth-century employers, resulting in a distrust of the effectiveness of negotiations and a conviction that equitable settlements only followed the use of power.

The outbreak of war in 1939 came only sixteen months after the ending of the economic dispute with Great Britain. Farmers had not had the chance to build up the numbers of their stock or to apply sufficient fertilisers to restore the fertility of their fields. They did benefit by higher prices but the increase in the agricultural price level was not remotely comparable to that of 1914-20. It was, however, notable that many of them seized the opportunity to reach agreement with their bankers over debts that had been outstanding since the early 1920s. Mortgages were paid off and farmers regained good credit standing. From a banking point of view, this was good so far as it went but there was little inducement, in the absence of fertilisers and feeding stuffs, to farmers to borrow to finance further production. In the manufacturing sector, there were equal difficulties.

Many of the then new tariff-based industries were badly affected because they were so dependent on imported raw materials. Many of them indeed were then little more than final processors, sometimes no more than packagers, of goods that had been imported in a nearly finished state.

This situation produced paradoxical, if temporary, results. Imports, whether of raw materials or of finished goods, decreased as the war went on. Exports were limited on account of the difficulties of production but they did not plumb the depths of imports. In 1943 and again in 1944 there was actually a surplus in the balance of visible trade. An immediate result was that the deposits of all the banks, and not least those of the Bank of Ireland, were substantially increased. This was to continue after the end of hostilities because it was so long before raw materials again became available and the normal channels of trade were re-opened.

All this was reflected in the Bank's balance sheet. Deposit and current accounts totalled £34.8 million in 1938, the last full year of peace: they were £66.2 million at the end of 1946. Between the same two years investments rose from £21.1 million to £45.9 million. On the other hand, discounts and advances rose only from £14.8 million to £19.4 million. Declared profits went from £303,000 to to £351,000.

Nothing like these figures had ever been seen before: the Bank was now operating on a quite unaccustomed scale. Perhaps it should have been more widely accepted that this abundance of funds was a transient phenomenon, the result of years of forced saving. The moneys thus accumulated would be quickly used to replenish the shortages of capital and consumer goods. This did not happen as quickly as was then expected, but clearly, when it did happen, the savings that had been piled up in the banking system would be quickly drawn down.

This process began in 1947. The position, however, was confused by growing controversy concerning the proper use of the banks' external assets (that is, their holdings of British gilts and treasury bills) and the proper relationship of the currency with sterling, particularly after the devaluation of 1949. Another factor was quite new, the rôle of the Central Bank which had begun its operations in 1943. In the post-war years its annual report relentlessly denounced the pace at which wartime savings were being dissipated. Further again, the decision of government to initiate a programme of public investment, announced in 1949, indicated that the state would become a regular claimant on the resources available for investment. This was also quite new. Even during the war, a surprisingly large proportion of public expenditure had been defrayed out of current taxation. The capital liabilities of the state, which had stood at £61 million in March 1939 were £79 million in March 1945.

The Bank participated fully in the revival of activity as normal trading conditions returned. That revival proved to be less substantial, at least in the decade that lay directly ahead, than was then hoped. Nevertheless, advances reflected the new conditions. They amounted to £30.9 million in 1948 which was not only another increase from the £27.1 million of the previous year but was also substantially ahead of anything previously recorded. However, they grew without any appreciable pause to £37.7 million in 1952. A check after the severely deflationary budget of that year was followed by renewed growth to £43.8 million in 1955. The severe depression of 1955-7 interrupted the cycle again. Thereafter the revival of business confidence following the adoption of the first programme for economic expansion was reflected in another expansion which brought advances to £47.1 million in 1959.

The programme of public investment was an important influence in these vicissitudes. It provided an injection of purchasing power into the economy on a scale which had been unthought of in the pre-war years. But, as became increasingly apparent, the investment was directed primarily towards renewing and extending what was then called the 'infrastructure' of the economy, towards roads, houses and hospitals. Its effect on the capacity to export was not great while, granted the community's propensity to import (another phrase then in fashion), it swelled the volume of payments going out for consumer as well as for capital goods. The situation was made still worse by the sharp increase in world prices as a result of the Korean War in 1950 and, later, by a succession of bad years in agriculture.

The effect of these developments was that the deficit in the balance of payments persisted long after the wartime deficiencies had been made good. As matters then stood, any payments deficit was met by drawing down the external assets of the banking system which, although there were fluctuations, were gradually reduced as time went on. Two other matters affected the situation. The progress of public investment entailed borrowing by the state on a scale hitherto unknown. The banks were invited to underwrite these loans and also loans floated by state companies and local authorities. Certainly this was accepted as part of their public responsibilities but it led to recurrent bargaining as to the issue price and the rate of interest that should be offered. These discussions took up much time and inevitably placed the banks in an invidious position.

A further issue in this unhappy period concerned the interest rates that should be charged and paid by the banks. After 1945 this became a recurrent controversy. The principle on which the banks then acted was that Irish rates should move in sympathy with rates in London. This flowed from the then ease of movement of money from one country to the other. More than that, it was a matter of the ease of movement from one branch of a bank in the Republic to another branch in Northern Ireland or vice versa. It was assumed that if Irish deposit rates remained for long below the comparable British rates there would be a flow of deposits, particularly of the larger deposits, out of the Irish banking system. The traditional practice was described by the Banking Commission in paragraph 307 of its majority report:

> the Irish Banks' Rate moves at 1 per cent above Bank of England rate when the latter is below $5\frac{1}{2}$ per cent, and at one-half of one per cent above Bank Rate when that rate is at $5\frac{1}{2}$ per cent and over.

In general it might be said that the Irish rates rose and fell more slowly than the British but they followed the same trend upwards or downwards.

This had been unimportant during the long period between 1932 and 1951 when bank rate remained untouched at a historically low level. Thereafter, British changes were closely scrutinised in Ireland, particularly by governments which were now regular borrowers. Matters came to a head in 1955 when a heavy payments deficit had developed in Ireland and there was also a sharp fall in the value of British gilts. At the beginning of the year bank rate was advanced in two stages from 3 per cent to $4\frac{1}{2}$ per cent; in Ireland, representations by the then government ensured that the rate for larger deposits was increased by one-quarter of one per cent and that all other rates were left untouched. This situation lasted until January 1956 when freedom of action was restored to the Irish banks. The net external assets of the Irish banks had stood at £116 million in March 1955. 'By the end of 1955, however', to quote the report of the Central Bank for 1955-6, 'the net external holdings of the commercial banks had been reduced to a level barely sufficient to support the existing liabilities within the State.' It was no wonder that in 1955, for the first time, the banks were forced to re-discount exchequer bills, which in its own way was a landmark in the evolution of the present credit system of the Republic.

To return to a point already made: all the banks were engaged in these controversies over the price and quantity of credit. Several were more seriously affected than the Bank of Ireland. But the Bank was in a particularly difficult position. It had, so it believed, a special responsibility. It was, after all, its Governor who was the *ex officio* leader of those delegations of bankers who were summoned to Upper Merrion Street. These transactions, not to put it any further, distracted attention from more commercial matters.

The year 1955, however, was the lowest point. The later years of the decade showed better trading returns, though the improvement was purchased dearly by the special import duties which, imposed to discourage imports, also discouraged the import of raw materials and led to severe unemployment and emigration. There were, however, already signs of an improving economy. Even in the otherwise depressing year of 1955, the Governor (T. F. Hennessy) could note the increasing business of the foreign exchange department. This was to be a matter for comment several times in the following years. It marked the beginning of a quite new trend in Irish trade. Hitherto, ever since statistics were first published in 1924, Irish trade had meant Anglo-Irish trade. From this time onwards, a growing proportion of exports were directed elsewhere than to the United Kingdom while increasingly, imports came direct from their country of origin. This was not the only sign of change. In 1961 the Governor (Gerald Wilson) noted 'the new and welcome feature' of a marked expansion in the export of manufactured goods. It recalls the outlook of the time that he believed it possible that exports in 1960 might be found to have reached the hitherto incredible level of £150 million.

In the same speech the Governor noted the foundation 'with our associates' (the Hibernian and the National City Banks) of Foster Finance. Banks in the United Kingdom had already entered the field of what was still called hire-purchase but the Bank was the first to form its own wholly-controlled subsidiary. It proved an immediate success and its network of offices rapidly spread all over the country.

Four years before, the Governor's speech had dealt with a matter which, in earlier decades, would have been considered to be a grave reverse to the fortunes of the Bank. The Central Bank Act of 1942 had provided for the gradual retirement of the consolidated bank notes issued under the Currency Act 1927. During 1956, the Bank surrendered the last of the note issue to which it was entitled.[2] That there was remarkably little fuss about it provides an ironical contrast to the anxieties created by the re-allotment of bank note issue in 1927. Values were already changing.

The rapid growth of the early 1960s provided the Bank with every opportunity to increase its business. Advances rose from £39.6 million in 1958 to £58.2 million in 1963. These figures now look puny against the inflation-swollen returns of more recent years; but the rate of expansion was unequalled in Irish experience at that time. Other rates were not so promising. In 1963 the Governor (A. C. Crichton) stressed that 'there were danger signals on the horizon, not least the steeper increase in the consumer price index which rose by about 4% in 1962 compared with 2.8% in 1961'. But at the time it was reassuring to note that declared profits had risen from £540,970 in 1958 to £720,026 in 1962.

There was in fact a remarkable recovery of the economy during 1957, partly as a result of the brutally effective special import levies and partly because of a fortuitous up-swing in the export of cattle. The recovery, once apparent, was to persist until the coming of the first programme for economic expansion brought a reinforcement of confidence and a new spirit of enterprise.

Up to then there had been little or nothing in the record of the Irish state to suggest any capacity for sustained growth. The first government had given priority to agricultural production: the second government had applied itself to building up manufacturing by tariff protection. Both efforts, though in many ways contradictory, had been successful up to a point, but they were frustrated by the conditions of the 1930s. The war inhibited progress in both agriculture and industry. Throughout the early and middle fifties the highest emigration for seventy years reduced the population to lower levels than those recorded in the last days of British rule. It was hard to see that the national income had increased in any substantial degree during the period between 1922 and 1957. On the contrary, what might stand as the symbol of the time was that, even in money terms, the national income of 1956 was lower than that of 1955. The most depressing reflection of all was that Ireland appeared to be untouched by the resurgence of production, employment and prosperity which marked Western Europe in that decade.

But the early sixties saw a remarkable change. The economic indices, always excepting a still depressed agriculture, pointed upwards in production and trade while emigration fell steadily and population began at last to grow. The economy became diversified, not simply in the sense that manufacturing expanded but that more foreign firms began to explore the possibility of setting up in Ireland. All this may have been due to the continued increase of world prosperity; a great deal of it might be traced to the First Programme, the adoption of which gave confidence that public policy was at last pointed in the right direction. What could not be doubted was the new feeling of confident acceptance of change. The contrast between the mood of 1956 and that of 1961 is remarkable; and it may encourage a later generation through a new experience of depression.

For their part, the banks had had only too much experience of working in a stationary state. Their balance sheets at once reflected the beneficial results of the new departure. But the new buoyancy brought its own problems. The stringencies of the fifties had brought some signs of strain in the banking system. If the economy were now to be renewed and expanded, it seemed safe to predict that the banking system might need renewal as urgently as any other of its components.

All banks were conscious of the criticism, however little they may have accepted it, that there were too many bank branches up and down the country, that the country was over-banked. This criticism had been made directly in the report of the first Banking Commission in 1927; it had been revived from time to time since then. It could be pressed further — that there were not only too many bank branches, there were too many banks. In the stagnant past it had been possible to ignore such claims. An altogether new situation was now developing and, granted the passion of the sixties for mergers of all kinds of businesses, might lead to the matter being raised in a much more urgent form. Already two of the eight associated banks had passed into British control: in 1917 the Westminster Bank had acquired the Ulster and the Midland Bank had acquired the Belfast. There was nothing to stop an extension of this process. Moreover, granted that Ireland was moving into closer association with the world outside these islands, it could happen that an American or a European bank might follow the example set by the Midland and the Westminster. In its report for 1964-5 (p. 18) the Central Bank had noted that

> Economic advancement, assisted by external capital and enterprise, has attracted the attention of banks and other financial institutions abroad.

The Central Bank was primarily concerned to advertise discreetly that 'consultation with the Central Bank is a proper preliminary step in connection with any proposal for the entry of an external institution into banking business in Ireland'. But it was plain to all, and not least to the Irish banks, that such an entry might be made by way of a takeover.

The Bank of Ireland had no need to fear for its own continued existence. That was safeguarded by an Act of 1929 (number 4 of the private acts of 1929). Summarising that measure F. G. Hall had noted:

> Furthermore, the Bank was prohibited from purchasing or acquiring control of any other bank, whether inside or outside the Saorstat, without the written consent of the Minister for Finance. It was also provided that the Bank could not be absorbed 'by any bank, corporation, trust or other company whatsoever'.[3]

But it could not disregard the possibility that other Irish banks would be taken over and operated so that it would be faced with enormously strengthened competition.

This was not the whole picture. The Bank had shown admirable results in the depressed years and it continued to do so as the business cycle at last climbed upwards. This had been achieved without any great changes. Indeed the only changes were those that were routine, such as the succession of Governors and of J. M. Harkness to the general managership in 1956. To some, however, there seemed reason to fear that the Bank was not securing its proper share of the new growth, either in resources or in advances. If that process were allowed to continue, its position would be seriously damaged. In one sense, its long history was a handicap. It had been the nearest thing that the country had had to a central bank: there was now an active and expanding Central Bank. Precisely on account of its past semi-official status, the Bank was not regarded everywhere as a truly commercial bank. However assured its position still was, it was in some danger of coming to get the worst of both worlds.

It may be said that the best refutation of these fears was provided by the Bank itself. By a long way, it was the first Irish bank to strengthen its position by judicious mergers. These were not designed so as to seize a predominating position. That might arouse fears of a monopolistic situation. The aim was rather to build a structure which, in the first place, would provide security in a changing country and then to reorganise its business and decisively expand the accepted concept of banking.

The first step concerned the Hibernian Bank which was one of the oldest of Irish banks, having been founded in 1825, and which possessed sixty-three branches. In 1958 discussions were initiated between the Bank (represented by the Governor, John A. Ryan and his immediate predecessor Hugh Kennedy) and the Hibernian Bank (represented by its chairman, Mr C. M. O'Kelly). A statement dated 28 August announced 'agreement in principle upon a scheme to facilitate a co-ordination between the services rendered by the two banks'. This agreement was implemented before the end of the year. Shareholders of the Hibernian would receive £1 Bank of Ireland stock for every one Hibernian share of £4 (£1 paid up). This was accepted by 97 per cent of the shareholders of the Hibernian, voting in terms of the value of their holdings. The Bank of Ireland increased its capital stock by £500,000 so as to enable the entire paid-up capital of the Hibernian to be acquired on the basis of this agreement. The consent of the Minister for Finance was sought and given. The accounts of the two banks were merged in the Bank's return for 1958.

This was the first step towards a new Bank of Ireland. The second concerned the National Bank. This was a more complicated transaction. The National Bank had been established in 1835. Its head office was in London and since the 1850s it had opened a number of offices in England and Wales. It was a member of the London clearing house since 1858. In Ireland it possessed 135 branches. Negotiations between the Bank and the National progressed with goodwill on both sides, but there were two major difficulties — the future of the English branches of the National and the position of that bank as a member of the London clearing house. Both of these were solved, largely through the good offices of the Bank of England.

The proposals for a new structure were announced on 17 November 1965. A new subsidiary of the National was to be formed to be incorporated in the Republic, and to which all the Irish business would be transferred. On completion the shares of the new Irish subsidiary would be owned by the Bank while the shares of the National Bank, representing the English business, would be owned by the National Commercial Bank of Scotland. Shareholders of the National Bank would receive for each ordinary share 36s. 6d. in cash and £1 Bank of Ireland Loan Stock. This represented a payment of 56s. 6d. for each National share, a value which might be set against the market value which between January and November 1965 had fluctuated between 31s. 9d. and 43s. 6d. The total consideration reached £16,950,000 of which £12,200,000 was found by the Bank and £4,750,000 by the National Commercial. The Bank raised roughly half of its purchase price by the creation of loan stock, £3.6 million out of investments and £2.6 million by the repayment by the British treasury of its indebtedness to the Bank.[4]

In March 1966 the scheme was adopted by the shareholders of the National Bank. In favour there were 3,953 casting 3,359,429 votes; against, 483 casting 348,110 votes. The necessary legislation in England, the National Bank Transfer Act, became law in March 1966 and in Ireland the consent of the Minister for Finance was received.

The acquisition of the Hibernian and the National transformed the organisation of banking in Ireland. The process was completed in August 1966 with the fusion of the Munster and Leinster, the Provincial and the Royal Banks into Allied Irish Banks. In 1965, it may be added, it was announced that the Midland Bank had acquired the Northern Bank.

Two other matters may be dealt with here. It will be remembered that in 1945 the Irish banks were well supplied with external assets (British gilts, treasury bills and other balances in London). They were under no operational necessity to need the assistance of the Central Bank which indeed at that time possessed comparatively exiguous uncommitted external assets. During the war the banks had maintained small balances with the Central Bank against the possibility that an emergency issue of

Plate 83
The 1969 Court of Directors, comprising the joint boards
of the three constituent banks in the Bank of Ireland group.
Donal S. A. Carroll, the Governor, is in the chair

currency notes might be required. They had no inducement to increase those balances after the war, granted that the Central Bank was precluded from paying interest on assets in the general fund. The Central Bank Act 1964 removed this prohibition but the change did not lead to any great increase in the balances still maintained. Gradually, however, these balances evolved from being balances for the clearing (which since 1958 had been settled by cheques drawn on the Central Bank) to being the means of settling transactions between the Central Bank and the individual banks.

A new situation was created in 1968 by the Basle Arrangements for the support of sterling which afforded protection against further depreciation to official holdings of sterling. Clearly they did not cover the important holdings of sterling possessed by the commercial banks. In late 1968 and again in 1969 the commercial banks transferred the greater part of their sterling assets to the Central Bank. This was effected by the establishment of reciprocal credits, the Central Bank crediting the banks with Irish currency and the banks crediting the Central Bank with the same amount of sterling. All banks, of course, retained some sterling for their business in Northern Ireland and in Great Britain.

This change affected all Irish banks. A second development concerned the Bank of Ireland only. The Central Bank Act 1971 provided for the transfer of the exchequer account from the Bank of Ireland to the Central Bank. This proviso took effect on 1 January 1972, thus ending a responsibility which the Bank had discharged under a long series of British and Irish governments since its foundation in 1783. The transfer had long been agreed. It was all the more acceptable because it suited so well the image of the commercial bank which the board was anxious to strengthen.

This seems the appropriate place at which to note the close and fruitful relationship which grew up in these years between the Bank and the Central Bank of Ireland. In less crowded times, the transfer of the sterling balances and of the exchequer account, not to mention the first letters of advice on lending policy (which will be considered later) would each have been the event of a decade. That they were effected so easily was due to careful consideration and co-operation. They were not the only examples. In 1965 the import levies introduced by the British government seriously threatened the interests of all Irish exporters to Great Britain. It was plain that the special circumstances of Anglo-Irish trade had been overlooked in the urgency of the situation. A method by which the new charges on Irish exporters might be financed by the banking system was suggested by the Bank to the Central Bank and the Department of Finance. It was welcomed and approved and put into operation in so short a time that the effects on exports were minimal. It was no wonder that when the Governor of the Central Bank, Dr Maurice Moynihan, came to retire in 1969 the Governor of the Bank should say to the General Court that:

> We would like to pay tribute to his contribution and to express our deep appreciation of the courtesy and consideration which we have received from him over the years. There have been many occasions in these past years when divergent views existed between the banks on the one hand and the government on the other. His tact, deep understanding of the issues and his wisdom invariably resolved the difficulties and contributed much to reconciling opposing views. The monetary sector of the economy must develop, but to do so, there must be a mutual understanding of technical problems and objectives and Dr Moynihan has created an atmosphere where much progress will be possible in the years ahead.

In the next year the Governor retired. Dr Carroll's summary of his term of six years compressed a great deal into a very short sentence: 'They have been eventful years, at times worrying, at times greatly satisfying'.

Mergers with the Hibernian and the National, important though they were, did not go to the heart of the changes that were contemplated. The most important lay out of public sight. They have always been associated with the McKinsey Report which was received by the Bank in October 1965. It is clear that the manner and sequence in which changes were made owed a very great deal to that report. It is fair to recognise that the Bank was already aware of the need for re-organisation and had already made some progress towards satisfying the new needs of its customers. Even the decision to call in McKinseys was itself a proof of new thinking. At that time the Bank was the first on this side of the Atlantic to make the approach. It was not until some years later that its example was followed by the Bank of England.

The first report set out most of the guidelines for what was to follow. The principal aims were, first, to transform the group of three banks into a single entity. This was bound to be a lengthy process, granted that each bank had its own style of management and its own mix of customers and customers' needs. There was all the more reason to get started on the job and at the same time to avoid the constant danger of hurting old loyalties and habits, both of customers and of staffs. The second was to eliminate barriers between management and staff. In turn this called for a great deal of delegation on a scale which was largely unknown in the traditions of each of the banks concerned. It followed that the area of personal responsibility and accountability would be greatly increased at all levels of staffing. Inevitably, there had to be assured leadership from the centre through what amounted to a revolution in the concept of what were the really important things in the business of banking and how they should be tackled. Therefore a greater continuity of leadership had to be provided.

This led to a reassessment of the duties of the Governors and directors. Hitherto the Governor had held office for two years and was succeeded by the Deputy Governor who had been elected as Deputy when the Governor went into office. In future the Governor's tenure of office would be extended: thus, Dr D. S. A. Carroll held office from 1964 to 1970 and his successors, Mr J. A. Ryan and Dr W. D. Finlay have acted for six years each. A retiring age for the board was introduced. This was the more necessary because the board was temporarily swollen by the inclusion of the directors of the Hibernian and National. The retiring age became operative in 1970. At the same time, the principle of diffused responsibility was honoured by the introduction of members of operating management to the board. Finally, the function of the Court was to be changed from an executive body charged with decision-making to being the body charged with the formulation of policy.

The lending power of managers was drastically increased, in some cases quadrupled; the term 'agent' was abandoned in order to mark their greater freedom and responsibility. At the centre of the management structure was the new Group Managing Director, Mr Ian Morrison. At the next level was the Chief General Manager who had four General Managers, with responsibility for specific geographic areas. Each General Manager had a number of Assistant General Managers in charge of the branches in their area. Henceforward the emphasis was to lie on individual responsibility rather than on government by committee. It followed that seniority was no longer the sole, or even the most important, claim to promotion. These changes were summed up in the speech of the Governor at the Bank's General Court in February 1966:

> The various businesses within the Group will operate as separate units, each with its own Chief Executive, co-ordinating through the Group Managing Director. We intend to develop a group executive which will be responsible for the provision of various management services to the operating units and which will recommend new policies to the Court of Directors.

The implementation of this policy has involved the creation of a remarkable number of companies designed for specific purposes. The accounts of the Bank for 1981-2 show a total of twenty-seven wholly-owned subsidiaries within the state, seven subsidiaries within the state in which the Bank has a controlling interest, fifteen wholly-owned subsidiaries incorporated outside the state in which the Bank has a controlling interest. Among these, mention should be made of two. Bank of Ireland Finance derives from Foster Finance; the name was changed in 1974. It is concerned with instalment credit and has two subsidiary companies in Northern Ireland. Another of its subsidiaries has thirty-seven branches in Great Britain. The Investment Bank of Ireland, another wholly-owned subsidiary, was founded in 1967, and deals with merchant banking, company finance, pension fund management and investment advice.

Another form of expansion has been the establishment of branch offices in England, West Germany and the United States. The first of these dates from 1971 and their number is still growing. They have greatly assisted the business of the Bank by attracting resources, strengthening links with foreign concerns beginning operations in Ireland, and assisting the increasing diversification of the export trade. On the other hand the number of Bank branches in this country has remained almost stationary in the last ten years. This is surprising in view of the considerable increase in business activity, but it is in line with the experience of the other associated banks. In sharp contrast, there has been a notable increase in the number of branches of the building societies and the Agricultural Credit Corporation in the same period. In 1982 the Bank had 7,370 employees in the Republic, 700 in Northern Ireland, 771 in Great Britain, fifty-six in the United States and three in West Germany.

These are matters of organisation, but it must be remembered that the new departure went very much further than a matter of re-organisation. The personal and psychological effects were at least as important. Two points only need be taken to indicate what was involved. This was not simply the re-organisation of a single institution. It concerned the staffs of three quite different banks, each different from the others in its customs, its traditions and its sense of how things should be done. All these differences had to be reconciled. At the same time, officials in each bank were asked to perform a major task of adjustment. They were asked to take responsibility, to break out of the ordinary and time-honoured procedures. Nothing in their careers had suggested that such demands would be made upon them. It was a very great deal to ask of them. The re-adjustment was bound to take time. It was a great triumph for everybody concerned that it was so successful.

These changes were revolutionary in quite another sense. They represented the introduction of a new concept of banking. A number of factors, quite distinct in themselves, led to this change: the sudden and quite unprecedented growth of the economy, its increasing exposure to international influences, and the new emphasis on the structure and methods of management. The function of a bank was no longer passive, accepting savings and placing them on deposit or in considering favourably or unfavourably applications for accommodation. The new function lay in seeking out customers and ascertaining their needs which, in the changing environment, would go far beyond purely financial requirements. It was for this reason that in the general re-organisation place was found for so many specialised services besides those already existing: investment management, financial control, marketing and others. Banking was now moving beyond its traditional boundaries.

This represented a breakaway from the older view of the business of banking as akin to the professions. It went without saying that the accepted virtues of reliability and integrity retained all their importance. If anything their importance was increased because they were now to be exercised in a changed context. Banking was more and more concerned with marketing. It had to find out what the customer wanted (not always easy when the owner of a developing business was not clear what his priorities were) and to decide in consultation with him what form of assistance would be most useful. The new approach was expressed by the Governor under whom these changes were made. Speaking to the International Banking Summer School held in Dublin in 1968, Dr D. S. A. Carroll said:

> The board needs to know the trends of growth in resources and the sources from which they may be expected to come; it needs to know the likely demand for accommodation, the sectors of the economy which will require it and the pattern of pay-back by borrowers. . . . The emphasis in the boardroom is changing from a predominant concern about the affairs of individual borrowers towards an overall concern for the effect of the economy on the bank and the effect of the business of the bank on the economy . . . Today a commercial bank must seek out and compete for resources and must take an active posture in relation to customers. It must concern itself to assess what assistance or guidance will be most beneficial to the individual customer.

These were the goals which the Bank set itself to achieve as it settled down in 1968 to realise the potentialities of the mergers. The expansion of its activities during the 1970s has been remarkable: the potentialities have been realised to a greater extent and with more success than even an optimist could have then expected. Equally, not even the most hardened pessimist could have foreseen the problems that would have to be faced, the persistence and aggravation of inflation, the entry into the European Economic Community, the oil crises of 1973 and 1979, the world depression and the far-reaching change in the basis of the Irish currency. The last-named factor provides a striking example of how developments outside the control of the banking system can affect its operation. In 1968, the traditional parity of the Irish pound with sterling still survived: the financing of Anglo-Irish trade presented no technical difficulty. In 1979, Irish adhesion to the European Monetary System was followed almost immediately by the breakaway from the sterling parity. Ever since, the Anglo-Irish exchange rate has fluctuated. As a result (and indeed also on account of the growing trade between Ireland and the other members of the Community), the Bank now employs in its foreign exchange department as many officials as were employed for all purposes by the Hibernian Bank before the merger.

Membership of the Community has had other results to which the Bank has responded. It presented agriculture with an immensely widened market: it also meant that this country became an even more attractive location for industrial investment by countries that were not members of the Community. For agriculture a team of agricultural advisors, all graduates in agriculture with special training in management and economics, was assembled to enable the Bank to provide the service which farmers needed in the new conditions. Lending to agriculture (not including dairy produce) rose from £42.8 million in 1972 to £415.8 million in 1981. A special unit was set up to deal with the needs of the growing agri-business sector.

For industry, a corporate and international department was established which was specifically geared to assist in servicing large corporate customers and the increasing number of multinational customers. This move recognised the highly developed and increasingly specialised needs of large commercial customers. Lending to the manufacturing sector rose from £33.5 million in 1972 to £245.6 million in 1981.

In addition to this traditional form of lending, the Bank developed a number of important new lending instruments. The most important of these were leasing and preference share financing, both of which were forms of tax-based lending. These forms of lending enabled the Bank to pass on the benefit of a reduced tax payment in the form of lower interest charges to industry. These forms of lending became an important part of the incentive package offered by the Industrial Development Authority to industry setting up in this country. They had a neutral effect on the after-tax profits of the Bank as compared with traditional forms of lending and tax payments but they ensured that the Bank could compete effectively for a new and growing form of business while adding to the attractiveness of Ireland as a location for industrial development.

These forms of lending were developed against a background of increased control of credit by the Central Bank. The control of credit is of course one of the prime responsibilities of a central bank. In Ireland, the Central Bank's first step in this direction was taken in 1965 when the first of a series of letters of advice on credit policy was addressed to the associated banks by the Central Bank. (The associated banks are the Bank of Ireland, Allied Irish Banks, the Ulster Bank and the Northern Bank, which have a special relationship with the Central Bank under the Central Bank Act 1942.) In 1971 the Central Bank also addressed advice to the non-associated banks. (Very generally, these are subsidiaries of the associated banks, branches of North American banks, subsidiaries and affiliates of British banks, a number of other Irish banks and banks from other Community countries.) The mode of advice has varied according to circumstance; sometimes liquidity ratios have been prescribed but, more generally in recent years, ceilings to the growth in lending have been set. Whether the advice given for any year is restrictive or not will obviously also depend on the existing or expected trends in the economy. It is, however, to be noted that financial institutions such as the Agricultural Credit Corporation, the Industrial Credit Company and the building societies are not subject to such advice. The consequence must be to affect to some extent the ability of each and all of the associated banks to provide credit, and the figures already noted for the expansion of the Bank's advances in agriculture and manufacture must be read with this limitation in mind. The same effect flows from the frequent injunction, in itself comprehensible, of the Central Bank that the associated banks should give a low priority to personal borrowers who consequently have been forced to look for credit outside the traditional channels.

There is one other problem which the Bank of Ireland shares with other associated banks. The continuance and growth of inflation throughout the last two decades has meant that loans, advances and investments grew increasingly quickly, and the need to retain proportionately higher levels of profit became acute to a degree never hitherto contemplated. If retained profits could not be increased then the total balance sheet would become disproportionately large relative to the capital employed.

The problem appears dramatically in the accompanying table. In the forty years between 1922 and 1962 the total increase of assets was 106.7 per cent. The increase of capital needed to underpin this growth was modest. Capital represented 8.3 per cent of total assets in 1922 and, after an increase of only £4.5 million, was 8.1 per cent of total assets in 1962.

Balance Sheet Year	1922	1962	1972	1982
	£m.	£m.	£m.	£m.
Capital and Reserves	4.4	8.9	46.7	305.8
Loan Stocks, Floating Rate Notes and Minority Interests	–	–	8.7	45.4
Deposit, Current and Other Accounts	41.0	98.9	647.3	4631.0
Notes in Circulation	7.6	1.1	4.0	18.1
Other Liabilities	–	.7	6.6	72.8
TOTAL	53.0	109.6	713.3	5073.1
Liquid Assets	6.6	14.3	137.2	1328.1
Investments	30.3	37.3	141.5	540.6
Advances to Customers	15.5	56.8	414.1	3083.5
Premises and Equipment	.6	1.2	20.5	120.9
TOTAL	53.0	109.6	713.3	5073.1

It will be plain from what has gone before that the disproportion between capital and assets had been notable only towards the end of the forty years ending in 1962. The next ten years, 1962 to 1972, saw the balance sheet total increased by 550 per cent. In spite of an addition of almost £46 million to capital the capital adequacy ratio fell to 7.77 per cent. The next decade, 1972 to 1982, saw an even greater disparity. Total assets rose by 611 per cent and although capital was increased by £296 million, the capital adequacy ratio fell further to 6.9 per cent.

This trend highlighted a second problem: that the traditional method of measuring profit had become seriously misleading. If management decisions and dividend decisions continued to be based solely on the information provided by the accounts, the Bank would be exposed to serious danger. Business might be taken on which would be attractive in appearance but loss-making in real terms: dividends might be paid which might look justified by the accounts but would be, again in real terms, a distribution of the basic capital of the Bank.

To overcome these dangers the Bank decided to produce a statement of the year's results to reflect changes in the purchasing power of money. This was in 1975 and was by any standards an early attempt to report the true situation. Later amended, the statement was repeated until 1981. In that year the Bank presented its results under the current cost convention. To do so was an important innovation: it recalls the fact that the Bank was also a leader when it disclosed its reserves in the accounts for 1971-2.

At this point a very summary account of the development of the Bank since 1922 may be appropriately ended. In times that are so uncertain and so quickly changing, there is no date, no particular decision, that can be used as a suitable conclusion. Like all institutions of its kind, the Bank must engage in a continuing process of self-questioning to determine the contribution that it can make to the prosperity of Ireland and how it can be best organised and directed to that end. So it has been in the past, so it will be in the future.

References

1   M. Fogarty, *Report of banks inquiry*, Prl. 1850, p. 65.
2   The Bank continues to issue its notes in Northern Ireland.
3   Hall, p. 363.
4   This dated back to the earliest days of the Bank. The consideration for the act establishing it and for its charter was that the Bank should lend the government a sum equal to the subscribed capital. It was neither negotiable nor redeemable. From the Bank's point of view it was an unrealisable asset; and from everybody's point of view it was a clear anomaly after 1922.

Plate 84

The foreign exchange dealing room in Baggot Street

Plate 85

Plate 86

This page and overleaf: the Bank's New York office

Plate 87

Plate 88

Reflections on a Bicentenary*

F. S. L. Lyons

MORE than a hundred years ago, Walter Bagehot posed the crucial questions which must be asked and answered in evaluating any financial institution.[1] 'The main point', he wrote, 'on which one system of credit differs from another is "soundness". Credit means that a certain confidence is given, and a certain trust reposed. Is that trust justified and is that confidence wise? ... To put it more simply — credit is a set of promises to pay; will those promises be kept? Especially in banking, where the "liabilities", or promises to pay, are so large, and the time at which to pay them, if exacted, is so short, an instant capacity to meet engagements is the cardinal excellence.'[2] In explaining the key rôle of the Bank of England in the money-market, Bagehot noted that despite some critical moments, especially in the early nineteenth century, faith in the Bank had remained firm. 'Somehow', he observed, 'everybody feels the Bank is sure to come right.' 'Most men', he added, 'would think as soon of "winding up" the English nation.'[3]

It is not fanciful to transfer these remarks, *mutatis mutandis*, to the Bank of Ireland. Throughout its history its probity and stability have given it such a special place in our affairs that in writing of it we are as justified in calling it simply 'the Bank' as English commentators are when they refer to the Bank of England in the same terms. Nor is the parallelism fortuitous. Dr Whitaker has shown in his essay how closely the Bank of Ireland was modelled upon its famous forerunner, although the exigencies of politics and economics in Ireland delayed its coming until nearly a century later than might have been expected. It fulfilled some of the functions of a central bank, as did also the Bank of England in its larger sphere, but these functions were necessarily affected by the fact that the Bank of Ireland had to operate in an environment which was both semi-colonial and also shaped by uneven economic development.

Nowadays, it has become a commonplace of our economic history to point to the undeniably significant advances that were made in the Irish economy during the eighteenth century, but it has also to be remembered that these advances were by no means all-embracing. In a predominantly rural country there was still much poverty and insecurity and even in the towns, although there was a striking increase in the money supply, this was not matched by a corresponding improvement in the machinery for dealing with it. The coinage was still in a chaotic condition, and banking in any modern sense was relatively undeveloped and largely confined to enterprises founded by merchants or land agents with surplus cash. Such individuals used their balances partly to lend money on the security of bills of exchange which they purchased, and partly, by the buying and selling of such bills, to ease the transfer of money between different parts of Ireland and between Ireland and England. Since most of these 'bankers' also issued their own notes without any effective control, it was not surprising that whenever the economy faltered — especially whenever the harvest failed — they should falter too. Between 1759 and 1793 there were only four or five private banks in Dublin and only a handful of others were opened outside Dublin in

*I wish to thank Professor W. J. L. Ryan for reading and commenting on this essay. All views therein are, of course, my own, as are any errors.

the same period.[4] Even so, these probably sufficed for the volume of business needing to be transacted at that time and in a commercial sense the coming of the Bank of Ireland did not initially make a substantial difference. 'The Bank of Ireland', says a leading modern authority, 'in no way revolutionised Irish banking . . . The bank grew slowly in the first ten years of its existence. To a large extent it simply re-discounted bills . . . Its rôle was subsidiary. The fact that it took bills made it easier for the other institutions in the London market to discount extensively.'[5]

Nevertheless, by its very nature the Bank had exclusively some kinds of business from the beginning and it quickly added to these. Not only was it laid down in the act of parliament establishing it that its paid-up capital of £600,000 would be lent to the treasury at 4 per cent (both the amount and the percentage being changed on subsequent occasions), but from the outset it was ordained that all public funds were to be paid into the Bank. From this it was a natural progression that it should assume the management of the Irish national debt which, with the onset of the French wars in the 1790s, became a major preoccupation. As Dr Whitaker points out, its importance as an issuer of reliable bank notes was speedily recognised, and this, together with its efforts to solve the coinage problem, made it an early and vital force making for equilibrium in the system. Furthermore, it had an additional stabilising rôle in its management, or attempted management, of the exchange rate between the English and Irish pounds. For most of the eighteenth century, as Dr Whitaker reminds us, the rate was stable at thirteen Irish pounds to twelve pounds sterling, but when the Irish pound followed sterling off gold in 1797 there ensued a period of fluctuations not dissimilar in some ways to the one the modern Irish pound has been experiencing since the break with sterling in 1979. With the restoration of the old thirteen to twelve ratio in 1821, the Bank resumed for another few years its attempt to stabilise the exchange rate as best it could. Its methods may have contributed to the general deflation of the economy which set in after Waterloo — though in Ireland this was also partly a consequence of depression in England which reduced Irish markets — and it must have been with a sense of relief that, with the amalgamation of the two currencies in 1826, the Bank saw this burden at least lifted from it.

One consequence of the bad times, particularly in the crisis year of 1820, was that the frailty of many of the private banks was cruelly exposed and some of them crashed. The episode illustrated a certain ambiguity in the Bank's own position which was to haunt it for many years. On the one hand, it was a commercial enterprise, competing with other banks and doing much the same sort of business as they did. On the other hand, by reason of its seniority, its chartered status, and its close relations with government, it was a kind of sheet-anchor of the banking system and accepted — at first, perhaps, a little grudgingly — a responsibility to act as a bank of 'last resort' for its rivals when, as in 1820, they were face to face with ruin. This did not prevent the collapse of sixteen out of the thirty-one banks then functioning in Ireland, but the Bank's intervention undoubtedly prevented the disaster, bad as it was, from becoming total.[6]

One of the ways in which the Bank had helped to support the economy as a whole—apart from the accommodation given to individual banks — had been by increasing its note issue to take up the slack when so many of the private bank notes had been withdrawn from circulation or ceased to be acceptable. It was therefore ironic that the first inroad into the Bank's monopoly — the act establishing it had provided that no other corporation or body of persons exceeding six in number could issue notes payable on demand, or for any period less than six months—came in the very year after the crisis. By an act of parliament in 1821 providing for an increase in the Bank's capital stock to £3 million, it was also laid down that banking firms could be established anywhere in Ireland outside a radius of fifty Irish miles from Dublin (without limit on the number of members) and that such banks would be free to undertake all kinds of banking business, including the issue of notes payable on demand. Here was a clear indication that the Bank would have to face increased competition in the future; this was speedily confirmed, after some further changes in the law, by the emergence within a very short period — 1824 to 1836 — of the joint-stock banks which were to become a familiar part of the scene right down to our own day.

In some ways the Bank was ill-equipped to meet this competition. It had been cushioned for too long by its monopoly, it was forbidden by the terms of its foundation to lend money on the security of land, and it omitted, or disdained, to pay interest on deposits. Moreover, it had the reputation of being a Protestant institution and with Daniel O'Connell's rise to fame on a platform of Catholic emancipation in the late 1820s, this was an exposed position to occupy. It is true that, so far as its directorate was concerned, the Bank eventually circumvented the sectarian clauses of its charter, for although the act of emancipation in 1829 did not in fact remove the existing prohibitions on Catholics being appointed directors or being entitled to vote at stockholders meetings, the Court decided to behave as if they had been removed. All religious tests ceased to be applied in practice from 1829 and in 1830 Stephen Grehan was appointed as the first Catholic director, others being regularly appointed from that time onwards, even though the offending oaths which had debarred Catholics in the past were not formally abolished until the Bankers (Ireland) Act 1845. So far as its staff was concerned, however, the Bank remained largely Protestant (in effect, Church of Ireland) at least into the early years of this century.

It is probably true to say that this ascendancy flavour was more of a political than a commercial liability, and it scarcely became even a political liability until home rule became a real possibility in and after the 1880s. If, as appears to be the case, the Bank entered rather hesitantly upon the battle of competition with the fledgling joint-stock banks, this was for reasons other than its religious isolation. It was tardy (perhaps because of the monopoly within the fifty-mile radius) in opening new branches and those it did establish were not at first so well managed as, for example, those of the Provincial Bank; its refusal until 1864 to pay interest on deposits put it at a disadvantage with rivals, such as the National or the Provincial, which did so from the start; it lacked a London power-base such as the National possessed; and it was not as good at parliamentary lobbying as others were, a defect perhaps connected with the fact that the Court of Directors was drawn mainly from the ranks of Dublin businessmen and lesser landowners who lacked familiarity with, or even access to, the corridors of power in Whitehall and Westminster.

Such comparisons can, of course, be misleading. Despite its conservative approach to the market-place, the Bank remained essentially the point of reference for the other Irish banks and even when they were trying to outdo it, they looked to it for advice and leadership in good times, as well as for support in bad times. This continued to be forthcoming even when the Bankers (Ireland) Act 1845 withdrew its monopoly within the fifty-mile radius and left it as just one (although much the largest) of six note-issuing banks. Indeed, after 1845 its leadership rôle in Irish banking seems actually to have become more pronounced. It remained the principal channel for the import and export of specie, it developed a note-clearing system in Dublin and followed this by devising efficient machinery for the clearing of cheques. More and more it was becoming the bankers' bank, while still remaining the government's bank as well. This latter function may in fact have been a mixed blessing, for if it conferred prestige it also involved exertion which was progressively less well rewarded in the late Victorian period. There is even a case for arguing that the £2.6 million which it compulsorily lent to the government at 3 or $2\frac{3}{4}$ per cent might have been much more profitably employed and that it was a major handicap to be obliged to maintain a reserve several times larger than those of its commercial rivals. The Bank itself, admittedly, seems to have been more inclined to blame the fact that from its foundation it had been prohibited from lending money for land mortgages as a prime cause of its relative uncompetitiveness, but though this prohibition was removed in 1860, the irony that so often seemed to attend its nineteenth-century activities soon asserted itself here also, for within twenty years lending to hard-pressed landlords on the security of their estates became about the last business a responsible banker would wish to get involved in. Nevertheless the Bank by no means absented itself from the felicity of what Professor MacDonagh sees as the golden age of Irish banking, the period from the late 1850s to the late 1870s. It shared, as he says 'moderately', in the wave of prosperity that broke beneficently over the country in those decades, which, in practical terms meant that while during that period Irish banking business doubled, with profits doing likewise or better, the Bank's business and profits increased by only 60 per cent.

This sedate but solid progress, though less glittering than that of some of the Bank's rivals, was more than sufficient to maintain its prestige as leader. This prestige, it is important to realise, extended from the centre to the circumference, from head office to the smallest branch. After a slightly amateurish start the Bank's administration and staffing were radically overhauled in the middle years of the nineteenth century. This, as Professor MacDonagh describes it, was a process of 'centralisation, professionalism and uniformity'. The outcome was not merely increased efficiency in the Bank's performance at every level, but a widespread conviction among the Protestant middle class that service with the Bank was one of the most desirable ambitions a young man could hope to achieve. True, the early years of a bank official could be decidedly penurious, but if he survived that harsh apprenticeship he could be sure of a reasonable competence even if he never rose above the status of a clerk, and if he advanced to the middle or senior grades he was decidedly a cut above his opposite numbers in most other comparable careers.

No doubt similar developments were occurring in other banks — for 'bank service' was highly regarded by the Catholic as well as the Protestant middle class — yet the prestige of the Bank of Ireland as an institution cast a reflected glow upon its local agents (they were not called 'managers' until the reorganisation of the late 1960s) up and down the country. Branches were founded in small or medium towns; this often occurred just at the period — the last quarter of the nineteenth century — when clubs and societies for games or other activities were beginning to transform provincial Ireland. It became an essential part of a bank official's duty to play a prominent rôle by holding office in these clubs and societies, (a banker was almost invariably treasurer), and often providing them with the continuity without which they could scarcely have survived. The doyen of the banking corps, so to speak, was by common consent the agent of the Bank of Ireland. As the son of the manager of another bank in a small west of Ireland town as late as the 1930s, I can myself recall the almost automatic deference that was accorded to the agent. It was he who set the tone for his own and other officials, he who gave a cachet to this or that social occasion, even he who suggested which funerals merited a full turn-out by the banking community, the purity of the deceased's credit-worthiness being, of course, the main criterion.

Yet, although the Bank did to a large extent impose its imprint upon provincial society, there can be no denying that its quintessentially Protestant character isolated it in a way that was not true, for example, of either of its later associates, the National Bank and the Hibernian Bank. This was not necessarily an impediment to business during the late nineteenth and early twentieth centuries, and even in the rural areas the Bank got at least its fair share of the accounts of the small farmers who in growing numbers were becoming the owners of their farms. Moreover, there were clear indications, as Professor MacDonagh shows, of a policy of 'de-Anglicanisation', in the appointment of Catholic staff from about 1850 onwards, in the provision of loans to Catholic clergy and institutions in the last quarter of the century (a detailed survey would probably carry that date still further back) and in donations at all times to Catholic as well as to Protestant charities.

Where the isolation occurred was in the political sphere. While Professor MacDonagh is no doubt correct in characterising the Victorian Bank as 'Protestant' rather than 'unionist', and in suggesting that its active participation in politics was limited to what was necessary to maintain its status and well-being, with the rise of the home rule movement, and still more with the revival of militant republicanism in the early years of the new century, coming events began to cast an unmistakable shadow. It was not only, as Professor MacDonagh himself says, that the Court of Directors were 'unionist to a man', and that the great majority of their staff were also of that persuasion; it was that there was a world of difference between operating under the umbrella of the Act of Union and operating when that umbrella was disintregating in the revolutionary gale blowing through Ireland between 1914 and 1922. Or to change the metaphor, it was comparatively easy for the Bank to adopt a liberal stance when the *status quo* was intact, but it was quite another thing for it to retain its traditional poise when the ground was heaving under its feet.

The predicament that faced the Bank with the approach of independence and its eventual achievement for the twenty-six counties (the Irish Free State) in 1922 is clearly brought out by Dr Fanning. Essentially it was the predicament shared by all who had banked too heavily — in all senses — on the continuance of the British connection. Once the majority of Irish Protestants and unionists had secured their own future under the devolved government accorded to Northern Ireland, the remainder in the rest of the country, the 'southern unionists' in the language of the time, found their interests increasingly disregarded by a British government intent on extricating itself from as much of the Irish problem as it could, and at the the same time at the mercy, as they saw it, of the new and untried regime that had taken power in Dublin.

With hindsight we can see now that these fears were exaggerated, though at the time they seemed justifiable enough, especially when the Civil War of 1922-3 threatened the very existence of the Irish Free State. Like that other institution across the street, Trinity College, Dublin, the Bank felt under siege, and again like Trinity, its instinct was to look to the British government for guarantees of survival. It would be possible, indeed, from the minutes of the Court of Directors, and from those of the board of the College, to construct a kind of antiphonal lament echoing from one side of College Green to the other. But while both were worried about many aspects of the future, the Bank had one particular cause for alarm, which was a clear case of the sins of the forefathers being visited upon their descendants. When in 1802 the Bank had acquired the old parliament house, there had been a stipulation 'that the two chambers of parliament shall be effectually converted to such uses as shall preclude their being again used upon any contingency as public debating rooms'. As Dr McParland demonstrates in his essay, the Bank simply ignored this proviso. The House of Lords remained, and remains, intact, and if the House of Commons disappeared as such, it was to meet the Bank's own internal needs and not to guard against any recurrence of oratorical splendours.

Yet, as nineteenth-century nationalism developed, the restoration of 'the old house on College Green' became one of the most abiding clichés of popular rhetoric. When in 1913 home rule really did seem about to materialise, the Court of Directors took this rhetoric at its face value and for the next ten years was in a fever of anxiety lest its head office should be sequestered without due compensation or adequate alternative accommodation being provided. It is a measure of its desperation, as well as of the influence it could still bring to bear as late as 1920, that in the face of bland British suggestions that it trust to the goodwill of a future Irish government, it yet managed to have inserted into the Government of Ireland Act of that year safeguards to secure it both alternative accommodation and compensation for whatever change might be forced upon it. These safeguards were not only worthless, since the act never operated in 'Southern Ireland', but also dangerous, since for the Bank to have started life under an Irish government depending on a guarantee from the British government would have been to show itself isolated and alien and therefore an object of suspicion.

The true path forward was to demonstrate that it had a part to play in the making of the new state and that it was willing and ready to do so. This was in fact what happened, though not without some regretful backward glances across the Irish Sea, and only after the Irish government had indicated in no uncertain manner that it needed the Bank of Ireland and was prepared to work with it. Relations were opened between the provisional government and the Bank in January 1922 when the Bank was asked to act as the government's financial agent and to arrange for credit of £1 million. This, as Dr Fanning rightly stresses, was the first clear evidence of something which became plainer almost month by month, that the new regime, however revolutionary in a political sense, was in economic and financial matters dedicated to continuity rather than to change. Symbolic of this fact was the Bank's belated realisation that the government, far from serving it notice to quit College Green, had apparently never even considered this as a possibility.

Even so, it took time for the Bank to adjust to the hectic and largely uncharted world in which it found itself. Dr Fanning has shown, indeed, that it could on occasion act with the Irish government in frustrating the machinations of the British treasury — for example in blocking the proposal to transfer the register of British government stock maintained at the Bank in Dublin to its principal office in Belfast — but it still felt uncertain about the financial viability of the Irish Free State and when pressed, together with the other banks, by the government for loans running into millions of pounds, looked longingly towards Britain for guarantees. These pious aspirations were rebuffed with about equal severity in both countries. The British made it clear that they had no power to intervene and that even if they had, the Irish banks would deprive themselves of all influence in Ireland if they were seen to be going constantly hat-in-hand to London. In Dublin, William Cosgrave, head of the government after the deaths of Arthur Griffith and Michael Collins, made it brutally clear, not just to the Bank of Ireland but to the banks collectively, that his administration was all that stood between the country and anarchy and that he must have the means to carry it on and especially to pay the army upon which the whole frail structure depended.

Once this lesson had been learned, and by 1923 it had been, the way was open for a much friendlier and more constructive relationship. It was made the easier for the Bank, and indeed for all the banks, by the agreeable discovery that the Free State government, both the political leaders and their financial advisers, were monuments of fiscal and financial rectitude. And although after the advent to power of de Valera in 1932, his economic policies caused some tremors in banking circles, it soon emerged, despite the dire prophecies of the *Irish Times* that if Fianna Fáil took office 'the Free State's carefully fostered prosperity will wither', that nothing fundamental would change.[7] Thus, although during the inter-war period two Banking Commissions examined the banking system — in 1926 and between 1934 and 1938 — neither of these effected any major alteration in the status or functioning of the Bank.

To this generalisation there is, however, one exception which in time became a significant exception. It had been noticeable that when the new state was being set up, some of the commercial banks had made efforts to persuade the government to divide its business among them and thus to end the Bank's exclusive position as government banker. That manoeuvre had come to nothing, but the idea was voiced again during the Banking Commission's proceedings in 1926, though once more to no avail. That it failed once more was possibly due to the realisation that it would not be easy to divide the spoils among the hunters, but a more cogent reason for not pursuing the matter may well have been a growing feeling that in modern conditions the coupling of government and commercial business within the same institution was not ideal either for government or for the institution. In 1922, indeed, the then Governor, W. P. Cairnes, had incautiously admitted as much to Professor T. A. Smiddy, economic adviser to the provisional government, even going so far as to say that the best contemporary opinion was that 'you could not have one and the same bank undertaking the proper duties of a state bank ... and at the same time acting as an ordinary competitive, commercial and industrial bank.' In this he was undoubtedly out of step with his own Court of Directors and when the subject came up at the Banking Commission of 1926, the Bank strongly and successfully resisted any attempt to undermine its special position.

Yet that same 1926 Commission did make one recommendation which pointed the way to a quite fundamental change, soon afterwards embodied in the Currency Act of 1927. This was to set up a Currency Commission consisting of three banking members, three members nominated by the government, and a seventh member, the chairman, to be chosen by the other six. The main function of the Currency Commission was to be the issuing of legal tender notes, backed one hundred per cent by a reserve composed of gold, British legal tender or sterling balances, or British securities maturing within twelve months (this last limitation was removed in 1930). The Currency Commission's capital was subscribed by the eight banks then operating within the state — the Bank of Ireland, the Hibernian, the Munster and Leinster, the National, the Northern, the Provincial, the Royal and the Ulster — and participation in the consolidated note-issue was shared between them.[8]

The Banking Commission of 1926 had discussed the desirability of establishing a fully fledged central bank, but had rejected the suggestion as unnecessary in the conditions prevailing at that time.[9] All the same, the appointment of the Currency Commission was a first tentative move towards a form of *étatisme*, however modest, and when a second Banking Commission sat between 1934 and 1938, it inevitably turned its attention to the possibility of expanding the Currency Commission's functions so as to make it in effect, and even in name, a central bank. It was not intended that the banking system as a whole should be changed: indeed Professor Meenan has summed up the extremely conservative majority report as a 'recommendation to leave things as they were'.[10] But the pressure towards the creation of a central bank was irresistible, even though the legislation needed to wind up the Currency Commission and establish in its place the Central Bank of Ireland was not passed until 1942. Its powers were more extensive than those of the old Currency Commission (they were to be extended much further over the years) and its capital, its organisation and its management were more tightly controlled by the government. In the immediate sequel it did not much impinge upon the ordinary commercial operations of the banks, and the Bank of Ireland, perhaps rather to its surprise, was allowed to retain the exchequer account for another thirty years. One might, indeed, go further than this and suggest that the increasing concentration of the non-commercial side of banking into the hands of a centralised and specialised agency was positively beneficial to the extent that it enabled the banks to devote themselves with less distraction to their more profitable activities.

No doubt the Bank shared in this development, but it still retained a special position over and above its handling of the exchequer account. By virtue of its antiquity, its size, its prestige, it had always been the natural leader of the commercial banks and this position was if anything enhanced in the difficult years leading up to independence. One of the problems facing all the banks at that time was the growth of a more articulate demand among their staffs for certain concessions, following the formation of the Irish Bank Officials' Association in 1917. The immediate question was whether to recognise the Association at all, and if so what action to take on its request for arbitration on salaries and conditions of work. Despite an early and almost instinctive reaction against recognition, wiser counsels prevailed and in 1920 not only was the IBOA effectively recognised, but an arbitration award was accepted. This, as Professor Meenan demonstrates in his essay, was only the beginning of a long and often difficult chapter in the history of labour relations within the industry, but the close co-operation between the banks in a hastily assembled 'standing committee' led to a unanimous decision to form a permanent body of the same name, the IBSC. Although this body had no formal constitution, the Governor of the Bank, or in his absence the Deputy Governor, presided at meetings, the appointment of a secretary was left in the hands of the Governor and directors of the Bank, and the committee met habitually at College Green. This meant that in the negotiations between the banks and the government which were necessary from time to time, the Governor had a distinctive rôle as leader of the bankers, though this did not prevent ministers from dealing with him direct whenever they so wished.

To this informal recognition of the Bank's primacy among the commercial banks

Plate 89

An ICA group attend one of the Bank's 'Focus on Farming' courses at An Grianan, Co. Louth

Plate 90

Almost a quarter of the Bank's private sector lending is to farmers

Plate 91

In addition to direct loans to farmers, the Bank provides
finance for agribusiness enterprises such as this skim milk
powder processing plant

must be added the legislative recognition it received when in 1929 a private bill to amend the charter was approved by the government and passed into law. Essentially the Bank of Ireland Act achieved three main objectives. First, it provided that the Governor, Deputy Governor and at least three-quarters of the directors should be domiciled and resident in Saorstat Eireann (as the state was then officially designated). Second, not only was the Bank prohibited from purchasing or acquiring control of other banks without government permission, but it was itself protected from being taken over by any other institution. And finally, its powers were greatly extended. It could act as an 'issuing house' for the promotion of companies, guarantee or underwrite an issue of shares, hold shares or establish subsidiary companies, and guarantee contracts or grant indemnities. Above all, and in the sharpest contrast to the terms of the establishing act, it was empowered to purchase or carry on any business, and to enter into partnerships. Taken together, these provisions not only guaranteed, as Hall put it, 'that the Bank would continue to carry on business as an independent Irish institution, without in any way being dictated to or influenced by any other interest', but also ensured that in its commercial rôle it would be even more fully integrated into the life of the community than before.[11]

The full implications of this were not to be worked out for perhaps another forty years. In the short run — between the act of 1929 and the end of the Second World War the main impression conveyed by the Bank and by its rivals alike was certainly one of stability, but hardly of creative thinking. This was not surprising in view of the depression, the Anglo-Irish economic war and the distorted conditions that prevailed between 1939 and 1945. Professor Meenan has put his finger on the essential difference between that remote period and the adventurous decades of the 1960s and 1970s. In those earlier years, he says, the Bank, like its rivals, was passive, not active, in its attitude. 'It reacted to change as best it could, and indeed with a reasonable amount of success. That it should seek to guide, much less create, these changes, was not yet part of its approach to business.' In this it reflected the society it served; as Professor Meenan also remarks, the tendency of customers — particularly of rural customers — was not to use the banks in any dynamic way, but rather as receptacles for savings, a tendency illustrated in the banking system as a whole by the very high proportion of resources — 82 per cent in 1932 — which were held in the deposit accounts so dearly cherished by the farming community. So ingrained was this saving habit, Professor Meenan indicates, that towards the end of the 1930s, despite the depression and the Anglo-Irish economic war, the banks owed more to the farmers than the farmers owed to them.

This small, intimate, conservative way of doing things presupposed a close relationship between the branches of the Bank and their customers up and down the country. This was not in itself new, for we have already seen the roots of that relationship being established far back in the nineteenth century. But in one profound yet unadvertised way, the relationship was all the time becoming even closer. Quietly and steadily the Bank was losing the Protestant and unionist affiliations which it had maintained right up to the moment of independence and perhaps for a few years afterwards. In its recruitment of staff the Catholic element became steadily larger and ultimately predominant. The same was true of the Court of Directors where it would seem that the proportion of Catholics to Protestants changed from approximately one-third around 1939 to approximately two-thirds in the 1970s. The process cannot be too precisely documented for the excellent reason that the Bank was no longer thinking in those terms — a healthy institution does not keep a sectarian ledger. And it is difficult to say how much was policy and how much was the outcome of the natural course of events. An increasing Catholic representation on the Court of Directors and the recruitment of a predominantly Catholic staff would in any case have become inevitable with the striking decline of the Protestant population of the twenty-six counties in the decades after independence. So far as there was a policy in this matter it was the natural and pragmatic policy of a business concern which was anxious only to establish the maximum compatibility between its staff and its customers. But whatever the causes of the change, the results were nothing but beneficial to the Bank, removing the last traces of a minority, in some senses alien, institution and identifying it much more closely with the country it sought to serve.

This adaptation was well advanced by the time the war broke out, but the long isolation of Ireland throughout the six years of conflict, while it reinforced the 'cosiness' of the Irish economy, also underlined its lop-sidedness. The closure or reduction of markets and the shortage of imports led to reduced economic activity and restricted demands for credit, while deposits continued to grow. The consequences were seen in the contrast between the Bank's discounts and advances, which rose only slowly from 1938 to 1946, and the total of deposit and current accounts which almost doubled in the same period. There was something essentially impermanent about this faster growth in resources than in lending, for it was obvious — more obvious perhaps in retrospect than at the time — that resources which had been built up in a near vacuum would quickly be run down when the chance came to replenish capital and consumer goods.

When that began to happen, around 1947, there ensued a hectic phase of expanding credit which soon dissipated the wartime savings. And since an increasing part of that credit was absorbed by the government for building houses, hospitals, roads and other elements of the economic and social infrastructure — all much needed, but not directly contributing to the country's capacity to earn its way by developing its exports — the most significant effect of this expenditure was suddenly to inject into the economy a large element of purchasing power, with predictable inflationary results. But at the same time, as if to emphasise that Ireland was so placed as to suffer the worst of both worlds, its continuing dependence on Britain, not only for trade but in such matters as interest and exchange rates, meant that some at least of this early post-war inflation was also imported.

The unprecedented heavy borrowing by the state, state companies and local authorities placed considerable strains upon the banking system. So too did the vertiginous ups and downs of the economy in the late 1940s and throughout the 1950s. In the former case the banks accepted the necessity of underwriting state borrowing as a duty to be performed, however unpalatable it might be in some instances, but inevitably, as Professor Meenan points out, this involved them in controversy about the issue price and the rate of interest to be offered. And in the latter case, the interest rate to be charged and paid by the banks in their ordinary commercial dealings was also frequently controversial, the more so since rates were effectively governed by what happened in London. All the banks were caught up in these arguments, but the Bank bore the brunt of them, since the Governor was the *ex officio* leader of those melancholy deputations that made the pilgrimage, or obeyed the summons, to Government Buildings in time of crisis.

In both its official and its commercial rôles the Bank coped with the immediate problems of the post-war world efficiently enough, but in retrospect those problems seem like a rest-cure compared with the difficulties it was to face in the 1980s. In between however, there occurred a kind of economic miracle, even if one not so permanent, so radical or even so miraculous, as it was at one time the fashion to assume. The development and expansion of the 1960s is a familiar story, and its outlines have been clearly charted in this book by Professor McAleese in relation to the banking system and the economy as a whole, and by Professor Meenan in relation to the Bank in particular. Helped partly by a broadly favourable world economic climate, at least until the oil crisis of 1973, and partly by a constructive government policy based to a large extent upon Dr Whitaker's famous report, *Economic development*, and on the [First] *Programme for economic expansion* which derived from it, both published in 1958, those years saw a transformation of the Irish economy. It was a transformation characterised by the change from a predominantly agricultural to a predominantly industrial basis; by the almost doubling of living standards (measured by GNP *per capita*) between 1960 and 1970; by the reversal of the traditional demographic pattern from steady decline to modest but sustained growth; by the attraction of a large foreign-owned element into Irish industry which was highly export-oriented; by the diversification of Irish exports and the country's entry into the European Economic Community; by a growth in industrial output of 6 per cent annually between 1961 and 1973; above all, perhaps, by the generating of a mood of confidence almost if not quite unparalleled in Irish history.

This heady experience was not, of course, without its dangers. 'The net effect', Professor McAleese comments, 'has been to leave the Irish economy more prosperous than ever before. It has also become more vulnerable.' Prosperity has increasingly depended on exports, and further increases in living standards must depend upon export *growth*, of which a large proportion has been derived from foreign-owned firms operating in Ireland. The capacity to expand exports has unfortunately been much impaired by the mushroom cloud of inflation, especially in the late 1970s and early 1980s.

Both the prosperity and the vulnerability confronted the Bank with major problems. On the one hand, there were unprecedented opportunities to be seized. On the other hand, trading conditions, once deterioration had begun to set in after 1973, became perhaps more difficult than in any previous period. To exploit the opportunities and to guard against the hazards required from the Bank a much more positive and wide-ranging response than any it had previously made in its entire history. That response took a double form — structural reorganisation and a rethinking of the whole nature of the business in which it was engaged. Reorganisation had both an external and an internal aspect. Given the tendency of the 1960s to go for growth through mergers of one kind or another, it was not perhaps altogether surprising that the Bank should have turned in that direction. But there were arguments more weighty than fashion. It was arguable — and had been argued for decades — that the country was 'overbanked', that there were not merely too many branches but also too many institutions. In a word, that unity, or some form of it, was strength. There was, too, always the possibility of an invasion of the intimate world of Irish banking by takeovers from outside. This had indeed already begun to happen when in 1917 the Westminster Bank had acquired the Ulster Bank and the Midland Bank the Belfast Bank, and there were other possibilities on the horizon. An extension of this process might easily pose a threat to the Bank. Not a threat to its independent existence, for that was safeguarded by the act of 1929, but a threat in terms of greatly increased competition. One way of meeting such a threat, and of preparing for more intense competition if it should materialise, was to counter size with size.

How the Bank dealt with this situation is well described by Professor Meenan. The link with the Hibernian was forged in 1958 with remarkable rapidity, a happy conjunction which would have astounded the Hibernian's founders, vociferous as they had been in 1825 that banking facilities were being withheld from a large section of the community, 'owing to the political and religious preferences of the Bank of Ireland'.[12] This was followed by the more complex transaction which brought together the Bank and the National Bank and which was satisfactorily concluded in 1966. With the completion of this important business the Bank assumed its modern shape. It was an essential element in the reorganisation of the Irish banking system, but not the only one, for in 1965 the Midland Bank had acquired the Northern Bank, and in 1966 the Munster and Leinster, the Provincial and the Royal Banks came together to form Allied Irish Banks.

Even before the merger with the National had been completed, the Bank had begun to turn its attention to an internal reorganisation which would probably have been desirable in any event, but was now urgently necessary in view of the greatly increased size of the business. The process began with the commissioning of a survey from McKinsey & Co., a firm of management consultants with an international reputation. While it is by no means a universal law that the adoption of reports from management consultants leads invariably to increased efficiency, the Bank had the courage of its convictions and was in fact the first institution of its kind on this side of the Atlantic to undertake such a reassessment. That it was implemented so success-fully owed much to the then (and present) Governor, Dr D.S.A. Carroll and the then Group Managing Director, Mr R. I. Morrison, sometimes described respectively as the 'architect' and the 'builder' of the reorganisation. The prime objective, of course, was to transform the group of three banks, with their various other interests, into a coherent and mutually sympathetic whole. In any circumstances this was bound to be a difficult task. Each institution had its own style, its own loyalties and attachments, and individuals would not have been human if they had not wanted to ensure that change should affect their lives and careers as little as possible. In any close association of businesses which have proud traditions of independence there is bound to be a transitional period while senior officials who have been bred to the old ways work their time through to retirement. At the same time, new recruits have to be quickly absorbed into an organisation which will catch their imaginations and offer them proper scope for their abilities. It was thus an important aspect of the post-McKinsey changes that a deliberate effort was made to lower barriers between management and staff. In psychological terms this was a wise response to an age of declining deference and burgeoning informality. In terms of efficiency it was desirable in that it led to much more delegation and therefore to a higher degree of responsibility for many younger men. Side by side with this, as Professor Meenan points out, went a reshaping of the duties of the Governor and directors, the introduction onto the Court of members of the operating management and the adoption of a retiring age for directors. In general, the message was that mere seniority was no longer the royal road to promotion.

In purely business terms, the Bank, while ever mindful of its traditions, has in these recent years been in the forefront of innovation in many different ways. It has been fertile in the creation of new companies, either wholly owned or with a controlling interest, inside and outside the state. It has been adventurous in founding branches in Britain, and in extending its activities to West Germany and the USA. It was a pioneer in disclosing its reserves in the accounts for 1971-2. It has been vigorous in finding fresh customers and fresh kinds of business, and it became, as Professor Meenan puts it, 'more and more concerned with marketing'. It was, in short, taking a new view of banking which was consonant with, and indeed complementary to, the new and much more open economy within which it had to work. The opportunities, at least while the good times lasted, seemed almost limitless and one initiative followed hard upon another, with the creation of a special unit to promote agricultural business, of a corporate and international department to deal with the large corporations and the multinational concerns which were becoming so significant a part of the Irish scene, and of an operations department to handle computerisation and other aspects of modern technology. The change of scale which these and other initiatives engendered — combined, of course, with the effects of inflation — was colossal. Lending to agriculture (excluding dairy produce) rose by nearly ten times between 1972 and 1981 and to industry by about eight times during the same period.

Nowadays, however, it is not sufficient for a great institution like the Bank simply to transact its business, however successful and diversified that business may be. It is necessary also to contribute to the quality of life in the society which it serves and in contemporary terms that can mean many things. It can mean simple contributions to deserving causes, it can mean the support of various kinds of research, it can mean the encouragement of the arts, it can mean filling, in a hundred different ways, the gaps left either by individual initiative or by state aid.

When the Bank was founded, and for a century and a half after that, this important function was understood, though perhaps only to a limited extent. Dr McParland has paid tribute to the Bank's long tradition of enlightened patronage (to use the old term) of the visual arts, going back even beyond its occupation of the parliament house in College Green. Once that splendid building had been acquired it became a matter of intense pride to preserve it in a proper state, and anyone who has admired the results of the recent restoration and cleaning of the exterior will bear witness to the impressive *pietas* with which the Bank has discharged this most important duty — a work which, as Dr McParland says, 'has set new standards of architectural restoration in Ireland'. True, he also says that after it had so skilfully and elegantly adapted the parliament house in the early 1800s, the Bank rested on its laurels for the remainder of the nineteenth century. Its branches, sober and decorous as they so often were, did not add much architectural distinction to the Irish townscape and although there was a slightly more venturesome air about some of its early twentieth-century creations, nothing in the previous history of the Bank could have prepared even the most optimistic observer to anticipate the new head office in Baggot Street. Both in the quality of design and in excellence of materials, it is a most notable addition to the architecture of Dublin and, as Dr McParland so convincingly demonstrates, the application by its architect, Mr Ronald Tallon, of the ideas of Mies van der Rohe to an Irish setting is both exciting and in most aspects brilliantly successful.

Head office fittingly symbolises the new, progressive Bank which it houses, but it does more than that. It also contains the notable array of paintings and sculptures which amount to the most important collection of modern Irish art (together with some important foreign works) to be assembled during the 1970s. Begun by Ronald

Tallon and continued by Neil Monahan, it is an indispensable summing up of the best of what was being done in Ireland at that time. But this was only one, if the most important, aspect of the encouragement of the arts to which the Bank had committed itself in bad times as well as in good. Thus, it has not only made space available in Baggot Street for numerous exhibitions (some of them perhaps more distinguished as good causes than as fine art), but it has also supported music and the theatre in a variety of ways.

Nor is this simply an élitist predilection for arts with a limited appeal to the general public. In its most recent statement of accounts, the Bank stressed its policy of contributing to the welfare and development of the communities within which it operates. It has done this in a great variety of ways, supporting, to take only a few random examples, research and development in the universities and other educational institutions in different ways, religious and charitable organisations, environmental projects, sporting clubs and events, hospitals and medical research. In one quarter of a recent year more than sixty causes or institutions were helped in one fashion or another. And in the year ending 31 March 1982, the Bank contributed more than half a million pounds. Of the total of its 'social contribution', 49 per cent went to education, 22 per cent to religious and charitable causes, the same amount to environmental and cultural causes, and 7 per cent to hospitals and medical research.[13]

This generosity is all the more remarkable — and all the more valuable — because it is given during a recession. In hard times hard cases multiply and already the Bank has had to warn applicants that there are now so many contenders for the limited amount available that most will be disappointed. It could not be otherwise, for the Bank cannot single-handed take up burdens which neither private nor public benefactors have been able or willing to carry. In the last analysis the Bank must earn sufficient profit to sustain its activities and maintain a capital base that meets the Central Bank's requirements for adequacy. It has, therefore, to set a boundary to its 'social contribution' and the marvel is that it has been able to do as much as it has in the peculiarly bleak economic climate of the last few years.

It is hardly necessary to rehearse again the background to the present depression which Professor McAleese has so clearly analysed. We are all only too familiar with at any rate the symptoms, although there may be room for argument about the order of priority of the many causes. Even the most casual observer will be aware of the rapid inflation, the high rates of interest, the steadily increasing unemployment, the unsustainable levels of budgetary deficits and government foreign borrowing, the decreasing competitiveness of Irish products in both the domestic and foreign markets and the unavoidable prospect of a fall in living standards over a period of years.

It is not surprising in the circumstances that the annual statements of the Governors of the Bank have been exceptionally doom-laden of late. A bicentenary is no occasion on which to parade a catalogue of domestic woes, many of which we must hope will soon be of historical interest only, and it is proper to record that even the gloomiest statements contain ample evidence of the resilience and resourcefulness of the Bank in these most difficult times. Management must look beyond its immediate concerns to the broad trends discernible in the economy as a whole, and Governors' statements tend to address themselves as much to these broader issues as to the actual operations of the Bank. They are, of course, issues which are common to the banking system in general, or at least to the associated banks, but precisely because the Governor is at the head of the Bank of Ireland his statements carry a peculiar authority and receive correspondingly wide attention. It may therefore be worth while — if only to indicate to remote posterity how things were in the bad old 1980s — to mention briefly some of the recurring preoccupations of these years.

One, particularly stressed by the Governor in 1980 and 1982, was the need to improve labour relations within the industry as a whole. Major stoppages in the banks send ripples through the entire economy and the more closely interlocking that economy is the greater the damage that closures of the banks can cause. The emphasis laid by Dr Finlay on the development of orderly procedures for consultation and negotiation was valuable, not only for the Bank in its own operations, but for the country generally in both its international and its domestic business.

A second preoccupation has been with the situation arising from the fact that within the last decade the regulatory function of the Central Bank has greatly intensified through its power (conferred by the Central Bank Act 1971) of licensing and supervision of the commercial banks, through its authority to issue guidelines as to the amount of credit individual banks can extend, and through the rule that its approval must be obtained for changes in bank interest and bank charges. These are substantial constrictions and Professor McAleese, like Clive of India, might stand astonished at his own moderation when he says: 'Although Irish banks are in private ownership the notion that they are in consequence free to do as they like is quite at variance with reality.' Regulation, even intense regulation, by a central authority is unavoidable in times of financial stringency, but it would have been accepted more philosophically save for two things. The first is that the regulatory powers of the Central Bank have not been applied uniformly. Certain banks have been subject to lower liquidity ratios. Other institutions — the Post Office, building societies and Trustee Savings Banks for example — have been subject to less draconian regulations concerning taxation, disclosure of interest on deposits and the growth in their lending. Inevitably, there has been a sense of adverse discrimination among the associated banks and this has been given trenchant expression on more than one occasion in Governors' statements. Second, the fact that government borrowing escapes Central Bank control means that monetary policy must operate on bank lending to the private sector. The effect upon the banks and their customers is very serious, since the inevitable consequence is that at moments of crisis it is the private sector that is squeezed most severely.

A third, and perhaps the most important, handicap under which the banks have had to labour concerns the way in which the rôle played by their profits has been consistently misunderstood. As Dr Finlay put it in 1980: 'The Bank must look to the growth in its real profits to meet the demands of capital adequacy and pay a reasonable dividend. Unlike industrial companies which enjoy the benefit of stock relief, banks are not granted any tax allowance to increase their capital as backing for their deposit liabilities which expand rapidly with inflation. It is therefore a misconception to regard profits as surplus over and above the Bank's requirements.' Capital had to be increased in proportion to maintain the ratio of capital to total liabilities at the 6.5 per cent level required for prudential reasons by the Central Bank, and the principal source of the additional capital was retained profits. It was therefore not true to say, as some critics were apt to do, that profits retained in the Bank were 'lost to the community'. As Dr Finlay stated, in the nine years ending 31 March 1980 rather less than 14 per cent of the Bank's profits had been distributed to stock holders as dividends. The remaining 86 per cent was put to work in the economy by lending to government, local authorities, state bodies and the private sector.[14] Admittedly, the Bank's case was not helped by the tradition of presenting the accounts on the basis of the historical cost accounting convention which consistently overstated the true profits and made no provision for the capital required to maintain the continuity of the business at current prices. After several years in which it also provided a truer measure of profit than that provided by the historical cost convention, the Bank in 1981 opted for presenting its accounts in accordance with the current cost accounting convention. These changes gave a progressively more accurate picture of the true profits and in adopting them, the Bank was once again a major innovator.

This did not prevent it, and the other associated banks, from continuing to be a target for criticism on the two grounds that their profits were excessive (even though they were not so judged by the Central Bank) and that they did not fully discharge their liability to corporate taxation. These accusations were firmly refuted by the Governor in his 1982 statement. But in that same statement he drew attention to the likelihood that these two 'serious misconceptions' might have underlain the arbitrary levies imposed by government on the banks of IR£5 million in the July 1981 budget and of IR£20 million in the March 1982 budget. Such levies, as he pointed out, had serious implications not only for the banks but for other businesses that either had already been or might be so affected in the future. 'There is', he said, 'understandable unease that similar arbitrary measures might be applied whenever enterprises succeed in achieving the level of profitability that is necessary to ensure survival and to finance expansion of jobs and output. The restoration of business confidence requires a stable tax structure within which enterprises can plan for expansion and development. The established criteria for an effective tax system do not include arbitrary and variable imposts.'[15]

Nevertheless, important, even vital, as such considerations were to the Bank, the main thrust of most recent Governors' statements has been towards the dangers of inflation coupled with, or rather inseparable from, the serious over-spending and foreign borrowing by successive governments. Another way of putting this is to say that, like other institutions, the Bank, while doing its considerable best to weather the storm, was ultimately at the mercy of forces which were outside its control. Both Professor McAleese and Professor Meenan have made this point in different ways and both would certainly agree with Dr Finlay's conclusion in his statement of 1980: 'no bank can prosper independently of the community which it serves'.[16]

While this is entirely true, it needs perhaps to be taken one stage further. One has to ask on what does the economic health of the community depend, which alone will make it possible for it and for the Bank to prosper? In part, certainly, on international and market forces from which, in a time of world depression, a small open economy cannot expect to be exempt. But it also depends to a large extent on the will of the community to survive and to recover. There are steps which can be taken to regain control of the situation, but they require political leadership with the capacity to present hard choices to the electorate and to impose unpopular remedies. Hitherto, we have been pursuing the politics of seemingly infinite expectation on the basis of resources which are only too painfully finite.

At the time of writing, there are signs that the Irish people, having looked over the edge of the abyss towards which they have been careering in recent years, have begun to recoil from the chaos they have glimpsed. That out of the shock of recognition will come a new realism and a new resolve may as yet be only a pious hope, but it is the last, best hope of this small piece of earth.

We are fortunate as a nation in our banking system and that system has itself been fortunate in the leadership it has received from the Bank of Ireland over the past two hundred years. I commenced this essay with a quotation from Walter Bagehot emphasising the creation of confidence and trust as the criterion which must always be applied in assessing any responsible financial institution. When I was casting about for a conclusion to the book I asked the present Governor if he would express for me his views about the past, present and future of the Bank. In kindly responding to this request he began by stressing the balance that must be preserved between tradition and heritage on the one hand, and innovation and leadership on the other. He emphasised also that the Bank cannot thrive unless the society it serves thrives, and that it must be ready at all times and in every adversity to support its customers with funds, with fresh ideas, with new technology. And then echoing Bagehot's actual words, he added: 'The very essence of banking is confidence and trust, earned by the way the bank has done its business in the past.' Thus deep speaks unto deep across the centuries and the Bank, as it celebrates its bicentenary, still demonstrably steers by the same principles which have guided such great institutions at all times and in all places.

References

1   Walter Bagehot posed his questions in *Lombard Street*, first published in London in 1873. The quotations which follow are taken from the 1892 edition.
2   Walter Bagehot, *Lombard Street*, p.22.
3   *Ibid.*, p.42.
4   Hall, pp.9-14; L.M. Cullen, *An economic history of Ireland since 1660*, London 1972, pp. 72-3.
5   L. M. Cullen, op. cit., p.95.
6   Hall, pp.127—33.
7   Cited by F.S.L. Lyons in F. MacManus, ed., *The years of the great test, 1926-1939*, Cork 1967, p.102.
8   For a convenient summary, see James Meenan, *The Irish economy since 1922*, Liverpool 1970, pp. 216-20.
9   Banking Commission 1926, *First interim report*, p.16. One of the minority reports, however, by J. J. McElligott, had taken a different view.
10   James Meenan, op. cit., p.222.
11   Hall, pp.363-4.
12   Hall, p.138.
13   *Report and accounts for the year to 31 March 1982*, pp.21-2.
14   *Report and accounts for the year to 31 March 1980*, p.13.
15   *Report and accounts for the year to 31 March 1982*, p.6.
16   *Report and accounts for the year to 31 March 1980*, p.16.

Select Bibliography

The essays in this book are based mainly on primary sources, of which easily the most important have been the archives of the Bank of Ireland. References to primary sources are from the Bank's archives except where otherwise stated and abbreviations have been given when possible. A key to these abbreviations will be found at the beginning of the book. Apart from Dr Fanning's essay, where the nature of the topic required detailed documentation, our policy in general has been to be sparing with footnotes, though appropriate references have been included whenever these seemed necessary. What follows is a short, alphabetically arranged list of works which may be helpful to readers who wish to explore the subject further.

Bacon, P., Durkan, J. and O'Leary, J., *The Irish economy: policy and performance, 1972-81*, Dublin 1982
Bagehot, Walter, *Lombard Street*, 2nd ed., London 1892.
Barrow, G.L., *The Emergence of the Irish banking system, 1820-45*, Dublin 1975
Clapham, Sir John, *The Bank of England*, 2 vols, Cambridge 1945
Crick, W.F. and Wadsworth, J.E., *A hundred years of joint stock banking*, London 1936
Cullen, L.M., *Life in Ireland*, London 1968
———, *Anglo-Irish trade, 1660-1800*, Manchester 1968
———, *An economic history of Ireland since 1660*, London 1972
———, *The emergence of modern Ireland, 1600-1900*, London 1981
Cullen, L.M. and Smout, T.C., ed., *Comparative aspects of Scottish and Irish economic and social history, 1600-1900*, Edinburgh 1977
Dillon, Malcolm, *The history and development of banking in Ireland from the earliest times to the present day*, London and Dublin 1889
Fanning, Ronan, *The Irish Department of Finance, 1922-58*, Dublin 1978
Feaveryear, A.E., *The pound sterling*, London 1931
Fetter, F.W., ed., *The Irish pound, 1797-1826*, London 1955
Freeman, T.W., *Pre-Famine Ireland*, Manchester 1957
Gibson, N.J. and Spencer, J.E., ed., *Economic activity in Ireland: a study of two open economies*, Dublin 1977
Gilbart, J.W., *The history of banking in Ireland*, London 1836
Gregory, T.E., *Select statutes, documents and reports relating to British banking*, London 1929
Hall, F.G., *The Bank of Ireland, 1783-1946*, Oxford and Dublin 1949
Kennedy, K.A. and Dowling, B.R., *Economic growth in Ireland: the experience since 1947*, Dublin 1975
Lynch, P. and Vaizey, J., *Guinness's brewery in the Irish economy, 1759-1876*, Cambridge 1960
Meenan, James, *The Irish economy since 1922*, Liverpool 1970
———, *George O'Brien*, Dublin 1980.
Moynihan, Maurice, *Currency and central banking in Ireland, 1922-60*, Dublin 1975
Munn, C.W., 'The coming of joint-stock banking companies in Scotland and Ireland', in D. Dickson and T.M. Devine, ed., *Ireland and Scotland 1600-1800: parallels and contrasts in economic and social development*, Edinburgh 1982
———, Unpublished article, 'Bank finance for industry: Scotland and Ireland, 1820-1850'. Thanks are due to Dr Munn for making this available
O'Brien, George, *Economic history of Ireland in the eighteenth century*, Dublin and London 1918
———, *Economic history of Ireland from the Union to the Famine*, London 1921
O'Hagan, J., ed., *The economy of Ireland: policy and performance*, Dublin 1981
O'Mahony, D., *The Irish economy*, 2nd ed., Cork 1967
Riordan, E.J., *Modern Irish trade and industry*, London 1920
Sayers, R.S., *Modern banking*, London 1938
———, ed., *Banking in the British Commonwealth*, Oxford 1952
Schumpeter, J.A., *History of economic analysis*, New York 1954

Index

Entries in **bold type** denote illustrations.

219

221